Timothée Parrique is an economist originally from Versailles, France. He holds a PhD in economics from the University of Clermont Auvergne and the University of Stockholm and is currently a researcher at Lund University in Sweden.

Claire Benoit is a translator and a lawyer practicing immigration and tax law. She lives between Brooklyn, NY, and Paris, France.

SLOW DOWN
OR DIE

Timothée Parrique

SLOW DOWN OR DIE

THE ECONOMICS OF DEGROWTH

*Translated from the French
by Claire Benoit*

Europa Editions
27 Union Square West, Suite 302
New York NY 10003
www.europaeditions.com
info@europaeditions.com

Copyright © Éditions du Seuil, 2022
First publication 2025 by Europa Editions

Translation by Claire Benoit
Original title: *Ralentir ou périr: L'économie de la décroissance*
Translation copyright 2025 by Europa Editions

All rights reserved, including the right of reproduction
in whole or in part in any form.

Library of Congress Cataloging in Publication Data is available
ISBN 979-8-88966-101-6

Parrique, Timothée
Slow Down or Die

Cover photo: Brett Sayles/Pexels

Cover design by Ginevra Rapisardi

Prepress by Grafica Punto Print – Rome

Printed in the USA.

CONTENTS

INTRODUCTION
The Economy, a Matter of Life and Death - 11

1
THE SECRET LIFE OF GDP
Between Phenomenon and Ideology - 19

2
THE IMPOSSIBLE DECOUPLING
The Ecological Limits to Growth - 50

3
MARKET VERSUS SOCIETY
The Social Limits to Growth - 83

4
FALSE PROMISES
The Political Limits to Growth - 107

5
A BRIEF HISTORY OF DEGROWTH
From Objection to Growth to Post-Growth - 137

6
A Transition Pathway
Degrowing the Economy - 166

7
A Societal Project
Toward a Post-Growth Economy - 191

8
Controversies
12 Critiques of Degrowth - 210

Conclusion
Deserting Capitalism - 235

Notes - 243

Acknowledgements - 273

SLOW DOWN
OR DIE

INTRODUCTION
The Economy, a Matter of Life and Death

Custom would have me start this kind of book by observing the extreme gravity of our situation. I could serve up the usual inventory of ecological cataclysms and their social consequences, choose a few shocking statistics, and embellish with an anecdote or two to capture the reader's attention. But why waste time? Everybody knows there is a crisis without precedent in the history of humanity. Each day, the environmental collapse[1] we now face inflicts its crop of disasters, and few by now would dare deny the crushing responsibility of our species.

Welcome to the Anthropocene. Coinciding with the start of the Industrial Revolution, it is the name scientists gave to that period "during which human activity is considered to be the dominant influence on the environment, climate, and ecology of the earth."[i] It is thus humankind as a whole (*anthropos*), the rowdy hominid family, that bears responsibility for the apocalypse: a general sin that gives us each equal cause to blush, and whose expiation can only be collective.

All of humankind, really? In 2021, the richest 10% of households in the world owned 76% of the world's wealth and snatched more than half of all income, that is, 38 times more wealth and 6 times more income than the poorest half of the world's population.[ii] Worse yet: the richest 1% (only 51 million

---

[i] Per the definition in the *Oxford English Dictionary*.

[ii] According to the "World Inequality Report" (2022, pp. 26-27), the top

people) have captured 38% of all of the wealth generated since 1995, while the poorest half have only gotten 2%. Same thing in a country like France, where the wealthiest decile owns nearly half of the country's wealth and takes a third of all income.[iii]

With the right to riches comes the right to pollute. The richest 10% in the world are responsible for half of all greenhouse gas emissions.[2] Wealth and emissions are almost perfectly symmetrical. This "pollution elite"[3] pollutes four times more than the poorest half of humankind.[iv]

The injustice of this "planetary apartheid"[4] is twofold: the rich pollute and the poor suffer. The Somalian fisherman who sees his fish supply dwindle and the sea level rise has probably never taken a flight; he has contributed neither to the warming he inherits, nor to the overfishing. Nevertheless, he will be among the first to pay the price, and he will pay it in full. It is the most vulnerable populations, starting with those in the poorest countries, who drink polluted water, breathe toxic fumes, live by landfills, endure floods and heatwaves, etc. The notion of the Anthropocene masks profound inequalities: even if we all belong to the same species, we are not equal, neither in our

---

10% of the global wealth distribution represent 517 million people with an average monthly income of €7,300 and an average net worth of €550,900. They own 76% of the world's wealth and earn 52% of all income. The poorest half of the world's population includes 2.5 billion individuals; they earn on average €230 per month and own on average €2,900 in assets. This poorest half owns only 2% of the world's riches and receives only 8% of global income.

[iii] According to the "Rapport sur les riches en France" (2022, pp. 12-13), the richest 10% of French people—those with a minimum monthly income of €3,765 (4.5 million people) and a minimum net worth of €607,700 (2.9 million people)—own 46% of the nation's wealth and receive 28% of all pre-tax income.

[iv] According to an Oxfam report ("Confronting carbon inequality," September 21, 2020), half a million people have already used up 56% of the carbon budget that would limit warming to 1.5°C, while the poorest 2.5 million have only used 4%.

responsibility for nor in the dangers we face from the ecological catastrophes of today and tomorrow.

Let's say it plainly: ecological disintegration is not a crisis, it's a beating.[5] Climate change is a "slow violence,"[6] a diffuse violence, a decay that grinds gradually and out of sight, primarily affecting the most impoverished populations today, but that will, little by little, creep up the social ladder. This situation has nothing to do with some supposed human nature; rather, it is the symptom of a specific social structure, narrowly aligned with a certain global political vision. At least, that is the argument I will present over the course of this book: the primary cause of ecological derailment is not humanity but capitalism—the hegemony of economics over all else and the frantic pursuit of growth.

Let's forget, then, the *Anthropocene* and opt for the terms *Capitalocene*, *Econocene*, and *GDPocene*.[7] Let's cut to the chase: the economy has become a weapon of mass destruction. Economist Serge Latouche echoes Hannah Arendt and speaks of a "banality of economic evil":[8] a system that orchestrates the massacre of the living while diluting the culpability of those responsible. Everyone diligently goes about their task, justifying their actions by telling themselves that if they didn't do it, others would.

How many bankers are rushing to invent new toxic financial products and how many engineers are hard at work designing superyachts? How many executives lay off staff because of "the economy"? How many advertisers promote harmful and futile products? How many slaughterhouse workers mechanically brutalize and kill animals? How many lobbyists lie to protect fossil fuel interests? I've got bills to pay, they might say when reproached for destroying the world. If I don't do it, someone else will.

This violence is an emerging phenomenon—a sort of spontaneous disorder that no one directly anticipated, yet is, absurdly, sustained by our most innocuous social behaviors. One must pay back a loan, pay a bill, satisfy the shareholders, make money; we are hostages of a system that predetermines behaviors we would otherwise consider immoral.

Would we lend our friends money with predatory interest rates? Would we devise ad campaigns to pressure our loved ones to buy products they do not need? Would we decide to lay off a friend because someone on the other side of the planet can work for less? No, obviously not. If the cobalt mine were in my backyard and my children worked in it, I would think twice before upgrading my phone.

But we don't have a choice. The economy imposes itself on us via certain rules we are expected to respect: a price, a work contract, a mortgage, accounting principles. The problem is not the existence of the economy itself (all societies have always organized their productive activities in one way or another), but the rules that we give it and the central objective that drives it: *growth*. Whether it's individual income, company profits, or a country's GDP, it seems that in economics, *more* is always synonymous with *better*.

What is growth? The word is everywhere but never really explained, let alone deconstructed. A magic bullet in election campaigns, an unfailing answer to families' despair, it has so penetrated the imaginary of our contemporaries that no one hesitates to share their opinion on the matter. Yet, few people know not just what growth is and how it is measured, but also its complex links to nature, employment, innovation, poverty and inequality, public debt, social cohesion, and quality of life. Born from an accounting concept in the 1930s (the Gross Domestic Product), growth has become a myth with a thousand connotations. Progress, prosperity, development, protection, innovation, power, happiness—growth is no longer just an indicator, it is a symbolic vessel filled with collective and individual projections.

Green growth, circular growth, inclusive growth, blue growth; fifty shades of growth but always growth. The influence of this growth matrix on our collective imagination is such that rather than consider the consequences of our economic model on the planet, we worry about the impact of global warming on GDP. It's the world turned upside down. We can easily imagine our planet in all sorts of *Black Mirror*-esque dystopias, but to imagine an economy where we produce less than we do today is considered heresy.

Growth had, once upon a time, a clear function: to revive the American economy after the Great Depression, produce the equipment necessary for war, end famine, eradicate poverty, sustain full employment, or rebuild Europe. Measuring it allowed us to evaluate our progress toward these various goals. Over the decades, the indicator became the objective: growth for growth's sake, no more underlying aim. But production for production's sake is an objective without substance. We, living in countries envied by the rest of the world, continue to sacrifice our time and resources to produce and consume more, even though we have nothing more to gain—and so much to lose—by insisting on increasing our GDP. Like a young adult who, having just finished their growth spurt, is determined to keep getting taller, without understanding that, past a certain age, growth is no longer measured in inches.

As I write these words, every added inch is earned with pain. The Earth is overheating, societies are burning out, and GDP is becoming a sort of "countdown to doom."[9] A terrifying countdown because it's exponential: the bigger the economy, the faster it grows. Growth at an annual rate of 2% doubles the size of the economy every thirty-five years. We are on a bus speeding faster and faster toward a cliff, and we celebrate every added mile per hour as progress. It's madness. Maximizing growth is like stepping on the accelerator with the absolute certainty of dying in a social and ecological collapse.

We could use terms like *soft landing*, *downsizing*, *degrowth*, *de-escalation*, *descent*, *harmonization*, *restraint*, or some other analogy. The challenge ahead of us is one of less, lighter, slower, smaller. It is the challenge of restraint, frugality, moderation, and sufficiency. But it is also a matter of soft-landing, not crashing; a diet, not an amputation; a slowdown, not a hard stop. We know we must slow down, and now we have to imagine how to intelligently plan this transition so that it happens democratically, in the interest of social justice and well-being.

To do so, we must free ourselves from the "mystique of growth,"[10] meaning we need to denaturalize economic growth as a phenomenon. We urgently need to lend a critical eye to practices we have normalized[11] as natural and universal. Should every company make a profit? Should we let the markets decide what we produce? Should a government aim to increase its GDP? The argument I will defend here is that growth is not a destiny but a choice.

The implications of this thesis are more important than they appear: if growth is not caused by human nature but by certain socially constructed institutions, then it is possible to imagine an economy that can function without necessarily producing and consuming more. This is the aim of this book: to imagine *degrowth* as a transition toward a *post-growth* economy.

Here is the twofold definition that will guide us throughout the book: "degrowth" as a *downscaling of production and consumption to reduce ecological footprints, planned democratically in a way that is equitable while securing well-being*. Degrowth, to what end? Answer: toward "post-growth," a *steady-state economy in harmony with nature where decisions are made collectively and wealth is equitably shared, allowing us to prosper without growth*.

The challenge that awaits us is threefold: understanding why the growth-driven economic model is a dead end (the rejection), outlining the framework of a post-growth economy (the projection), and conceptualizing degrowth as a transition to get us there (the journey).[12] Throughout the coming chapters, this book advocates a simple yet radical idea: growth has become an existential crisis. From here on out, our survival depends on our ability, or inability, to change our economic model.

1
THE SECRET LIFE OF GDP
Between Phenomenon and Ideology

Economists sing its praises, politicians worship it: economic growth is our mantra, "the perpetual quest" of our economic policies, as the French Ministry of the Economy's website openly proclaims.[1] The true barometer of our modern societies, Gross Domestic Product (GDP) controls the weather. It's the number to know, the one heads of state repeat over and over again to justify their rank among great nations and that most of the press discusses seven days a week. Everywhere and in concert, whether we're poor, rich, tenants, landlords, workers, or civil servants, we're supposed to tout and pray for that vaunted growth.

But what is growth? An increase in GDP, some would say. But what else? Defining growth as an increase in GDP is like describing heat as an increase in temperature; it's a description without explanation. Like dark matter for physicists, growth has its own secrets that economics textbooks do not reveal. Yet, unveiling them is necessary to understanding its role in the crisis we now face. Because if growth has become the main driver of social and ecological unsustainability, understanding and demystifying it is our only escape.

THE ANTHROPOLOGICAL ECONOMY

To talk about *economic* growth, we have to define—or rather redefine—what the economy is and what it's for. The "sphere of market exchange" only captures a tiny part of our lives. Imagine the economy instead as an iceberg; what goes on in stores, factories, or government agencies—what we know how to quantify, the economy that the GDP measures—is only the tip of a much larger structure.

Our way of understanding and studying the economy is the result of a series of exclusionary choices. National accounting consists in taking inventory of certain activities; we include so-called "economic" production (primarily market activities) and we exclude everything else (e.g., ecosystem services, mutual aid, volunteer work). But this division is merely a methodological convention. Just because some statisticians decided it's too difficult to integrate pollination and reciprocity into national accounting doesn't mean they have no value. *What counts cannot always be counted, and what is counted does not necessarily count*—a phrase all economists should learn by heart.

To start, let's take the iceberg out of the water and expand our definition of the economy to *the social organization of need satisfaction*. The term actually comes from the Greek *oikonomia*, the management of the household (*oikos*, house, *nemein*, to manage). Hunting, fishing, harvesting, industry, craftsmanship, cryptocurrency, flea markets, public hospitals—every human community forms an economy once it organizes itself collectively with rules and procedures to meet its needs. This is a fundamental starting point: the economy is first and foremost a form of mutual aid; it's about doing together what we could not have accomplished alone.

The economy I would call "anthropological" is not measured in euros, but in kilograms of raw materials used, in joules of energy mobilized, in hours of labor. Before even mentioning money, which is only an intermediary form of value, the economy is about *time*, *effort* (energy), and *matter*. These are the three principal sources of value, the primary flows without which no economy (no matter its system of organization) could exist.

Now let's divide all economic activity into five big groups: *extraction*, *production*, *allocation*, *consumption*, and *elimination*.[i] By *extraction* I mean the mobilization of a natural resource—I cut down a tree in the forest. *Production* then transforms this resource into a product—I use the wood to build a chair. *Allocation* (from the Latin *allocare*, to place) transfers this good, either by donation (I give the chair to a friend), reciprocity (I lend it to a friend), distribution (I give it to a collective body that then distributes it to someone), or sale (I exchange it for money in a market). *Consumption* is the act of using, which can be individual (the person who winds up with the chair sits on it) or collective (to sit on a public bench)—this is the need satisfaction stage. Once the chair loses its utility, we will consider it waste and get rid of it (*elimination*).

These five fundamental activities form the perimeter of the anthropological economy. Their purpose revolves around a concrete goal: to satisfy *needs* in the broadest sense of the word, that is, everything a community could possibly want, whether essential or superficial. This is a second important point that we often forget: the economy is a means, not an end. The ultimate purpose of an economy, if indeed there is one, should be to advance our "capabilities for flourishing,"[2] to improve our quality of life, our existence. An economy is supposed to *better* manage finite resources, but this goal of *economic efficiency* (the careful management of limited resources) is only a means to achieve *economic sufficiency* (that is, having enough of everything we need and want).

---

[i] This terminology can too easily confine us to a specific relationship with nature. *Extraction* implies a form of pillage and *elimination* suggests discarding waste into an environment separate from ourselves. Certain pre-modern communities were animated by a less violent cosmology, one that should make today's Western economists think: what if we thought of "extraction" as a "loan" from mother nature that we must eventually repay?

Our definition takes clearer shape: the economy is thus the *collective organization of contentment*, or at least of its material conditions. An economy that does not satisfy the needs of its participants—or at least of the vast majority of them—is useless (and we will see that this is the case for whole swathes of contemporary capitalism). Because what is the use of collectively organizing to extract, produce, allocate, consume, and eliminate if it does not allow us to live more fully? This is a radical starting point, because in several chapters it will lead us to admit that the pursuit of infinite economic growth is an absurd goal—in Sisyphus's image, life spent pushing the heavy boulder of the GDP.

In his "matrix of fundamental needs," the economist Manfred Max-Neef catalogs nine types of need: subsistence, protection, affection, understanding, participation, idleness, creation, identity, and freedom.[3] According to Max-Neef, we satisfy these needs through four existential strategies: being, having, doing, and interacting. The need for subsistence, for example, requires *being* in good health, *having* decent housing, being able to rest (the *doing*), and being able to fully participate in social life (*interacting*). We work in order to produce what our family or others need or to pay our bills (the need for subsistence), to socialize (the need for participation, for affection), to learn (the need for understanding), to be considered a useful member of the community (the need for identity), to undertake new projects (the need for creation), etc.

According to economist Amartya Sen's "capability approach," poverty is not the lack of money but the incapacity to satisfy a need.[4] Well-being flows from what people are capable of doing with the means at their disposal. Poverty is therefore plural: to find oneself without shelter is to be *subsistence*-poor; without access to work, *participation*-poor; without skills, *creation*-poor; without free time, *idleness*-poor, etc. And the same goes for wealth. We can be *affection*-rich by being close to those we love, *participation*-rich in a stimulating group environment, *identity*-rich through language, religion, or custom, *protection*-rich thanks to an expansive social safety net, etc.

Our quality of life depends on the consonance between our needs and the means at our disposal. Money, for example, is only one means among many, and it is primarily what it allows us to buy that determines its capacity to satisfy our needs. This is an essential point: what counts, in the end, is not "purchasing power" but "living power."[5]

For a long time, most economists defended the idea that human needs were limitless, thereby justifying the fantasy of perpetual growth. But take a moment to ask yourself: which of your needs are really infinite? Material needs are quickly satisfied. Enough food for a balanced and diversified diet, enough space and comfort for decent housing, enough clothing to dress, enough pavement to walk on, etc. Most immaterial needs follow the same logic of sufficiency: enough friends to feel socially fulfilled, enough freedom to undertake projects, enough free time to do what we feel like doing, sufficient access to education and to culture, etc. We can therefore refine our anthropological definition of the economy by presenting it as the *social organization of need satisfaction*.

The satisfaction of most of our needs takes on a collective dimension, even if we don't realize it. Even the most solitary activities, like reading this book, depend on a host of collective activities. Therefore, and here is the essential point, the satisfaction of our needs can be realized under different social configurations. We can feed ourselves with what we grow in our garden or what we buy at the corner store. We can seek care in a public hospital or in a private clinic. Needs like protection and participation can be satisfied through socio-economic institutions like social security or civic service. Other needs flow from the interaction of several elements: *idleness*, be it made of dreams, games, or parties; the *affection* that flows from our relationships with humans and non-humans; and *identity*, sometimes tied to our person, to our job, or to the customs of our community.

The economy comes in as a supply system that, through extraction, production, allocation, consumption, and elimination, enables the satisfaction of needs. This cycle takes place on three different time horizons: well-being in the present, that well-being's resilience to shocks, and the sustainability of this supply system in the long run.[6] An economy that satisfies today's needs at the expense of future needs is an economy doomed to collapse (it is *unsustainable*); same thing for an economy that collapses at the slightest crisis (*fragile*), or worse yet an economy that cannot even satisfy the present needs of its participants (*useless*).

The economy so defined is universal in the sense that it contains the diversity of all systems that have ever existed. The chair can be made of wood, plastic, or iron; built at home, by a for-profit private company, a cooperative, or a public enterprise; it can be gifted, lent, exchanged, or distributed (the four modes of allocation: donation, reciprocity, exchange, and distribution); it can be consumed individually, collectively, in every way and for every possible and imaginable reason; then repaired, recycled, discarded, or destroyed.

The different forms of capitalism, from the liberal market model to the social-democratic model by way of Asian capitalism, the different forms of communism, from Soviet bureaucracy to Cuban decentralization, as well as feudal and tribal economies, and the hunter-gatherers that came before them: all of these communities have extracted, produced, allocated, consumed, and discarded in one way or another to try to meet their needs.

The History of GDP

This anthropological economy is not the economy we hear about in the news. How did the quasi-totality of the economic iceberg find itself plunged underwater? About a century ago, the national accounting revolution gave birth to what has now become the matrix of economic life: GDP.

Its invention goes back to the Great Depression of the 1930s in the United States.[7] With entire industries in agony, a flood of bankruptcies, a stock market collapse, and an employment rate in freefall, the economy was in cardiac arrest. The American government was desperately trying to stimulate activity, without really being able to evaluate the effectiveness of its interventions. In 1932, Simon Kuznets, a Russian-American economist who had arrived from the Soviet Union in the early 1920s, was tasked with developing a national accounting system—a sort of inventory of economic activities. Kuznets had a brilliant idea: aggregate all production in an economy into a single number, the Gross National Product (GNP), ancestor of the Gross Domestic Product. In other words, Kuznets invented a kind of blood pressure monitor to take the pulse of the whole economy. Useful, since it allowed for evaluating the effectiveness of public interventions. If it went up, that was good—you had succeeded at resuscitating the economy. If it didn't move, no impact—you needed to continue the resuscitation and try something else. If it kept plummeting, that was worse.

Once the 1929 crisis had ended, the government continued to use this measuring instrument, which would prove essential to organizing a spectacular surge in arms production during World War II. In 1953, the United Nations published the first international accounting norms, following Kuznets's methodology, thus making GNP a global indicator—with the exception of the Soviet Union, which preferred to use "Net

Material Product" and "Gross Social Product"[ii] before accepting the United Nations framework in 1988. In the 1990s, Gross National Product (GNP) became Gross *Domestic* Product (GDP), no longer measuring economic activities on the basis of their nationality (all French units of production, even those located abroad, contribute to the French GNP) but based on their location (only those situated in France, whether French or not, contribute to the French GDP).

These statistical conventions have essentially stayed the same to this day, despite five revisions in 1960, 1964, 1968, 1993, and 2008. The official document that explains how to calculate GDP defines it as the "sum of the gross value added of all resident institutional units engaged in production."[8] Value added is defined as "the value created by production," or more precisely "the contribution of labor and capital to the production process." GDP growth is therefore the increase from one period to another of the sum of value added produced by an economy.

It's impossible to estimate this value added without defining the scope of "economic production." And it is in the choice to include or exclude certain activities within the measurement framework that today's vision of the economy takes shape. Here is the definition the national accounting system gives for activities admitted into the economy's perimeter: "an activity, carried out under the responsibility, control and management of an institutional unit, that uses inputs of labor, capital, and goods and services to produce outputs of goods and services." This includes marketable and monetizable activities, along with certain non-market activities whose monetary value is easy to gauge.

[ii] Developed in the 1920s, the "Gross Social Product" measured the total value of the production of physical goods (public services and activities were not included), and allowed one to calculate, by subtracting intermediate consumption, the "Net Material Product."

GDP is thus the solution to one gigantic addition equation, as if an enormous calculator summed up all the value added by production considered economic. This addition can be done in three different ways.[9] We could sum all *value added* (sale price minus intermediate consumption, meaning the purchases necessary to the production of the good or service); or sum all *expenditure* (the purchase price of a product intended for consumption); or sum all *income* (remuneration of employees and operating surplus). As these three aggregates are, by convention, accounting equivalents (the consumption and spending of some are necessarily the production and revenue of others), the different methods of calculation lead to the same figure: GDP.

We talk about *Gross* Domestic Product and not *Net* Domestic Product (NDP), because the former does not take into account the "depreciation of capital," in other words, the loss in value of certain production factors like the deterioration of roads, the electrical grid, or buildings. If we include only machinery and infrastructure in *capital*, the difference between GDP and NDP is negligible. However, if we broaden the concept of capital to include nature (*the depreciation of natural capital*) and even the health and well-being of workers (*the depreciation of labor*), GDP growth may be offset by the degradation of ecosystems and individuals it has caused—we'll come back to this.

Kuznets's idea may very well be brilliant, but it would be wrong to think that GDP's strength stems from its conceptual simplicity or ease of calculation. Most economists don't know how this figure is calculated, a task mastered only by a handful of specialized statisticians. Its construction relies on so many hypotheses that interpreting it proves no less perilous. To rejoice at an increase in GDP without understanding how it is calculated is like rejoicing at the sight of a stocked fridge without knowing what's inside.

The Boundaries of GDP

Seeing governments' reckless infatuation with using Gross National Product in public policies, Simon Kuznets, its creator, sounded the alarm. As early as 1934, he declared to the U.S. Congress that "the welfare of a nation can scarcely be inferred from a measure of national income," and would go on to say: "Distinctions must be kept in mind between quantity and quality of growth, between its costs and return, and between the short and the long term. Goals for more growth should specify more growth of what and for what."

The indicator indeed has several limitations.[iii] GDP is but a selective and approximate estimation of production, and only assuming a certain conception of value. It measures not the anthropological economy, but a simplified and quantifiable representation of it. Of course, national accounting statisticians had no choice at the time; to be able to measure the economy, they had to shrink its perimeter according to the data available. Let's put ourselves in their place: it's hard to add up physical quantities measured in baskets of leeks, tons of hand sanitizer, and hours of massage therapy. To estimate production as a whole, GDP adds up these goods and services based on the monetary value they hold in the market.

This method is imperfect. First of all, outputs with no monetary equivalent are not accounted for, or only partially so. GDP measures *exchange value* but not *use value*. Kuznets's decision to assess products by their price forces us to exclude everything that does not have one. If I publish an open access book on the

---

[iii] This critique of indicators is not new. In France, it was developed in the late 1990s through the work of Dominique Méda, Jean Gadrey, Florence Jany-Catrice, Isabelle Cassiers, Patrick Viveret, among a dozen other thinkers gathered around FAIR, the Forum pour d'Autres Indicateurs de Richesse (the Forum for Other Indicators of Wealth). See: D. Méda, "Promouvoir de nouveaux indicateurs de richesse: histoire d'une cause inaboutie," Fondation Maison des sciences de l'homme, 2020.

web and a record number of people read it, because no one was paid to write it, it will not be accounted for in GDP. But if that book is commercialized and sees record sales, the book will be an asset in the eyes of national accounting. In both cases, the book and its readership are identical. But in the eyes of GDP, what does not give rise to a monetary transaction has no value. Caring for your children, cooking for your loved ones, organizing a community board meeting for your neighborhood—all of these activities, though they create value for society, are not counted in GDP.

All volunteerism, without which our society would be paralyzed, is excluded from GDP. Imagine what our society would look like without the 20 million volunteers that animate community life in France.[10] The world of sports would disappear overnight without all those who run amateur sports clubs. The Salvation Army, the Red Cross, WWF, Restos du Coeur, Secours Populaire, Action Against Hunger, Little Brothers of the Poor, Agir pour l'Environnement: organizations that could not be more economic (as they serve to satisfy needs) but whose activity is underestimated, ignored even, because a large portion of those who work for them do so as volunteers. Targeted marketing of useless products brings in GDP points, while taking care of a sick child or taking in an abandoned animal scores none.

The value of production in the public sector, though measured since the 1970s, is severely underestimated. Health, education, and public transportation are accounted for in GDP, but only up to certain quantifiable costs (mainly wages), and without taking into account their real value added, which is difficult to estimate without there being a sales price in the market. By contrast, we can easily calculate the value added of market activities by subtracting the cost of intermediate consumption from sales revenue, which includes the company's profits. Public sector value added is measured only in wages, while private sector value added is measured in wages and profits. Because of this bias, the same service contributes more to GDP if it is produced by a private company than if it is produced by a public entity, not only because private wages are often higher, but also because the private sector must remunerate for an additional factor of production, via shareholder profits.

Another criticism: this addition approach draws no distinction between the desirable and the detrimental. The GDP calculator has only one button and it's a "+." The production of a vaccine, of a smart fridge, of a speculative financial product, of antidepressants, or of hours of cleaning after an oil spill contribute to GDP in the same way: these outputs are added in according to their market value. A lavishly paid trader who speculates on food commodities "produces" more in the eyes of GDP than a childcare worker making minimum wage. The volunteer work of activists fighting to protect a forest has no quantifiable value, while the paid work of those who will raze it constitutes value creation in the national accounting sense. A private and more costly education system like the one in the United States will represent a greater contribution to GDP than a public system that is comparatively cheaper but better performing, like the one in Finland.

GDP is a quantitative indicator that informs us about the volume of cash flows. But since it tells us nothing about the positive or negative nature of the goods and services produced, its growth isn't necessarily good news. The statisticians who constructed GDP were actually the first to emphasize that it would never be an indicator of well-being. "GDP is often taken as a measure of welfare, but the SNA [System of National Accounts] makes no claim that this is so and indeed there are several conventions in the SNA that argue against the welfare interpretation of the accounts."[11]

Even for specific sectors or products, market values are bad at reflecting changes in quality. If the real price (meaning adjusted for inflation) of a computer turns out to be the same in the 1990s as in the 2010s, it will be counted exactly the same way in GDP, even if the more recent model is considerably better performing than the old one. What may seem like a subtlety proves problematic when applied to the measurement of entire sectors whose performance is fundamentally qualitative, like health or education.

Finally, the most damaging defect: GDP ignores nature. Its calculation protocol says so in black and white: "a purely natural process without any human involvement or direction is not production in an economic sense."[12] While bees spend hours tirelessly pollinating our agricultural outputs (an example of ecosystem production), they are excluded from the value added by agriculture recorded in GDP. A tree only has value when cut down and sold, but its own production by the biosphere and the services it renders throughout its life (producing oxygen, capturing carbon, cooling the air, stabilizing soil, protecting biodiversity, etc.) don't count. Or, according to an example in the United Nations' national accounting handbook, "the unmanaged growth of fish stocks in international waters is not production, whereas the activity of fish farming is production."

And if nature doesn't count, its destruction leaves no trace in the national accounting books. Forest fires will ultimately boost GDP through the spending generated to put them out. Even if ecological capital is thereby impoverished, the value added will have been recorded via the firefighters' wages and the gasoline sold to fuel their trucks. The latest ICPP report, when defining GDP, states that it is determined "without deducting for the depletion and degradation of natural resources."[13] By this logic, and to ecologists' great horror, exterminating the last members of an endangered species in order to sell them and eat them in a restaurant would increase the "value added" to the economy.

Economist Éloi Laurent aptly sums up the situation: "growth faithfully accounts for an increasingly insignificant part of human activity: goods and services but not their allocation; market transactions but not social ties; monetary value but not natural quantities"; GDP is "blind to economic well-being, blind to human well-being, deaf to social suffering, and mute on the state of the planet."[14] Conferences are regularly organized and reports regularly written to move beyond this indicator, but thus far without any notable effect: GDP continues to reign over the political governance of nations.

Growth: A Question of Size and Speed

We often compare the economy to a cake to be shared, and growth to a way of making it bigger so that we can each get a bigger piece. But GDP's notion of "product" does not mean accumulated wealth. GDP does not measure a *stock* of wealth (the total balance in a bank account or the number of fish in a lake) but a *flow* of wealth production over a given period (the money and fish added each year).

Since we cannot differentiate between monetary flows that enrich and those that impoverish (one of GDP's limitations), celebrating or decrying GDP movements is fallacious. Two people can bake the same cake in two different ways, one being a less experienced baker who will surely spend more time fixing their mistakes along the way and cleaning up the kitchen afterward. But the cake (wealth) will be the same, despite the two different baking styles (GDP).

What we call, perhaps too readily, "growth" is more like an intensification of *economic agitation* than an increase in total wealth. Picture a snow globe whose every snowflake is a monetary transaction. What GDP measures is the agitation of the flakes in the snow globe, a sort of measure of the monetary economy's effervescence. Accordingly, we can increase GDP in two different ways: by adding snowflakes to the globe, or by shaking the globe more vigorously. This yields two types of growth: one based on the *expansion* of the market economy's perimeter (the addition of snowflakes) and the other based on the *intensification* of the types of transactions that already exist.

Let's start with *expansive growth*. By the economy's perimeter, I mean the monetary economy's proportion compared to everything else (meaning, the line between the emerged part and the submerged part of the iceberg). Every time we transform something that was outside of the monetary sphere into a product that can be sold, the economy's perimeter expands.

A fish, which existed before being fished, will only add to GDP once commercialized. If you catch the fish yourself in order to feed yourself, that act of production will remain outside of the quantifiable economy. However, if you decide to sell the fish at a market, GDP will grow—or rather, swell—for there will be one more sale to record in the national accounts. Nothing has really changed—the fish is caught and eaten—but its commodification (the fact that it becomes a commodity sold in a market) inflates GDP.

Another example: the creation of Airbnb expanded the size of the monetary economy by transforming a service that until then had not been a commodity. An economy where all apartments are rented via CouchSurfing (a platform that connects hosts with people looking for free, short-term accommodation) would have a smaller GDP than an economy where they are all rented via Airbnb, all else being equal, while producing an at least equivalent use value.

Same thing in an economy where we take a taxi instead of getting dropped off by a friend, or where we use a paid dating app instead of chatting with someone directly. Once something gives rise to a new monetary transaction, it adds snowflakes to the globe. "Production" does not always mean "manufacturing." Here, the apartment is the same whether it's on CouchSurfing or Airbnb. It is not the resources that change but the social protocol that organizes them.

The second type of growth (shaking the snow globe more vigorously) is more intuitive: it's the existing economy running faster. If instead of changing phones every ten years, planned obsolescence practices force me to change phones every two years, the volume of value added/revenue/final expenses (the three ways of measuring GDP) increases. In this case, it's production that accelerates—we will have to manufacture five times more phones and mobilize all the resources required to do so.

This conceptual divide between *expansion* and *intensification* works in the other direction, too. The sphere of the market economy can *contract* if goods and services previously commodified are now produced outside of GDP's domain. When paid encyclopedias like Encarta gave way to Wikipedia, assuming the rest of the economy did not compensate for the dip, GDP decreased (even if the proliferation of knowledge, and so wealth in the larger sense, clearly increased). People continue to read and write encyclopedia articles, but this all happens in a sphere with fewer monetary transactions and barriers to access.

Just as an increase in GDP does not always represent the emergence of additional output (it could already have existed in the non-market sphere), a decrease in GDP does not necessarily mean that activities have disappeared—we could say they've merely exited the perimeter of the quantifiable economy.

The sphere of the market economy can also *slow down*. A pandemic hits and mask sales rise, pushing their contribution to GDP upward. Once the health crisis ends, the volume of masks declines, and so does their contribution to GDP. If I decide to stop eating meat or to stop flying, and these transactions are not offset by others, GDP drops. The same is true if I buy a train ticket for €100 to go hiking in the Auvergne volcanoes instead of paying €1,000 for a flight to visit Réunion Island. If we massively reduce working hours, or if we prohibit certain activities like advertising for the most polluting products, we will probably observe an *economic slowdown* due to the reduced agitation of these sectors.

Why attempt to deconstruct growth into multiple phenomena? It's a necessary exercise for demystifying a modern belief, according to which GDP growth is always progress and degrowth is necessarily undesirable, a belief that therefore suggests that we should always strive to "stimulate" the economy, and never to contract it or slow it down. When we are dealing with complex institutional changes, GDP as a compass obscures more than it enlightens. Nationalizing a healthcare system and capping housing and energy prices will reduce GDP, which isn't necessarily a bad thing, as long as indicators for health, well-being, and sustainability improve.

The growth and degrowth of GDP doesn't tell us much about the true performance of the economy. We can celebrate certain kinds of agitation when they serve to satisfy needs (producing masks during the pandemic, producing works of art, writing a book on climate change, etc.). We can denounce others that would be useless (certain forms of advertising, SUVs, gadgets) or even counterproductive to our well-being (the design of planned obsolescence, junk food). The same goes for lulls. Certain slowdowns in production feel like an amputation, leading to exclusion, unemployment, austerity, and poverty. Others are more like a diet: a situation where a community manages to satisfy its needs with less economic effort. This economic rhythm of more and less is not an inevitability but the result of social choices.

The Ingredients of Economic Activity

All activity, whether or not it is considered economic in the GDP sense, requires resources. Economists use "factors of production" to describe everything we use to produce, like energy, raw materials, ecosystem services, tools, labor, and institutions. The term "production" is used here in the largest possible sense: the mobilization of resources to produce a good or service that permits the satisfaction of a need.[iv] These factors can take a market form counted in GDP (paid workers' hours of labor and the electricity we buy, for example; these are the *emerged* factors of production) or not (nature, knowledge, and institutions; the *submerged* factors of production).

Nature and Tools

Let's start with the factor without which nothing could be produced: nature. All production mobilizes energy and raw materials, even the most dematerialized services. Computers consume energy, and we humans consume calories. It's impossible to make energy available without building machines made of materials, and it's impossible to grow food without water and soil. To these raw materials which are mobilized directly (materials and minerals, energy, water, land, and living beings) we must add others that contribute to production indirectly. Ecosystem processes like pollination, climate regulation, soil formation, the water cycle, genetic diversity—in other words, *ecological outputs* supplied by the living world and natural cycles—provide services without which it would be impossible not only to prosper, but simply to live. So, let's think of the economy as a metabolic superorganism that ingests energy and materials and expels waste.

Economists speak of "manufactured capital" to describe the tools, machines, and infrastructures used for production. A sushi knife, but also a hangar, a road, or a prison gate. Most economists worry little about the depletion of natural resources or the collapse of ecosystems because they think that ecological

---

[iv] To avoid productivist pitfalls and expand our economic imagination, we could even speak of *factors of satisfaction* in order to emphasize not the thing produced, but its utility.

factors of production can be replaced—economists say "substituted"—by human factors of production like tools, labor, and knowledge. Robert Solow was the first economist, in 1974, to propose this substitutability theory. "The world," he wrote, "can, in effect, get along without natural resources."[15]

The limitations of this theory are obvious: some natural resources are irreplaceable by human inventions. No machine can replace the Earth's climate or the circulation of ocean waters. Manufactured capital, being necessarily produced from natural materials, can never be a complete substitute for nature. We could pollinate using drones, but building these drones and powering them with electricity would require materials and energy (and these drones would likely be less effective than their biological alternative). In ecological economics, tools are thus considered a subcategory of natural resources—a hammer is simply a rearrangement of wood and metal that already existed in another form before being mobilized. The hammer itself, before becoming a factor of production, is already a final product that required tools for its construction, tools that were themselves produced in another process of production, and so on until the natural resource in the rawest state: something we would find directly in nature.

Working Time

Another indispensable factor of production: *labor* in the most general sense of the term. All production requires time and effort. Even the most automated production requires the construction, programming, and maintenance of machinery, a task that demands time and effort from somebody.

The labor capacity of an economy depends on its active population (excluding children, retirees, and people of working age who don't take part in the labor market), the productivity of labor per hour (which depends on what orthodox economists call "human capital," meaning the attributes of those who work:

skills, know-how, and all other attributes that facilitate production), and the cultural organization of labor, namely working hours. Like the living world and other earthly resources, labor is used either directly (an hour of work spent making a hammer) or indirectly (the hours of work spent developing an online tutorial that explains how to make a hammer).

As we will see in Chapter 3, labor is not an unlimited factor of production. There are only 24 hours in a day, only a small part of which can be mobilized to produce—these are the *available* working hours. Demographics are pretty much stable, at least in the high-income countries implicated in degrowth, and labor productivity is trending downward (we'll also see that its increase isn't always desirable).

If bees were to disappear, sure, we could pollinate by hand, but it would be hard to increase production every year, because sooner or later all available working hours will have been mobilized. The social limit of available working time is, after the ecological limit of natural resources, the second insurmountable obstacle for an economy seeking to grow perpetually.

Institutions

All production is enmeshed in a social infrastructure. It's difficult to produce without property rules to manage allocation, without money and a market to facilitate exchange, without credit policies to finance new projects, without legislation to guarantee participants' rights, without trust in oneself and others, or without a common language to communicate. Beyond a basic subsistence economy where each person produces what they need for themselves, production requires rules of organization, that is, *institutions* like laws and customs.[16]

Just as nature develops ecosystems, societies develop institutions, and both provide services without which production would be impossible. In the same way that trees in a forest absorb carbon and help regulate the climate (an ecosystem service), friends who comfort us after a tough day at work render a socio-system service, as they absorb distress and help regulate our emotions. In both cases, these services are emergent properties—of nature or of social interactions—which, directly or indirectly, affect our capacity to produce.

Technical Progress and Economic Progress

If we want to produce more hammers, we can either mobilize more resources or improve the production process to make it more efficient. This is technical progress. In economics, we often define it as an increase in "total factor productivity," meaning to produce more with the same quantity of factors of production, or alternatively to produce as much with fewer resources. If I notice that I am more productive in the morning because I write faster, and decide to write in the morning instead of at night, that's technical progress: I will produce more pages with the same quantity of work and energy, and with the same tools.

First point: *productivity* implies *production* and so, for economists, GDP. *Use productivity* in terms of satisfaction is too often reduced to *monetary productivity*, that is, the relationship between production estimated according to sales prices and manufacturing costs based on purchase prices, which are also monetary. In a world where prices do not incorporate social and ecological value (or do so poorly), an increase in monetary productivity does not necessarily signal an increase in use productivity.

Second point: under a conception of production that only takes into account the factors we buy (the price of materials, energy, tools, and labor costs), technical progress occurs as if by magic, a sort of alchemical transmutation that ignores the use of non-monetary resources. But if we broaden the production function to include social and ecological production, we realize that this progress isn't magic at all.

If I write faster, it could be because I'm better rested. But this rest is itself the result of production outside of the GDP economy. My productivity at work is indirectly determined by other, non-market factors outside of work (this will be the central thesis in Chapter 3). Same thing for ecological production. The bee is no magical apparition; it is made of matter, powered by energy, the result of information derived from millions of years of evolution, and co-exists with many other species in complex ecosystems that also require certain factors of production to exist.

Technical progress is only illusory if the increase in a (market) factor's productivity is achieved at the expense of another (non-market) factor's productivity. The advent of fertilizers, pesticides, and herbicides temporarily increased the yield from agricultural labor, but at the cost of losing biodiversity, soil fertility, and of putting workers' health at risk. The surplus in monetary production came with a decline in ecological and social production. What looks like technical progress in the traditional production function is, in reality, the substitution of one factor for another in an ecological production function. If we take all factors into account, we ultimately notice a loss in productivity and a technical setback.

This is an important point: market production as measured by GDP only accounts for some of the factors of production—those with a price. Total factor productivity is only counted if it increases the output's commercial value. To grow your tomatoes with less water, clean your house more quickly, or organize a walking bus to bring kids to school are economic innovations in the anthropological sense, because they facilitate the production of goods and services that contribute to the satisfaction of needs. Yet these are not the kinds of innovations that economists study.

The problem is that, for economists, technical progress measures exchange value and not use value. Let's imagine that an engineer invented a new production process that allowed us to produce a drill with half as much material, machinery, and labor. Production could therefore double (increasing GDP) without mobilizing new factors of production: the factors' productivity would have increased, resulting in "technical progress." Now imagine that someone invented a reciprocity network allowing objects to be shared among neighbors. Instead of having one drill per household, a single drill could be shared among three households. The need (to drill holes) would be better satisfied with fewer drills (decreasing GDP).

We are confusing two types of progress. On the one hand, there is anthropological progress, which allows us to better satisfy needs using fewer resources, and which resembles *economic progress* in the sense of the economy's original goal (meeting needs by the most parsimonious means possible, parsimony appearing here as a smaller volume of outputs). The other type of progress (the "technical progress" of economists) only takes monetary value into account, thereby creating the quantifiable illusion of enrichment. Often, however, this improved productivity only reflects the transformation of social and/or ecological wealth into financial wealth.

The Engines of Growth

There is no magic in economics. All the ingredients for producing exist before becoming factors of production. A tree could simply remain a tree without ever becoming lumber or an opportunity for ziplining, and my free time could very well remain as such without ever being mobilized for a paid job. A bicycle can be used either to go for a ride or to work, and our intellectual and cultural capabilities can be applied just as well to agriculture and industry as to chess and politics.

These factors can become productive in the anthropological sense, meaning they can participate in the satisfaction of a need: I grow tomatoes in my garden and give them to friends and family (I thus provide for a need without the value added of my labor being counted in GDP). But these factors can also be mobilized in a market production process: I grow tomatoes in order to sell them. Depending on the economic system in place, the market sphere will be more or less significant (prevalent in a capitalist economy where most factors of production are commodified, and less so in a tribal economy composed of decommodified common goods).

To explain economic growth, we must start by understanding the mechanisms that lead to the agitation of the market sphere, what I will call the *engines of growth*. Certain economies are more prone to growth than others (for better or for worse), due to their institutional structure—that is, the rules they set for themselves. To simplify, we can identify at least three major actors and engines of growth, according to the scale at which they drive accumulation: businesses (productivism), households (consumerism), and the state (which will later be described as *economism*).

First, there is the propensity of businesses to maximize their profits. The social responsibility of business is to increase its profits, neoliberal economist Milton Friedman used to say.[17] Businesses compete in markets, which pushes them to produce more and to create new products. The goal: to minimize costs and maximize revenue. Generally, the more a business sells, the more profit it generates, and the more it can reinvest in its production capabilities to further increase sales—a positive feedback loop (hence the engine analogy). This cultural selection for the most profitable eliminates businesses with low profit rates and favors those who manage to yield higher margins.

The second engine operates at the level of consumer behavior. In a society where everything is for sale, it's normal to want to make more money. To procure money, one must work for pay, grow the value of one's assets, or engage in any other activity likely to generate income. Whether individuals are motivated by the pursuit of happiness, by a positional competition for prestige, or by the repayment of consumer loans does not matter. Nor does it matter whether these behaviors result from spontaneous desires or are spurred by advertising and planned obsolescence. All these reasons lead to the same result: more purchases. For an economy to grow, it needs consumers who buy more and more. The more we buy, the more businesses make profits, the more businesses augment their production capabilities and can encourage consumption (second positive feedback loop).

The third engine of growth plays out at the state level. It's no secret: governments are in active pursuit of economic growth. The justifications are many: eradicating poverty, bringing down unemployment, reducing inequality, paying back debt, or maintaining well-being (even if the link between growth and these objectives remains to be seen—this will be the subject of Chapter 4), or simply "improving a country's attractiveness."

This pushes public authorities to facilitate the commodification of certain social spheres, in the hope that privatizing this infrastructure will unleash a virtuous cycle of GDP growth. By contrast, everything that might slow market agitation must be undone: we must raise consumer purchasing power, reduce business costs, and encourage corporate investment. The more the market sphere acquires importance in social life, the more the satisfaction of our needs depends on purchasing power and the good health of businesses, and the more the government is forced to accommodate its smooth functioning, which in turn facilitates the expansion of the market sphere (third positive feedback loop).

Economic growth in a market economy depends on three elements: consumers always willing to buy *more*, businesses always willing to sell *more*, and a government that supports the process as a whole. Each engine has its speedometer: individuals want to maximize their income, businesses their profits, and governments their GDP. While each process has its own mechanisms, together they form a positive feedback superloop. The more businesses are productivist, the more they engage in aggressive marketing strategies, encouraging spending; the more consumers are dependent on businesses to satisfy their needs, the more businesses gain power; and the more powerful businesses become, the more they can pressure public authorities. In this sense, growth is a structural element of today's capitalism, the default macroeconomic result of an economic system where every actor strives indefatigably to always get more.

The Ideology of Growth

Growth isn't only a real phenomenon, it's also a collective obsession. Just look at the omnipresence of GDP in discussions about health, ecology, education, and culture. It's impossible to invest in hospitals or schools without growth, in a world where "there's no magic money," according to Emmanuel Macron's quip.[18] Micro-economically, money is the *power to buy*, and macro-economically, GDP is the *power to act*. The prerequisite of profitability becomes an invisible barrier constraining thought and action. What leads to growth is desirable, and the rest is relegated to the realm of the unthinkable. Hence economists' reticence toward degrowth, "a dangerous utopia" according to Bruno Le Maire, because it would threaten the health of the economy.[19]

In France, government bodies implement "growth policies," and the Minister of the Economy is legally required to define "the proper measures to promote growth."[20] Our elected officials pass laws "for growth," like that of August 6, 2015, whose first hundred articles are titled "freeing activity." The use of the term "freeing" perfectly denotes the obsession: we must at all costs deregulate, privatize, and reduce the social and ecological frictions that limit growth. British law goes even further: since 2015, it imposes a "growth duty" under which "a person exercising a specified regulatory function must have regard to the desirability of promoting economic growth."[21] In short, do not ask yourselves what your country can do for you, but what you can do to make your country, or at least its economy, grow.

Growth as a grand narrative is a recent development. Retracing the use of the term "economic growth" over the period from 1890 to 1960, historian Daniel Hirschman notes that discussions on the subject emerged only after World War II.[22] Even after the concept of "national income" became established in the 1940s, the primary concern remained the economy's stability, not its growth. It was not until the 1950s that this new preoccupation appeared. Historian Matthias Schmelzer's work has shown, moreover, that the goal of growth was actively promoted at the time by the Organization for European Economic Cooperation, first in the United States in the early 1950s, then in the rest of the world, often against the will of politicians who did not see the point in endlessly boosting an abstract indicator that did not measure well-being.[23]

The novelty lay not in the desire to increase a country's wealth (a goal as old as time), but in the way in which it was measured and the emphasis placed on the speed of its accumulation. There had to be not just more, but more, faster. And this surplus had to be reinvested to become sur-surplus, and so on, thereby creating a dynamic of systemic accumulation. Accordingly, accumulation became an obligation, and so the utilization of each resource had to be optimal. It's the logic of "profit thinking" so dear to traders, but applied to the economy as a whole.[24] Thus was born the ideology of growth as a form of monetary monomania, an *economism*.

Economism is that vision of the world that applies the frameworks of contemporary economic analysis—neoclassical, capitalist, and neoliberal—to real life. An obsession with the economy, the primacy of the monetary over everything else, such that every human activity is subjected to a cost-benefit analysis. The economy has become the subconscious of our modern societies.[25] Every problem, be it social, cultural, political, or ecological, is subordinated to the will of the market. Is fighting global warming profitable? Do we have a financial interest in quarantining? Are there enough jobs in France to be able to welcome refugees? The economy in growth-at-all-costs mode thus imposes a "tyranny of monetary value," "disdain for everything that is not money."[26]

We could say it's the economy turned religion;[27] the cult of an abstract entity, "a mythological monster"[28] on whom we bestow realness and power. We cannot increase public spending, it would seem, because the markets would not allow it. This is a depoliticization of the economy, now naturalized as independent of the will of its participants. The economy is divine and it wants to grow. Today, we are confronted with the "idolatry of growth,"[29] in the words of Rowan Williams, former Archbishop of Canterbury. A GDP on the rise is considered common sense, a natural, inevitable, timeless, and universal state of affairs—a "mystique of growth"[30] that becomes the metanarrative of our modern societies, the very definition of progress, and the direction of history. It's the *spirit of growth*, to borrow from Luc Boltanski and Ève Chiapello's theorization of Max Weber's famous "spirit of capitalism."[31]

At the heart of this generalized obsession with growth: the belief that there is never enough, and that each accumulated asset should be reinvested into a new cycle of production. It's productivism without limit or destination—"to infinity . . . and beyond!" Countries, companies, and individuals do not strive to meet the thresholds of sufficiency, but rather to stay on an ascending path of accumulation. All sense of measure, restraint, sufficiency, and moderation become antimodern, like archaic customs from which we must be freed. *More* is always *better*. No individual ever complains about getting richer, no company objects to a rise in its profits, and no country is saddened to announce an increase in its GDP.

These capitalist behaviors have long been in competition with other ways of understanding human activity. What makes our society "capitalocentric"[32] is the hegemony of these behaviors over all others. Denis Colombi develops this thesis in *Why Are We Capitalist Despite Ourselves?*: "Oftentimes, without really wanting to, without even being aware of it, we act according to these principles, in a way that facilitates the infinite pursuit of profit and accumulation."[33] The *habitus* of growth becomes common sense in a society where everyone wears capitalist lenses and where the principle of profitability is institutionalized as an ethic. "In a capitalist economy, it would be rather difficult not to behave like a *homo oeconomicus*, not to calculate, not to rationalize, and not to participate, in one way or another, in the race for profit, given how the structures, infrastructures, and institutions that surround us are made for just that."[34] Practicing voluntary simplicity in an economy organized around growth is as difficult as playing *Grand Theft Auto* without committing a crime.

This mentality also affects our identities. Psychologist Harald Welzer describes economic growth as "the mental infrastructure" of our modern societies.[35] The obsession penetrates our ways of thinking and feeling, pervades our desires, hopes, and values, and shapes our identities and attitudes. Who would call it success to have less money in the bank at forty than they did twenty years earlier?

Entrepreneurship applied to existence itself, just as Michel

Foucault theorized in his analysis of emerging neoliberalism.[36] We ourselves become "factors of production," "human capital" that we must then use optimally to maximize the growth of our income. Philosopher Céline Marty provides a good summary of this internalization of the productivist economic rationale: "Do you feel rushed in the morning, guilty to have lingered a few more minutes in bed? Do you feel bad for having said no to happy hour with your colleagues? Do you feel guilty going to pick up your kids at 6 P.M. while your colleagues are still at work? Do you feel ashamed for hanging out on your couch, 'doing nothing'? That's because the world of capitalist labor makes us internalize its productivist imperatives, to its own advantage."[37]

Our obsession with growth is such that it dissolves time. In the space-time of modern capitalism, there are no hours or years, only euros. In this GDP-ified society, the present is defined by one level of wealth, the past understood as its reduction, and the future as its augmentation. Losing money is stepping backward; getting rich is moving forward. Just like Walt W. Rostow's phases of development:[38] countries with low GDPs are considered "under-developed," those experiencing growth are "developing," and those with the highest GDPs per capita are considered "developed." Time literally becomes money. Every hour spent with your children, playing chess, educating yourself, voting, etc. carries an economic opportunity cost: how much could I have earned if I had worked instead of letting my factors of production "sit idle"? Economic thinking thus infiltrates every social and ecological relationship, turning the world into a giant factory where everything is a potential factor of production.

Stagnation, by contrast, becomes modern societies' ultimate fear. We still talk about Japan's "lost decades" without growth. In Europe, the "Trente Glorieuses" (Glorious Thirty) were followed by the "mediocre twenty." We say "sluggish growth" and "secular stagnation" to refer to disappointing growth rates. A company whose revenue stagnates is considered bogged down, stuck in its race to success.

Eva Sadoun offers a cute analogy: "Financial markets function a bit like dating apps" and "financial indicators and GDP are like filters that enhance our impression of a certain company or country. In other words, on public debt Tinder, you have to project the image of a state whose GDP is growing and who is doing everything to keep it that way."[39] Countries with a stagnating GDP become untouchables while those that grow are hailed as economic miracles—the macroeconomic equivalent of those vaunted "unicorns" of which we know nothing besides their high market capitalization.

Of course, if stagnation is considered a failure, it's no surprise that recession is experienced as a catastrophe. When its GDP declines for several months, an economy falls into a "depression," a term that says a lot about the anxiety our societies feel at the absence of growth. Reducing your revenue is synonymous with bankruptcy, lowering your income is synonymous with bad financial planning, and a GDP in decline is every government's worst nightmare, like an economic wildfire come to burn the country's riches. Our phobia of slowing down plainly shows that we have erected the growth of GDP—this rudimentary thermometer from the 1930s—as a veritable model of civilization.

Yet the ideology of exponential and perpetual growth is a sociohistorical anomaly. Growth is the exception, not the rule. Human experience, be it biological, psychological, or sociological, is one of limits and finitude. In the world of the living, growth is always temporary, confronted with various mechanisms of self-regulation. It's a phase that, once complete, gives way to other dynamics. Facing a full ecological crisis and the imperative to reduce our consumption of natural resources, this "malady of infinite aspiration"[40] that Durkheim spoke of is a scourge.

2
The Impossible Decoupling
The Ecological Limits to Growth

Imagine a regular smoker, hospitalized with respiratory issues. After a consultation, a doctor tells them to quit smoking, at least until their condition improves. After another consultation, a different physician confirms that smoking is bad for the patient's health, but tells them that they can keep smoking anyway, because in the future—the second doctor is sure of it—certain innovations will allow us to dissociate smoking and cancer.

Should we pressure this person to stop smoking or, like the second doctor, trust in the future? Returning to our subject, we could ask ourselves a similar question: should we limit production—the tobacco—or believe that we'll be able to render it harmless to the environment? In other words: can we *decouple* economy and ecology, develop the former without destroying the latter? Far from being reserved for specialists, this question now lies at the heart of civilization's greatest challenges.

Green Growth and Decoupling

First, let's define the key terms of the debate, starting with the notion of *decoupling*. Two variables are said to be "coupled" if one changes proportionally to the other (for example, more of A means more of B), and they decouple from one another when they stop doing so.

When we invoke "green growth," decoupling refers to the dissociation between GDP growth (the economic variable) and environmental pressures (the ecological variable). By "environmental pressures" I mean the totality of consequences that human activity has on nature, whether through the use of resources (raw materials, energy, water, and soil) or its impacts on the environment (climate change, biodiversity loss, ocean acidification, air, water, and soil pollution, light pollution, noise pollution, etc.).

We often speak of *carbon footprint* (emissions measured in tons) and of *carbon intensity* (the carbon content of GDP) in relation to the climate, but there are many other interactions between the economy and ecology: the *footprint/intensity of materials, water, soil*, etc. There are also phenomena that are more difficult to quantify, like water pollution or effects on living species.

Then let's use *ecological burden* to take into account the totality of pressures that a society exerts on the nature that surrounds it. We will call a decoupling *partial* if the dissociation pertains only to certain pressures (for example, CO_2 emissions but not the use of raw materials, soil pollution, the impact on biodiversity, etc.), and we will describe it as *total* if it includes all components of the ecological burden.

Decoupling can also be *relative* or *absolute*. A *relative* decoupling, between GDP and greenhouse gas emissions for example, describes a situation where emissions per unit of production fall but not fast enough to compensate for the simultaneous rise in production over the same period. In other words: the ecological burden worsens as production increases, even if less quickly. In a case of *absolute* decoupling, however, GDP growth coincides with emission reduction. When decoupling is absolute, the ecological burden decreases without a corresponding decline in economic activities or, inversely, economic activities increase without a rise in the ecological burden.

Decoupling can happen in two different ways. We talk about decoupling *from the top* when the economic variable frees itself from the ecological variable. A boom of paid encyclopedias will increase GDP without really affecting real production (at least in the short term), and so the ecological burden. Inversely, a decoupling *from the bottom* describes a situation where the economic variable remains more or less constant while the ecological variable decreases. This could occur after the introduction of new, less polluting technologies, for example. When we talk about an economy's *carbon intensity* or *material intensity*, we relate an ecological footprint to GDP (same thing for *carbon productivity*). But according to the mechanics of this ratio, intensity/productivity can decline in the same way whether pollution decreases (decoupling from the bottom) or GDP increases (decoupling from the top).

Depending on the variables we choose, decoupling can be *local* if it only applies to a specific region (the decoupling of Australia's GDP from its water consumption) or *global* if it applies on a planetary scale (the decoupling of global GDP from the erosion of biodiversity across the world). It can also be *temporary* or *permanent*. Two variables that decoupled for a time can "recouple" later (this is known as *recoupling*). Temporary decoupling creates the illusion of victory but often just shifts the problem in time.

Let's recap: genuinely green growth, in the sense of sustainable development, would consist in an increase in production accompanied by a decline in the economy's total ecological burden. It would be growth backed by a *total* decoupling, one that is *absolute*, *from the bottom*, *global*, and *permanent*. And of course, the reduction of the ecological burden should be rapid enough to avoid exceeding "planetary boundaries."[1] Yet such green growth has, to this day, never existed.

Decoupling: Fake News

The decoupling theory is not new. It dates back to the 1990s and the empirical research of some economists[2] who, while studying the link between GDP and certain specific environmental impacts, discovered some rather optimistic bell curves. Optimistic because, according to their observations, ecological burden correlates to income only up to a point (the peak of the bell), after which the trend inverses—growth begins to green. What is known today as the "Environmental Kuznets Curve"[i] was born, and with it the hope of reconciling the economy and ecology.

In July 2019, six colleagues and I published a report assessing the state of research on decoupling. The document's title captures the result: "Decoupling debunked."[3] After going with a fine-tooth comb through hundreds of empirical studies on the link between economic growth and the use of materials, energy, water, greenhouse gas emissions, land use, water pollution, and biodiversity loss, it is clear that no study justifies the current faith in green growth. Decouplings, when they do occur, are predominantly relative, often temporary, and involve only a minority of environmental pressures. Even in the most significant cases of decoupling, the reduction rates are pathetic.

A year later, a group of sixteen researchers reviewed the entire body of literature on decoupling, 835 scientific articles containing no less than 1,157 studies.[4] This colossal analysis confirmed our findings. "We conclude," write the authors, "that large rapid absolute reductions of resource use and GHG emissions cannot be achieved through observed decoupling rates."

This conclusion has serious implications: the allegedly "green" growth celebrated by governments and international agencies has

---

[i] In reference to a similar bell curve that Russian-American economist Simon Kuznets had observed regarding the relationship between national income and inequality.

never really been so. In truth, as I will argue in this first section, the impression of any meaningful decoupling between GDP and ecological burden is an illusion, for at least five reasons: we only talk about carbon; we do not account for imports; decoupling is often only temporary; the orders of magnitude are far from sufficient; and we do not take into account the fact that this greening is partially explained by low rates of GDP growth.

Problem #1: we only talk about carbon

Decarbonizing isn't enough. Discussions around decoupling too often ignore the myriad impacts we have on the Earth system. Take biodiversity: according to the Living Planet Index calculated by WWF, the average population size of vertebrate wildlife declined by 68% between 1970 and 2016.[5] This means that, over fifty years, the populations of 4,392 different species were reduced on average by two thirds. Even more troubling, the latest report from IPBES—the Intergovernmental Panel on Climate Change's (IPCC's) equivalent for the study of biodiversity—states that 14 of the 18 categories of ecosystem services have declined since 1970, a 47% drop in the average health of ecosystems.[6] In France, the National Biodiversity Observatory fears a "significant regression in habitats and their diversity," finding that four out of five natural habitats are in a degraded state of conservation.[7]

As for the use of materials at the global level, the results are clear: there has never been an absolute decoupling. The global extraction of raw materials increased twelvefold between 1900 and 2015, with a constant acceleration since the start of the 21st century.[8] The material footprint of OECD nations as a whole doubled between 1990 and 2008, in direct correlation with economic activity, every 10% increase in GDP bringing with it a 6% increase in material footprint.[9] As for the material intensity of the global economy (the quantity of raw materials extracted per GDP percentage point), it increased by 60% between 1900 and 2009.[10]

Some countries are quick to congratulate themselves for having dematerialized, when in fact, they have simply relocated their industrial activities abroad. To take into account all the materials used by an economy, one must calculate its *material footprint*, meaning the total volume of raw materials associated with the goods and services consumed in the country (including the resources extracted beyond national borders). France's material footprint amounted to 17.1 metric tons of materials per person in 2018.[11] The government report "L'environnement en France" is clear on the issue: "If industrialized countries tend to show a certain decoupling between growth and the mobilization of materials, it is in part the result of a transfer of extractive and industrial activities to emerging and/or developing countries."[12]

Often, the decoupling of one pressure is achieved at the cost of recoupling another—or even many others. We can decarbonize the economy with low-carbon energy sources, electric cars, or biofuels, but at the cost of other impacts. Building wind turbines affects the soil, biofuels encourage deforestation, producing a 1 MW solar power plant requires nearly 3,000 tons of water, constructing a dam destroys habitats rich in biodiversity, manufacturing an electric car requires 6 times more material than a gas-powered car, and renewable energy sources demand 10 times more metals per kilowatt-hour than their fossil counterparts.[13] Here's a point we too often tend to forget: every form of production imposes an ecological burden that is multifaceted and systemic.

Let's be careful, then, not to decouple on the left only to recouple on the right. For example, the World Resource Institute[14] reported an absolute decoupling of greenhouse gas emissions in the United States between 2000 and 2014, with a 6% fall in emissions alongside a 28% rise in GDP, a reduction made possible by the transition from coal to natural gas. Not only is this gain likely to be temporary (as we will see), but it could also turn out to be offset by other kinds of emissions. In fact, the extraction of natural gas causes leaks, mostly of methane, a gas whose global warming potential is 28 times that of CO_2. A 2016 study found that methane emissions increased by 30% over the same period, more than canceling out the decrease in CO_2.[15] Same result in another study, which shows that if more than 3% of the methane emitted during shale gas extraction leaked into the atmosphere (the authors' current estimates range from 3.6% to 7.9%), natural gas's carbon footprint would rise to that of coal.[16]

Problem #2: we do not account for imports

It's easy to decarbonize a country's GDP if the products it consumes are manufactured abroad, and so recorded in the domestic emissions of the exporting country. A country that relocates the most polluting forms of production to places where they are less regulated (to a "pollution haven") does not really make its way of life greener, it simply offshores its consequences.

Indeed, most countries use *production indicators* that measure the ecological burden of territorial production—that is, domestic production. The few tons emitted during the production of a car in France will be added to the country's carbon footprint, and therefore to the average carbon footprint of the French people. But if you buy a car produced abroad, those tons will be attributed to the exporting countries, even if the car is used in France. To estimate an economy's ecological footprint, it is therefore better to use *consumption indicators* and thus include the totality of impacts linked to the products consumed in the country, regardless of whether they are produced within national borders or abroad. This is important because today a quarter of global production is exported, which explains why a third of greenhouse gas emissions[17] and 41% of the global material footprint[18] are linked to international trade.

This is the logic of *scopes*, often used by companies in

carbon accounting. Scope 1 includes emissions directly linked to production—that is, everything that is emitted at the time and place of production. Scope 2 adds the indirect emissions associated with the energy purchased by the company. Scope 3 extends this carbon budget to all other indirect emissions: those from the goods and services the company uses, its waste, the transportation of its raw materials, the construction of infrastructure that facilitates its supply, its financial assets and franchises, the use of the products it sells, etc. For example, Apple's carbon footprint in Scopes 1 and 2 represents less than 1% of its footprint in Scope 3, because the latter includes the emissions linked to the manufacturing of its products (70% of the total footprint), their transport (8%), and their use (22%).[19] We don't really talk about scopes at the country level, but the logic is the same: the more we restrict the perimeter of ecological responsibility, the easier it will be to "green" our economy—at least on paper.

The latest IPCC report identifies 32 countries that have experienced an absolute decoupling (GDP/greenhouse gas emissions linked to production), but the number of countries drops to 23 when emissions are measured based on consumption.[20] France is emblematic in this regard. On national soil (production indicator), we indeed have the impression that French emissions are falling—they fell from 548 metric tons of CO_2 equivalent (MTCO2e) in 1990 to 445 MTCO2e in 2018, a 19% decrease over the period.[21] But this trend is deceptive because, over the same period, France's carbon footprint (consumption indicator, the most inclusive perimeter, which includes the emissions of imported products) increased, going from 619 MTCO2e in 1995 to 663 MTCO2e in 2019—a 7% rise.[22] Even if we take into account a recent, more optimistic revision of these figures (605 Mt in 2019 instead of 663 Mt), we still must concede that it is more a matter of stabilization than a genuine decrease.

The same goes for material footprint. The quantity of materials used for national production decreased by 3.3% between 1970 and 2019.[23] But this decline only reflects the relocation of production of the most material-intensive goods and services. In fact, extraction abroad represented 65% of the French economy's total material footprint in 2018, a footprint that expanded by 8% between 1990 and 2019. Figures for France are hard to find, but in 2022 the Spanish government published a footprint study that considered sixteen environmental pressures.[24] The result: since 2013, the weighted index of these resource use indicators stagnated between 2013 and 2018 on national soil while it increased significantly in terms of footprint.

Let's add that these relocations are problematic, as the countries toward which we relocate use production technologies that are much more polluting than our own. The two countries France imports the most from are China and Germany.[25] The carbon intensity of production in these countries (0.46 kg of carbon per $ of GDP for China, and 0.15 kg for Germany) is well above that in France (0.09 kg of carbon per $ of GDP).[26] Shuttering a factory in France may reduce domestic emissions, but it will raise the total carbon footprint if the goods that factory produced are now imported from China or Germany (and the international transport of these products will add further emissions).

When Citroën relocates production of the C3 to Slovakia, the carbon footprint of production increases because 73% of Slovakia's energy is derived from fossil fuels, compared to just 55% in France, thanks to the significant role of nuclear power in French electricity production.[27] Moreover, Slovakia's environmental regulations are certainly not as strict as France's, meaning it is not only the carbon footprint that risks increasing but also other environmental pressures. And if the car is electric, it is very likely that the batteries were produced in Asia in factories powered by coal, once again creating the illusion that the production of electric cars is "green."

Problem #3: decoupling is often only temporary

Reducing the ecological burden in a growing economy involves not only achieving absolute decoupling but also sustaining that decoupling in time for as long as the economy grows. In other words, continuous economic growth requires permanent decoupling.

Yet, just as economy and ecology can decouple at a given moment, they often *recouple* shortly afterward. A few years ago, the International Energy Agency declared that decoupling was "confirmed" after observing the stagnation of global CO2 emissions from 2015 to 2016. But this decoupling was short-lived. It was primarily due to China abandoning some of its coal for oil and gas right as the United States was turning to shale gas. Since shale gas emits 30% less CO2 than petroleum and 50% less than coal, we might hope that such a change would reduce emissions. But the reduction potential from this energy transition is temporary; once it is complete, growth recouples with emissions, even if their volume is lower.

Even a total transition toward low-carbon energy will not fix the problem, because there will still be couplings—with materials, water, and land use, for example. Austria, Finland, and Sweden increased the share of renewables in their energy mix and reduced their emissions between 2005 and 2015. But once this shift is made, the increase in energy demand linked to a rise in production requires an expansion of energy infrastructure, and so additional pressures. This is indeed what happened. Austria reduced its emissions by 0.6% in 2006-2010 and by 1.6% in 2011-2015, but emissions then started to rise again, by 0.3% in 2016-2019. A similar story unfolded in Finland and Sweden; reduction rates accelerated between 2006 and 2015 but slowed back down immediately afterward.

Problem #4: the orders of magnitude are insufficient

The fourth problem with decoupling is that its rates are minuscule. A 3% rise in GDP paired with a 2% fall in CO_2 emissions constitutes, by definition, absolute decoupling, but the same goes for a 3% rise in GDP paired with a 0.02% fall in emissions. You don't need to be a climatologist to understand that the latter does us no good. Ecosystems do not give out points to those who "do their best," and they could not care less if we are "relatively more efficient." To change the course of an ecological crisis, we must not only reduce our total impact but also do so quickly enough.

And let's not forget that most ecological crises are caused by an excess of cumulative impacts over a long period. There is no point in reducing fish consumption by 3% after fisheries have reached a tipping point and collapsed. It will be too late. To be effective, decoupling must be significant enough *and* fast enough to avoid breaching a number of planetary boundaries (global warming, ocean acidification, the erosion of biodiversity, land-use change, the concentration of aerosols in the atmosphere, the depletion of the ozone layer, freshwater consumption, phosphorus and nitrogen cycles, chemical pollution). To put it plainly: if the rate of decoupling is too low, it is pointless.

Let's quickly do the math for mitigating climate change. France reduced its territorial emissions by 1.7% per year from 2010 to 2019 (8.1 fewer Mt each year).[28] Now, let's compare these numbers to France's climate goal, in accordance with the European goal to reduce emissions by 55% below 1990 levels by 2030. This would require a 4.7% reduction in French territorial emissions per year from 2022 to 2030, or 16 fewer Mt each year. That would be double the reduction observed from 2010 to 2019—an already ambitious challenge.

But if we want to limit warming to 1.5°C while leaving room for poor countries to develop, we must make an even greater effort. Without recourse to "negative emissions technologies," the necessary annual reduction must more than double: we need not 5% per year, but 10% to 13%[29] (for a sense of scale, the emissions reduction in France from 2019 to 2020 linked to Covid lockdowns was around 9%). Not in ten or twenty years, but starting today and for decades to come. France's carbon decoupling, even if it is one of the most pronounced in the world (as a result of low-carbon nuclear electricity), is far from sufficient.

On a global scale, the situation is even more troubling. The carbon budget we must respect in order to not surpass 1.5°C of global warming is estimated at 420 billion metric tons of CO2, which corresponds to about eleven years at the current emission rate.[30] Considering the fact that developing countries will have to use a part—and, if we respect principles of equity, the whole—of this carbon budget, even faster reduction rates are required in rich countries. We are far off target.

The situation is the same for the material footprint. From 1992 to 2019, France's material footprint increased by 8% alongside a 53% increase in GDP.[31] Optimists will speak of decoupling, but let's not forget that this decoupling is only *relative*, meaning that the economy's total material footprint continues to rise. In a situation where we must not stabilize but reduce this footprint, the decouplings historically observed are far from sufficient. In 2018 France's material footprint was 17.1 metric tons per person, while a threshold for sustainable resource use should not exceed 3 to 6 metric tons.[32] How do you divide the country's material footprint by four without reducing production and consumption? It is not reasonably possible, as we will see in the following section.

Problem #5: the growth rates are minuscule
According to an oft-cited study, 18 countries[ii] that experi-

---

[ii] Sweden, Romania, France, Ireland, Spain, the United Kingdom, Bulgaria, the Netherlands, Italy, the United States, Germany, Denmark, Portugal, Austria, Hungary, Belgium, Finland, and Croatia.

enced an absolute decoupling reduced their emissions by an average 2.4% per year between 2005 and 2015.[33] Not bad, if this reduction had been accompanied by growth rates of 2% or 3%. But no, these economies experienced a median growth rate of +1.1%. Denmark, Italy, and Spain lead the pack with annual carbon reductions of -3.7%, -3.3%, and -3.2% respectively. Yet it is difficult to call this "green" growth, because these economies' GDPs barely grew (+0.6% for Denmark's GDP over this period), or even shrank (-3.3% for Italy and -3.2% for Spain, a decrease proportional to that of their emissions).

The study's authors found that part of these 18 countries' reduction in emissions is explained by a slowdown in economic growth. "These reductions in energy intensity of GDP [the quantity of energy used to produce a given quantity of GDP] in 2005-2015 do not stand out compared to similar reductions observed since the 1970s, indicating that decreases in energy use in the peak-and-decline group could be explained at least in part by the lower growth in GDP." In short, we haven't really greened the economy, production growth simply slowed down. According to their simulations, "if GDP returns to strong growth [. . .], reductions in energy use may weaken or be reversed unless strong climate and energy policies are implemented."

It is all a matter of degree, and that is precisely the problem. Even in a situation where growth rates are sustainably low, we only manage to green a small part of GDP. Remember that with a 3% growth rate, the economy doubles in size every 24 years. The faster the growth, the more we must accelerate the reduction of the ecological burden. Every percentage point of growth thus complicates a task that would have been relatively easier (and less risky) with a lower volume of production.

Progress report: in the vast majority of countries around the world, growth is not green. The rare cases of absolute decoupling that we observe are usually short-term exceptions during periods of low growth, which address only a portion of environmental pressures and often overlook imports. And even in the best cases, the ecological reductions achieved through "green" growth are minimal. A disturbing truth for proponents of the decoupling theory: green growth is a myth.

An Unlikely Decoupling

The future is not written, some will say, and the historical absence of decoupling doesn't necessarily mean that it will not materialize tomorrow. Here is the heart of the controversy: is it plausible that sufficient decoupling between ecological burden and GDP growth could take place in the coming years? This is the question economists are debating today. According to my research, believing in it remains a risky bet, for at least five reasons.

Limit #1: the increase in energy spending
All production, directly or indirectly, requires resources, starting with energy. Some economists might say that energy represents less than 2% of France's GDP, making it a marginal sector. Let Australian economist Steve Keen respond, by explaining that without energy, workers would be nothing but corpses, and machines nothing but sculptures.[34] There is no economy without energy, and no energy without materials to build wind turbines, solar panels, or nuclear power plants (and of course, no materials without energy to extract and produce them).

We must therefore find this energy, which is no small feat, as the availability of natural resources depends not only on their absolute quantity but also on their quality and accessibility. We often hear about the gigantic flow of solar energy to Earth: 1.56×10^{20} joules per hour, enough in a few hours to supply all of humanity's annual primary energy consumption. A godsend for infinite growth? Far from it, because only a tiny fraction of this energy is usable, and capturing it requires significant quantities of materials. Some might argue that all we have to do is increase the rate of capture by developing new technologies, but this argument quickly hits its limits—we'll come back to it.

For now, let's just note an economic principle related to our capacity to mobilize resources: the principle of least effort. It is difficult to talk about "laws" in economics, but this axiom may be one of the most solid in the discipline. It's the metaphor of the low-hanging fruit. When confronted with a problem, we often look for the easiest solution first, the one that requires the least effort. Indeed, why bother extracting oil several kilometers under the ocean when we could find some a few hundred meters deep right nearby?

This principle aptly describes the history of our energy system. The options cheapest to extract are generally mobilized first, and in our case, have already been exhausted. Extracting those that remain becomes an increasingly complex process, more demanding in terms of technology, more energy-intensive, and so generally more costly and less profitable (let's also add: often riskier for the surrounding ecosystems). This is the case for low-concentration metal and mineral deposits, oil sands, deep offshore wells, and reserves situated in polar regions or near densely populated cities, like Paris's shale gas.

We can measure the difficulty of access. For energy resources, we talk about Energy Return on Energy Invested (EROI), which is the ratio between the amount of energy made available and the amount of energy spent to extract it. For example, an EROI of 10:1 for oil means that it takes burning one barrel of oil to extract ten others. The same applies to renewable energy. While a solar panel can capture energy during the twenty to thirty years of its lifespan, its manufacturing also requires a certain amount of energy. The ratio of usable energy to energy used is what we call the energy return on investment.

A falling energy return describes a situation where we must sacrifice more and more intermediate resources to obtain the same quantity of final resources. It's a kind of "energy cannibalism"[35] where energy infrastructure consumes an increasingly significant chunk of the energy it produces. Instead of investing a single barrel of oil to extract twenty (a relatively easy extraction), I have to sacrifice five to extract the same amount. The energy used to extract a barrel of oil is energy that will not be available to produce other things, and so a loss of potential growth.

The same is true for renewable energy. A solar panel will take some time to repay the energy that was necessary for its construction—this is known as "energy payback time." This delay, which depends on the method of production, the panels' efficiency, and their lifespan, places a limit on the growth of new panel manufacturing. Without constantly improving these three factors, it is not possible for an energy infrastructure, even a 100% renewable one, to sustain continuous growth in energy demand.

While an economy with a rising EROI can grow faster and faster because energy and materials are more and more readily available, an economy with a falling EROI will find growth increasingly difficult to achieve. The problem—and this is a direct consequence of the principle of least effort—is that EROIs are rarely on the rise, or at least never for long. If all economic activity requires energy and materials, and if more and more energy and materials are needed to extract them, then the increase in energy use becomes an obstacle to decoupling.

Today, energy returns are falling, especially those of fossil fuels. The EROI for global oil and gas production went from 23:1 in 1992 (burning 1 barrel allows the extraction of 23) to 33:1 in 1999, thanks to improvements in extraction techniques, but then fell to 18:1 in 2005.[36] Taking fossil and renewable energies into account, another study finds that the EROI of the global energy system dropped from 7:1 in 1995 to 6:1 in 2018.[37]

With regard to renewables, energy returns are stable but low. The authors simulate what would happen to the average EROI by 2050 if renewable energy sources were to reach 30% or 50% of the energy mix. In the first case, the average EROI falls from the current 6:1 to 5:1. In the second case, it plummets to 3:1. Remember: the lower the energy return, the harder it is to green economic activities. The same downward trend appears in another study,[38] this time focusing only on electricity: in a 100% renewable electricity scenario, the average EROI at the global level would fall from 12:1 in 2010 to 5.8:1 in 2050.

Materials face the same issues. The average concentration of copper in extracted ore went from 4% in the 1930s to 1% today, a situation shared by other minerals.[39] Lower concentration rates mean that larger volumes of material must be extracted and moved to obtain the same quantity of ore, which requires more energy (and has a greater impact on ecosystems). A 2011 report estimates that the extraction of materials now requires moving three times more matter than it did a century ago.[40] Today, this ratio continues to deteriorate. A dynamic all the more worrying given how much higher the mineral intensity of renewable energy is than that of fossil fuels—for example, 1 kWh of renewable energy requires ten times more metal than 1 kWh of fossil fuel.

The vise's jaws are tightening—not only do renewable energy sources have a lower EROI, but they also require more minerals whose concentration in deposits is diminishing. We would be wrong to think that a 100% green energy economy could grow forever. It is physically impossible, short of having access to an infinite supply of sufficiently concentrated material deposits, which is evidently not the case on Earth.

Limit #2: rebound effects
Wouldn't it be enough to produce more efficiently? Indeed, it is often said that green growth will be made possible by

efficiency gains, meaning by reducing the amount of energy and materials required for production. We tend to think that the more efficiently we deploy a resource, the less it will get used. What is less often said is that these efficiency gains give rise to "rebound effects": a situation where a technological or social improvement that allows us to use a resource more efficiently results in the intensification of its use. This is the "Jevons paradox," named after British economist William Stanley Jevons who in the nineteenth century demonstrated that improvements in steam engine efficiency were followed not by a decrease, but by an increase in the total consumption of coal in the economy.

The rebound effect can be *direct* when the efficiency gain is reinvested in the same activity; we buy a more fuel-efficient hybrid car but, for that very reason, we end up using it more often. If the rebound is less than the initial gain, it is called *partial*: a new car consumes four times less than the old and we drive it twice as much, reducing gas use by a total of 50%. A *total* rebound, by contrast, cancels out all gains. If, in the previous example, I multiply the distance the car travels by six, the total consumption of gas will go up, even though the new car is more fuel-efficient than the old. In France, the direct rebound effect related to engine efficiency and car usage is between 30 and 55%, which means that a third of the efficiency gains are canceled out by the increase in distances traveled (a *partial* rebound).[41]

The rebound effect can also be *indirect*; the money we no longer spend on gas thanks to a new, more fuel-efficient car will be spent on other activities that emit greenhouse gasses, like a plane trip. We can see here that these indirect effects affect strategies for both production efficiency and consumption restraint. As in the car example (a rebound from efficiency), cutting out meat reduces food expenses and creates savings that can potentially rebound in other areas of consumption (a rebound from restraint).

These rebound effects exist at the household or business level (the microeconomic level) but also at the macroeconomic level, where efficiency gains in one sector rebound across the economy as a whole. For example, the shale gas boom in the United States lowered the price of energy and so production costs, which encouraged companies to produce more, and thus emit more CO2. According to one study,[42] the macroeconomic rebound in the United States is 100%, meaning that all the energy saved through efficiency gains was used elsewhere in the economy. Same thing happened in France:[43] in less than two years, 101% of the energy savings achieved through eco-innovation and consumption restraint were used up. At the level of the economy as a whole, the rebound is total, which means that efficiency gains failed to reduce energy consumption.

These rebound phenomena appear in every sector. Even if internal combustion engines have become more efficient in recent decades, the emissions linked to transportation have never ceased to rise: up 9% from 1990 to 2019 in France.[44] While each individual car is less energy-intensive (a 22% improvement from 2005 to 2018 for gas vehicles), the overall vehicle fleet consumes more because there are more cars in circulation (a 44% increase in car sales over the same period).[45] We often laud the energy efficiency of using LED outdoor lighting instead of outdated light bulbs. However, according to a 2017 study, the energy savings are more than offset by an expansion of the surface area lit, itself permitted by the reduced lighting cost due to improved energy efficiency.[46] Looking at the use of 69 materials from 1960 to 2010, one study notes that only six of them experienced an absolute decline, four of which (asbestos, beryllium, mercury, and thallium) did so because of legal restrictions due to toxicity issues.[47]

Let's take another example. Proponents of 5G boast that relay antennas are more energy efficient. But to reduce energy consumption (and so decouple), the gains in energy efficiency must make up for the rise in data traffic. Based on past trends, this seems unlikely. In fact, data consumption increased from 0.7 gigabytes per connected computer in 2014 to 8 gigabytes in 2019. (Watching a movie in 8K will require 32 times more data than today's high definition.)[48] To avoid a total rebound effect from 5G, the energy efficiency gains[49] over the period would need to exceed a factor of 10.

This is a *direct* rebound effect, but it doesn't stop there. Many existing phones are not compatible with 5G, meaning that a widespread switch to this technology will require upgrading a large number of devices (there are nearly 65 million smartphones in France today). The problem is that a phone's usage represents only 20% of its total energy footprint, with the rest coming from its manufacturing.[50] A large-scale upgrade of smartphones in France would therefore increase the carbon footprint of the digital sector by a quarter[iii] (on top of the impact in terms of material footprint: it takes 70 kg of raw materials to produce a single smartphone, or 600 times the weight of the phone itself).[51]

Compared to the potential gains in energy efficiency, we realize that the shift to 5G will increase the digital sector's ecological footprint, both in terms of emissions and extraction of natural resources (with the associated destruction of ecosystems, water footprint, and various forms of pollution).[52]

Let's keep going: which types of production will benefit from 5G, and where will the profits and wages it generates be spent? In a globalized economy where money can be used to buy almost anything, all purchasing power is potentially polluting power. A capitalist economy is a little bit like a pinball

---

[iii] The carbon footprint of digital technology represents 2% of national emissions, or about 13.26 million metric tons of CO_2 in 2019. Producing 64.7 million smartphones at 55 kg/CO_2 per phone would generate 3.5 million metric tons of CO_2, which is 26% of the total emissions from digital technology in France.

machine: whether we spend or invest in clean sectors (which are often not very profitable), sooner or later the money will drop to the bottom, that is, toward the most lucrative activities. The euros spent at the local food co-op will fund wages, which will be used to cover gas costs, for example, or saved and thus indirectly invested in other extractive activities. If we want to reduce our total footprint while avoiding rebound effects, it is essential that we stop growing.

Limit #3: the ecological footprint of services
Another hope is that decoupling lies in the tertiarization of the economy, meaning the shift from extractive and manufacturing industries to services. The latter are indeed less ecologically intensive than primary and secondary activities like construction, agriculture, or industry (the industrial sector emits nine times more CO_2 than the tertiary sector for an equivalent value added).[53] That said, it would be wrong to think that a service economy could be completely dematerialized.

Firstly, to have an effect on the total ecological burden, tertiarization must translate to an *absolute* and not just *relative* reduction in primary and secondary activities. If these stay at the same level, with the addition of services on top of them, the impact of services will add to that of industrial and agricultural emissions. Hard to call that an "ecological transition"—it would just be a form of relative decoupling from the top.

The problem is that this tertiarization is already complete in most OECD countries; the services portion of GDP often exceeds 70% (industry represents 13% of GDP in France). What's left are sectors that cannot be dematerialized: transportation (31% of territorial emissions in 2019), industry, and especially heavy industry like the chemical, steel, and cement industries (19%), agriculture (19%), construction (17%), energy conversion (10%), and waste management (4%).[54] It is in these sectors that we find the quasi-totality of emissions.

Furthermore, services remain tied to other sectors. The development of new services adds to old activities instead of replacing them. We subscribe to Netflix *with* and not *instead of* a computer. Ostensibly "immaterial" products require material infrastructure. To eat out, you have to travel to a restaurant; we listen to music on devices; a massage parlor must be heated, lit, and of course, built; the internet cannot function without cables and energy.[55] Amazon makes profits "online" but the trucks that deliver those products and the packaging that protects them are very real. The expansion of services is difficult to accomplish without ecological pressures because it is part of a complex economy that grows as an integrated whole.

We often speak of digital technology as a boon, but is that really the case? Information and communication technologies emit 830 million metric tons of CO2 every year globally, or 4% of global emissions in 2020.[iv] One study even calculates that digital technology could consume up to 51% of the world's electricity by 2030, thus contributing to 23% of global greenhouse gas emissions.[56] The entertainment industry may be relatively less energy- and material-intensive than certain heavy industries, but it nevertheless remains heavily material. A team of researchers at the University of Bristol calculated that all the videos watched on YouTube in 2016 generated 11 million metric tons of carbon equivalent, or the annual footprint of the city of Frankfurt.[57] A report by the International Energy Agency estimates that watching one hour of content on Netflix produces between 36 g and 82 g CO2e, or the equivalent of traveling half a kilometer by car.[58] In *L'Enfer numérique* (*The Digital Nightmare*), Guillaume Pitron estimates the footprint of an

---

[iv] "Re-think your digital habits," Digital for Planet, December 2020. Digital technology runs primarily on fossil energy. A report by Greenpeace ("How Clear is Your Cloud?," 2012) declares that 39.4% of the electricity used by Facebook's data centers derives from coal (it's nearly half for Apple). But even once we fix this problem in an economy with 100% renewable energy, the question of raw materials and the consequences of their extraction will remain.

email to be between 0.5 and 20 g of carbon, or the equivalent of leaving a lightbulb on for one hour.[59] Kyle Devine (University of Oslo) and Matt Brennan (University of Glasgow) have discovered that, even if music has become almost completely digital, it is, in terms of greenhouse gases, more polluting than it has ever been: going from 140 million kg CO2e in 1977 to 157 in 2000 and 200-350 in 2016.[60]

The ultimate example: cryptocurrencies, the archetype of dematerialized value. The Cambridge Bitcoin Electricity Consumption Index reports that bitcoin is responsible for an annualized consumption of 131 TWh worldwide, or about a third of the electricity consumed in France in 2019. At the global level, the digital currency bitcoin produces 69 MTCO2e per year, the carbon footprint of Sweden.[61] The more bitcoin gains in value, the more mining operations intensify—a perfect example of a coupling between monetary value and ecological footprint that captures the situation at the macroeconomic level. Moreover, given that the majority of transactions in financial markets are conducted by algorithms that rely on machine learning, we also need to train these robots (according to a study out of MIT, training an artificial intelligence model emits as much carbon as five cars do in their lifetimes).[62]

And let's not forget the rebound effects: everyone working in the service industry spends part of their earnings on material products. What is more, while the carbon footprint of Facebook or X is smaller than an airline's, the ads we see on these platforms are often for highly ecologically-intensive goods. Growth in these companies' "immaterial" activity therefore means more material consumption through their employees' salaries, additional investment into other sectors via investments of their cash balances[63] and dividends paid to shareholders, not to mention all the purchases incentivized by online advertising.

In short, tertiarization rhymes with neither decarbonization nor dematerialization. In a 2019 study, a researcher at York

University in Canada reviewed data for 217 countries, covering the period from 1991 to 2017.[64] The results: deindustrialized economies have never really decarbonized. The tertiarization of an economy lowers its carbon intensity per unit of GDP (relative decoupling), but it raises the total ecological burden. Like any transition, the decoupling gains are temporary and, once tertiarization is complete, the growth of the service sector brings additional pressures.

Limit #4: the limits of recycling
Now let's talk about the circular economy. Some argue that green growth would be possible if all of the materials needed to produce new goods were extracted from our waste. It's a noble aim. An ecological economy should be as circular as possible, but this circularity runs up against at least three limits.

The first limit, and without a doubt the simplest: not all waste can be recycled. It's hard to recycle a barrel of oil once it's been burned. Fuels, incinerated biomass, food, fodder, and all dissipative materials (brake pads, fertilizers, pesticides, metals mixed into paint, microplastics, etc.) cannot be reused or recycled because they simply cannot be retrieved. For every 100 billion metric tons of resources extracted globally each year, 37 billion are irretrievable.[65]

Then there is waste whose recycling is too complex. Even for the most modular smartphone (the Fairphone 2 at the time of the study), only 30% of the materials are recyclable.[66] In 2018, European Union countries only recycled 38% of the waste from electrical and electronic equipment, only 8% more than in 2013.[67] The increasing complexity of composite materials and metallic alloys complicates their recycling, which explains why certain metals are almost never recycled (a state-of-the-art smartphone contains around fifty metals, while a phone in the 1990s contained fewer than twenty).[68] The same goes for products made of different plastics: only 9% of the total quantity of plastic produced has been recycled.[69] The smaller and more complex products become, the more difficult their recycling—another obstacle to decoupling.

Also, what is recyclable in theory is not necessarily recyclable in practice. Even if the technological process exists, the financial incentives aren't always there. Most solar panels are not recycled and end up in landfills (in 2016, solar panels represented 0.5% of all electronic waste, or 250,000 metric tons).[70] There are only a handful of sites in the world that recycle solar panels. Single-use plastics are a similar case: for the past thirty years, their global recycling rate has oscillated between 10% and 15%. Of the 130 million metric tons of plastic waste in 2019, 35% was burned, 31% buried in landfills, and 19% dumped directly into the environment.[71]

Moreover, with better recycling come rebound effects. In *Recyclage, le grand enfumage* (*Recycling: The Big Smokescreen*), Flore Berlingen notes that even though in ten years the collection of used electrical and electronic equipment leaped from zero to 50% of the total discarded, this was not enough to counter the rise in the quantity of equipment put on the market (+20% by weight, and +45% in the number of units).[72] Improvements in recycling are more than canceled out by the increase in replacement rates (a computer's lifespan was eleven years in the 1990s, today it has been reduced to four years;[73] a smartphone's lifespan in France is only two years).[74] In fact, if recycling rates rise at a slower pace than average product lifespans fall (as is the case today), the total footprint will increase.

The size of the recycling sector should give us pause. According to the Fédération Professionnelle des Entreprises du Recyclage, the sector's revenue in France is around 8.5 million euros, with 30,800 workers.[75] Investment in the sector is modest: 625 million euros in 2019. When we compare this to corporate marketing spending (media advertising revenue in 2019 was close to 15 billion euros),[76] it becomes clear that recycling rates are unlikely to keep pace with the rise in production, which is partly fueled by advertising and planned obsolescence.

And even if recycling rates were to reach record levels (say 90%), there would still be a significant loss of material (half of the materials would be lost after just 6 successive rounds of recycling), and the consumption of virgin raw materials would need to increase to satisfy demand.

The second limit: a strictly circular economy cannot grow perpetually. If the economy continues to grow, it will demand more materials than were available in previous periods. It's basic arithmetic: in an economy that uses more and more resources, the quantity of used materials that can be recycled will always be less than the quantity of materials required to produce more, even if we could recycle 100% of all waste without using any energy. Trying to make a circular economy grow would be like hoping to recycle the materials from the International Space Station to build two new ones, each the same size as the original.

In 2020, the global economy consumed 100.6 Gt of natural resources: 50.8 Gt of minerals, 10.1 Gt of metals, 15.1 Gt of fossil fuels, and 24.6 Gt of biomass.[77] Of this quantity, we saw that 37 Gt end up as irretrievable waste because they are dispersed into the environment (e.g., burned oil and biomass, which are recycled over long periods of time). Another 31 Gt are integrated into products with long lifespans like buildings and cars, and 32.6 Gt are thrown out. The majority of this waste (74%) is not recycled, leaving only 8.6 Gt of materials that can be reused as raw materials the following year. Even if humanity consumed only the same quantity as the previous year, it would still need to extract between 92 Gt (at the current recycling rate) and 68 Gt (assuming a 100% recycling rate) of new resources from nature. It is therefore mathematically impossible to produce more the next year using only the waste available.

The third limit: we cannot recycle to infinity. The laws of

thermodynamics remind us that perpetual movement is a physical impossibility. Every recycling process requires energy and, most of the time, new materials, which must also be recycled at some point, requiring the use of even more new materials, and so on ad infinitum. Recycling one ton of scrap metal spares us the equivalent of 57% of the CO_2 emissions required to produce one ton of primary steel.[78] However, the recycling process will still emit almost one ton of carbon equivalent. Energy consumption leads to increased energy spending, which hinders decoupling. The two factors limit each other: we cannot continue to expand our energy infrastructure without materials, and we cannot recycle new materials without expanding our energy infrastructure.

Since materials inevitably degrade over time (in keeping with the law of entropy), they can only be recycled a limited number of times before having to be used to make lower-quality products. Sooner or later, all recycling becomes *downcycling* (or "degraded recycling"). For example, plastic bottles can be recycled into plastic fiber for clothing, but not back into plastic bottles. The cellulose fiber in paper can only tolerate three to six recycling cycles, each time resulting in lower-quality products. The crucial takeaway from all this data is that an economy cannot simultaneously be circular and growing. Once again, it is not a matter of discouraging recycling, but of admitting that it will not allow us to green growth.

Limit #5: technological obstacles

"Show how innovation can be a solution to the ecological limits of economic growth." This was the essay topic given to students in France for the 2021 baccalaureate exam in economic and social sciences. A real trump card for proponents of decoupling, technology often closes the debate: decoupling will be made possible by technical progress. But for that to be true, such progress would have to prioritize eco-innovations, those innovations would have to replace polluting infrastructure, and all of this would need to happen at a fast enough speed.

First of all, not all innovations are green. Horizontal drilling and hydraulic fracturing are also innovations, as are the discovery of new routes for cargo ships in the Arctic, the development of new advertising techniques that incentivize consumption, and the invention of new toxic chemicals. These innovations create new problems or exacerbate old ones, thus hindering decoupling. What matters, then, is eco-innovation—the kind that minimizes the use of resources.

What is the magnitude of these innovations? Hard to say. A 2016 study analyzed the patents filed by automobile manufacturers in 80 countries between 1978 and 2005.[79] Distinguishing "green innovations" (which promote the development of electric vehicles) from "polluting innovations" (which promote the development of combustion engines), the study showed that the number of polluting patents has always been higher than the number of green patents. Even in 2005, when the difference was the smallest, there were twice as many polluting patents as green patents. Therefore, even if eco-innovation went from a few patents in the mid-1980s to over 600 in 2005, polluting innovation followed a similar growth trajectory.

According to this same study, the inertia of past investments is particularly strong: the more a company has invested in a technology, the more it will fund research and development activities centered on that technology. A "path dependency" leads companies that have substantially innovated in combustion engines (the majority of companies) to primarily invest in that type of vehicle, and not in electric cars. It's a positive feedback loop: the more polluting patents there are, the more companies invest in polluting innovation. This explains the impasse that electric vehicles are at in France, where in 2020 they represented only 0.4% of the vehicle fleet.

What we observe in the automobile sector can be generalized

to the economy as a whole. If companies are incentivized to innovate in order to lower their production costs, they will naturally focus on the most expensive factors of production. But most natural factors of production are practically free, unlike labor and machinery. Companies will innovate to be able to use less labor and less machinery, while concerning themselves proportionally less with their consumption of energy and materials.

A second reason for doubt: the replacement of polluting energy sources. It is not enough for new technologies to emerge (innovation), they must also replace the old ones in a process of "exnovation." What's the point of inventing new low-carbon technologies (electric cars and bicycles, solar panels, wind turbines, or heat pumps) if they cannot, in practice, replace their fossil fuel counterparts? To reduce the total ecological footprint, we must not just *innovate* but also *exnovate*.

The problem is that this process is slow and difficult. First, some polluting technologies are stubbornly resilient, even when they have become obsolete—the notorious "zombie technologies."[80] This is the case with diesel cars used for short distances in cities, for example, but also with oil heating, which is more expensive and more polluting than its alternatives.

Most polluting infrastructures (power plants, buildings, transportation systems, etc.) require heavy investments, which creates inertia around their replacement. A refinery has a lifespan of about 100 years, a thermal power plant 40 years, and an airplane and a car roughly 30 and 15 years, respectively, and heating equipment is replaced every 15-20 years. If I buy an SUV in 2025, it will be on the road until 2040. The urgency of ecological action is measured in years, not decades—it is therefore impossible to wait peacefully for polluting infrastructures to reach the end of their life.

The energy sector is a good illustration of this technological stockpiling phenomenon. Developing renewable energy is far from sufficient to curb the impact of fossil fuels. In the past, we have not so much substituted as added new energy sources.[81] One study finds that each unit of low-carbon energy has replaced less than one quarter of a unit of its fossil counterpart.[82] What we often describe as an energy "transition" is more like the layering of fossil, nuclear, and renewable kinds of energy.

Even if we were to decide to decarbonize the entire global energy mix, this process would take time. In France, seven to nine years elapse between the decision to install wind turbine parks and the start of operations, a delay as long as fifteen years for a nuclear power plant.[83] As a reminder: the latest carbon budget for 1.5°C announced by the IPCC will be exhausted in 11 years, if 2021 emission rates remain stable.

The International Renewable Energy Agency tells us that fueling continuous growth without exceeding the 2°C threshold would require the installation of 12,200 GW of solar and wind capacity by 2050—more than 8 times the current capacity.[84] One study showed that to decarbonize electricity in the United States by 2050, we would need to build energy infrastructure at a rate 14 times faster than those observed in the last half-century.[85] This massive transformation of the energy mix would also require a significant quantity of materials, and these materials are, for now, extracted and processed using oil.

The layering of technologies does not only concern energy. Computers did not lead to dematerialization: we now use computers *on top of* paper. The boom of synthetic rubber after World War II did not prevent the production and consumption of natural rubber from consistently increasing throughout the century. Likewise, the explosion of synthetic fibers like polyester and nylon did not replace the production of natural fibers; while global annual production of synthetic fibers went from less than 2 Mt in 1950 to more than 60 Mt today, production of natural fibers more than tripled, going from less than 10 to about 30 Mt.[86] Today we use far more wood than in the Middle

Ages, more coal than in the 19th century, and more oil than in the 20th century. Instead of replacing polluting technologies, innovation most often piles new techniques on top of the old.

A researcher at Washington State University assessed the impact of eco-innovation patents on the ecological footprint of the economy as a whole.[87] The study covers 35 countries (including France) over the period from 1982 to 2016. The results: a 1% increase in patents for environmental technologies is associated with only a 0.005% decrease in the ecological footprint, a marginal correlation (by comparison, each percentage point of GDP growth raises emissions by 0.2%). Expecting technological progress to green the economy is as naïve as thinking that buying a few diet books is all it takes to lose weight.

Let's move on to the third and final limit of the innovation trump card: the speed of technological progress. We should first note that, from a purely mathematical perspective, productivity gains can only reduce the ecological footprint of a continuously growing economy if they increase enough each year to compensate for the rise in resource consumption due to that growth. If my economy doubles in size every 35 years, I need to generate productivity gains of 100% over the same period just to keep the ecological footprint constant. Thus, the greater the annual growth, the more significant the annual productivity gains must be.

Yet the productivity gains necessary for our economies to completely decouple seem disproportionate when compared to those we have achieved so far. Relying solely on technology to mitigate climate change requires extreme rates of eco-innovation that have never before been seen—a risky gamble.

Take commercial aviation, for example.[88] Since the 1970s, its energy intensity—meaning the amount of energy consumed per passenger-kilometer—has declined by 80%. But that has not been enough to reduce the sector's emissions, because these efficiency gains were more than offset by a 1,236% rise in traffic over the same period. In the end, the aviation footprint tripled in fifty years, despite technical progress.

Let's take a more general example, with a scenario offered by British economist Tim Jackson.[89] Consider a hypothetical where the global economic growth rate is 1.3% per capita per year and population growth is 0.8%. If we take the average annual reduction in carbon intensity observed since 1990 (0.6%), we realize that carbon emissions would continue to increase by 1.5% each year (1.3% + 0.8% − 0.6% = 1.5%). To reduce emissions by 90% in 2050, carbon intensity would need to fall by 8% per year. Add the fact that improvements in global carbon intensity have slowed since the start of the century (from 1.28% between 1960 and 2000 to 0% between 2000 and 2014).[90] Even if we only consider rich countries, those that invest the most in eco-innovation, the rates not only remain too low to ensure technological decoupling, but are also declining (−1.91% from 1970 to 2000, and −1.61% between 2000 and 2014).

These declining rates should not be surprising. Technology is a process of diminishing returns. Because of the physical limits of technologies, there comes a point where it is no longer possible to improve their productivity, or only marginally so. Engines, wind turbines, and solar panels have a theoretical maximum efficiency that cannot be exceeded. Once we hit this threshold (which is impossible in practice, we can only get close), continuous growth will automatically restart the increase of its ecological footprint.

An empirical study of American patents from 1970 to 2005 shows that it is increasingly costly and difficult to innovate.[91] This is also true for eco-innovations, like those in solar energy, wind energy, or recycling. As research progresses, it becomes increasingly complex and costly for increasingly minor improvements.

Another study examines changes in total factor productivity

(how economists measure technological progress) from 1759 to 2015.[92] The result: the marginal returns on innovation are shrinking. This is also the case for the famous "Moore's Law" (today it takes 18 times more researchers to double the power of a microprocessor than it did in the 1970s), and the same trend applies to all fields.[93] Contrary to what optimists would like to believe, technological decoupling is becoming less and less likely because innovating demands more and more time and effort.

The hypothesis of a dramatic decoupling that allows us to green GDP and reconcile economic growth with ecological sustainability does not pass the numbers test. Instances of decoupling are rare—rare and deceptive because they are partial, temporary, often relative, and always of insufficient magnitude. It is hard to contest this result after the section on mitigation in the latest IPCC report laid the green growth theory to rest once and for all:[94] "absolute decoupling is not sufficient to avoid consuming the remaining CO_2 emission budget under the global warming limit of 1.5°C or 2°C and to avoid climate breakdown. Even if all countries decouple in absolute terms this might still not be sufficient."[95]

Can we do better? Given the arguments presented in this chapter, there is ample reason for doubt. But are we ready to risk ecological collapse to find out? Probably not. Let's return to the smoker analogy that opened this chapter. In their situation, reason would undoubtedly lead the patient to reduce as much as possible the primary cause of their pulmonary lesions. We can therefore reasonably believe that they would quit smoking—or at least attempt to (the restraint and degrowth solution). Why act differently when it comes to the ecological crisis?

3
Market Versus Society
The Social Limits to Growth

Production cannot go against nature, or at least not for long. That was the idea of the previous chapter: any economy that degrades its ecosystems is sawing off the branch it sits on. But that is not its only limit. All production processes rely not only on nature, but also on *nurture*—our capacity to care for ourselves and others. Without the entire social infrastructure that we maintain through non-economic interactions, market production would simply be impossible.

And just like the Earth's ecosystems, these *sociosystems* cannot grow indefinitely, because they depend on the time we devote to them and that time is fundamentally limited. Sooner or later, the exponential increase in market activity runs up against what feminist economists call the *reproductive capacities* of a society.

The Reproductive Sphere

Let's start at the beginning: "Who cooked Adam Smith's dinner?" asks Swedish journalist Katrina Marçal.[1] The answer: his mother. Without the generous Margaret Douglas to take care of him all his life, poor Adam would certainly never have become the intellectual we know today. In other words, the production of Adam Smith's work depended on the *reproduction* of his capacity to write, a task that fell to his mother. In this chapter, I will show that this dependency logic of the economic on the extra-economic applies to all forms of production. Behind every product hides a social infrastructure whose role is indispensable.

Take for example the book you are reading. The computer on which I wrote it, the time I spent on it, as well as the skills I applied (what economists call *factors of production*) explain only a small part of the final result. There is a whole series of other elements without which this book could never have existed: my friends, family, and roommates and their emotional support, the countless discussions with my colleagues, the invaluable comments from the army of proofreaders who generously enriched the text, the Kazakh hacker who gave me access to academic articles, the people who grew the food that kept me alive and those who helped me get around, or even the beauty of the Anglet beaches that accompanied me on my daily strolls. It's a long list. What is certain is that, left to myself in a desert with pen and paper, I would not have produced much of anything.

In feminist economics, these are called *forces of reproduction*.[2] The reproductive sphere encompasses everything that contributes to the care, maintenance, renewal, and improvement of our ability to work, and more generally to the smooth functioning of social life. It notably includes domestic tasks—the mutual aid within a family or among friends—but also reciprocity, informal work, volunteering, community engagement and activism, and, in general, all those small acts that foster collective life. On the one hand, there are short-term and recurring elements that reproduce the labor force, like food, housing, healthcare, clothing, and all the daily activities that keep us alive. On the other, there are the long-term elements related to education, culture, safety, and the quality of our environment.[3]

The reproductive sphere is actually much more vast than the productive one. The average day of a French person is composed of 2 hours and 32 minutes of professional activities and 40 minutes of study, 3 hours and 31 minutes of domestic activities, 12 hours and 14 minutes of personal care and rest (including 8 hours and 29 minutes of sleep), and 5 hours and 3 minutes of leisure.[4] The average French person therefore spends only 10% of their day working. If we exclude students, the unemployed, and retirees from this average to focus on employed people, we find that women work on average 4 hours and 10 minutes per day, and men 5 hours and 19 minutes—or only 17% and 22% of a full day. Employed women devote 3 hours and 43 minutes a day to domestic activities (employed men only 2 hours and 12 minutes) and almost 11 hours and 47 minutes to rest (including sleep), a figure similar to that for men. Domestic work, according to a 2010 calculation, represents between one and two times the duration of paid work, or between one and two thirds of GDP depending on the wage attributed to it.[5]

The basic premise of this chapter is the following: those who produce are themselves produced. For example, for a baker to be able to make bread, they need a recipe, ingredients, an oven, and energy (the *factors of production*), but also self-confidence, a rested and healthy body, a balanced mood, and a healthy environment (the *factors of reproduction*). A depressed baker would be as incapable of producing a baguette as a baker with no oven or flour. In other words: all economic activity relies on extra-economic activity.

Too often, economists' "production functions" only take into account what is used at the time of production, at the place where it occurs. In the baker's case, for example, the oven, the ingredients, and the hours spent at the bakery to make bread. But each factor of production (nature and tools, working time, and institutions) is itself the product of a process of production beyond the quantifiable economy—we could speak of *social and ecological production*. Imagine three concentric circles of varying sizes: the sphere of market production is embedded within the larger sphere of social reproduction, which is in turn embedded within the economy of the living world or sphere of ecological reproduction. Embedding means contact. What happens outside the factory affects what takes place inside, and vice versa, and what we too readily call "growth" is sometimes only the appropriation of value that already exists, un-monetized.

Thus, ecosystems provide services like pollination, water purification, or climate regulation—in Fritjof Capra's words, the biosphere is a "web of life."[6] In the same way, *sociosystems* deliver a multitude of crucial services: our parents educate us, our friends look out for us, a whole host of people—from caring neighbors to volunteers—take care of our health, our safety, and our well-being. It's a *web of social life*, a vital tissue both indispensable and fragile. We find these reproductive activities at the individual level (taking the time for a nap), the household level (my partner taking care of the kids so that I can take a nap), the community level (my work colleagues respecting my need to take a nap), and the societal level (a labor law allowing me to take a nap). Without this ability to rest and all the infrastructure that enables it, our productive capacity wouldn't last long.

The Economy's Time Budget

Like all productive activity, reproductive tasks take time. If the availability of energy and materials represents a biophysical limit to all human activity, the availability of time represents its social limit. GDP can grow exponentially to infinity (in theory), but the time available for production hits physical limits (24 hours per day), physiological limits (16 waking hours), and social limits (let's say between 5 and 7 hours of labor per day, depending on the conditions).

Capitalism never sleeps,[7] and that is one of its greatest

contradictions. More and more businesses organize themselves into rotating shifts with atypical hours to ensure constant production. We can optimize production up to a certain limit (soon we'll see that many of these optimizations are undesirable), but one thing is certain: no matter our mode of social organization, we will never work more than 24 hours a day.

Every economy therefore functions with a limited time budget. An hour spent devising online advertisements is an hour that will not be spent growing vegetables; and an hour spent in the fields is an hour less for helping the neighbor carry up her groceries or writing articles on Wikipedia. If the finitude of natural resources implies that no material production can grow indefinitely (the thesis of the previous chapter), that of available time implies that no production *at all* can grow indefinitely. So, we could say that economics consists in "collectively organizing the sharing of our finitudes."[8]

Though this logic may shock certain economists for whom time is infinitely expandable through technical progress, it resonates with our experience of daily life. Doing the dishes, caring for children, cleaning the house, gardening—all these tasks require time, and we are all used to allotting our hours to such and such activity, and to organizing ourselves with family, colleagues, and friends to share the workload. The division of labor is one of the most essential economic relationships, one of the many protocols for the careful management of limited resources. Why would this fundamental limit cease to exist at the macroeconomic level? It may disappear in certain simplistic economic models, but not in real life. A person has 24 hours a day at their disposal; and that holds true for all 67 million people in France.

With 30 million economically active people, and after subtracting eight hours of daily sleep and days off, the theoretical French workforce amounts to 145 billion hours a year. That is our total time budget. First, we need to divide it between the economy and everything else: how much time is required to produce the things that satisfy our needs (versus the time we would prefer to spend on leisure)? Then, within the economy, we will have to decide how many hours to devote to market production and to other forms of production. And finally, within the market economy, we will have to spread the hours available for production across different goods and services. The idea of endless economic growth suggests that all these activities can increase simultaneously, but that is false. Economic activity can gain in efficiency but will never completely escape the constraint imposed by its time budget.

THE MAGICAL FANTASY OF INNOVATION

Sure, some will say, but technical progress allows us to overcome this limit. One hour of work today produces more than one hour of work did a century ago, and that is because production techniques improved (we'll say that *labor productivity* has increased). An economy decoupled from the use of natural resources (that is, where growth would have no biophysical limits), and where all additional production is accomplished thanks to more efficient production techniques (that is, where growth would have no social limits) could indeed grow forever. But as we will see, this situation, which economists often fantasize about, is a pipe dream.

Let's start with the following question: do all productivity gains save us time? In a production function with two factors of production (labor and capital), any rise in production not due to the rise of these two factors is attributed to what economists call "technical progress."

For most economists, and since American economist Robert Solow's work on theories of growth in the 1950s,[9] technical progress is conceptualized as a quasi-magical "residual."

Technical progress is that part of production growth that cannot be attributed to a proportional rise in the use of the factors of production. If I work twice as long and produce twice as much, there is no technical progress. If I work 1.5 times as long and produce twice as much, the technical progress is 0.5—what we call "Solow's residual."

But this growth is not magical. I may be more productive because I am better rested, but how did I manage to get better rest? Rest is an activity in itself, one that requires resources to be performed (time, a calm environment, a certain psychological tranquility, and sufficient material comfort). Production rises not just thanks to technical progress, but rather thanks to greater activity in the submerged part of the economy. The "labor" factor of production depends on the "rest" factor of reproduction. If I work 1.5 times longer and produce twice as much because I am better rested, the 0.5 residual is not technical progress, it's rest time.

Another example, this time adding the ecological dimension: suppose that agricultural harvests increase after an influx of pollinating insects and micro-organisms in the soil. Agricultural returns would therefore rise without increasing the number of farmers and tractors. Is this really technical progress? Not really—it is simply an increase in a factor of production that wasn't considered in national accounting. Since insects and organisms are themselves produced by nature, the "capital" factor of production depends on the "soil fertility regeneration" and "pollination service" factor of reproduction. When we extend the production function to ecosystem and sociosystem services, we realize that no additional production appears by miracle. On the contrary, it very often requires the intensified mobilization of other factors.

What we call "innovation" is a form of production in its own right. Tools don't invent themselves. To have more efficient machines, you first need more creative inventors—and how do these inventors become more creative? They study, train, and often spend time imagining. And for that to happen, a whole host of people must work (even if they are not paid to do so) in order to create a fertile context for these activities. Facebook would surely never have seen the light of day if no one had taken care to educate Mark Zuckerberg, if he hadn't had the free time to think about it, and access to a computer and the internet (which also had to be invented)—in other words, if he hadn't benefited from an entire social infrastructure. "Just as DNA in itself would not suffice to generate an organism, blueprints cannot generate a technology," as anthropologist Alf Hornborg puts it.[10]

Does "Technical Progress" Really Save Us Time?

Another problem: the way in which most economists conceptualize production only takes into account a limited temporal and geographic perimeter. If I travel from A to B right now, I might have the impression that using a car instead of a bike will save me time, since the car is faster. But that is only true here and now.

To know if I, individually, have saved time, other factors must be taken into account, starting with the time it took to earn the income that allowed me to buy the car, but also the time lost in traffic jams, spent on car maintenance, etc. It is not instantaneous speed that matters but "effective speed."[11] In the 1970s, Jean-Pierre Dupuy, a civil engineer, concluded by this logic that "the automobile's effective speed [which he estimated at about 16 km/h] is, in general, less than that of a bicycle."[12] If we all drove Ferraris, we might drive really fast in the moment, but this gain would be more than offset by the extra workload required to produce Ferraris, which, I imagine, takes a lot more time than manufacturing a Citroën Ami. This is what philosopher Ivan Illich calls a "counterproductivity threshold": the car we initially invented to save time ends up slowing us down.[13]

The problem with this calculation is that it only considers my individual working hours. But to know if using a car allows us, collectively, to save time, we must also include the hours worked across the product's full life cycle: the time spent extracting materials, transporting them, manufacturing the vehicle, selling it, and recycling it, as well as all the hours of labor necessary to maintain the social infrastructure that supports these activities. Let's also add the time spent extracting the energy needed for it to function and building the infrastructure that enables its use (the roads, gas stations, garages, etc.). We must also include the time lost due to the "negative externalities" this production process generates: the extra hours spent cultivating land rendered less fertile by global warming, treating the illnesses caused by air pollution, road accidents, etc.

If we put all our outputs to a *time footprint* test, chances are that many of the innovations we consider time-saving would turn out to be terribly time-consuming on a macroeconomic scale. Here is the key takeaway: increasing our speed does not always save us time.

When I explain that I don't fly, and that it therefore takes me about thirty hours by train to go from France to Sweden, I am often told I'm lucky to have enough free time to make such a journey. Yet it is quite likely that the effective speed by plane is lower than that by train, at least for short distances. Those who fly from Paris to Bordeaux "save" (very little) time by wasting (a lot of) other people's time. To put it another way, some people (often the wealthiest)[14] accelerate momentarily, but only by slowing down the economy as a whole.

This is not technical progress; it is a shifting of production costs. As demonstrated in 1950 by economist Karl W. Kapp in *The Social Costs of Private Enterprise*, individuals privatize benefits (the ability to travel quickly, i.e. instant speed) while socializing part of the costs (the time lost maintaining the entire infrastructure that allows these people to fly, i.e. effective speed).[15] The moral of the story is (still the same): no infinite growth in a finite world; past certain thresholds, the speed of some is achieved at the cost of slowing others down.

The Social-Reproductive Contradiction

Far more often than we might think, the economy is a zero-sum game. Growth in the tip of the economic iceberg (the part measured by GDP) can only happen at the cost of a decline of potential growth in the submerged part. This is true for natural resources and time, as well as for goods and services. An apartment on Airbnb is an apartment that isn't on CouchSurfing, a barrel of oil burned to heat the trading floor is a barrel of oil that won't be burned to heat a party venue, and an article written for a paid subscription newspaper is one less article in a free encyclopedia. GDP growth is therefore an "opportunity cost" in terms of non-economic development.

When we think about "growth" in a developed economy, we should not picture the miraculous creation of wealth, but rather an increase in one thing at the expense of something else. Drawing an analogy with Darwinian theory, American economist Jack P. Manno talks about the "natural selection of commodities."[16] Different activities compete for a limited quantity of resources, including our time. In a capitalist economy, the market rewards what brings in the most money, thus disadvantaging non-market or semi-market activities like volunteering or cooperatives. Because their products are not sold (or at least, are much cheaper than their market alternatives), these reproductive activities are neglected by an economic system that prioritizes the most lucrative outputs. If I work 40 hours a week to be able to pay my bills, it's hard to run an association, write articles for Wikipedia, or launch a local currency.

Like a giant magnet, the most lucrative sectors attract the time and resources available. Today, people tend to want to work in sectors where salaries are high and to invest in sectors with high returns on investment. The more profitable an activity, the more it attracts investments (monetary, but also educational, technological, and institutional). This natural selection creates a brain drain, but also drains time and resources in general toward the sectors of the economy most prone to growth. How else can we explain that in France there are nearly as many real estate agents (249,400 people) as researchers (295,754 people)?[17] It is a tragic "waste of talent."[18] Over time, the sectors and commodities that succeed at capturing the most attention are constantly improved. At the opposite end of the spectrum, non-market alternatives in which we have collectively underinvested deteriorate. Like natural selection, it is a virtuous cycle for some (lucrative activities), and a vicious cycle for others (activities that are less—or not at all—lucrative).

An example: imagine you wanted to organize a local childcare exchange system among neighbors. Such a system can only work if it reaches a certain critical mass, with enough parents to ensure a rotation of care, and a sufficient level of trust, which involves getting to know the other parents and spending time with them. If some of the parents decide to put their children in private daycares, the system will no longer function properly. And the less the system works, the fewer parents will participate and invest their time and effort into improving it, and so the less the system will function. This downward spiral inevitably leads to the social equivalent of bankruptcy. In an economy where we commodify childcare services, the economic growth of private daycares will lead to the social recession of self-managed daycares. In other words, the opportunity cost of developing a market for childcare is the non-development of a potential non-market alternative.

According to Marxist geographer David Harvey, economic growth is therefore often accomplished through "accumulation by dispossession."[19] In his theory, the dispossession is direct: I dispossess you of something (land, natural resources, free time). But as we have defined it in this chapter, growth is also linked to indirect dispossession. It mobilizes certain resources that cease to be available for other activities. We could say that the market sector *dispossesses* the non-market sector of free time that could potentially have enriched it.

Why do non-commercial activities systematically lose the competition? First, the two spheres of production and reproduction rest on different logics. The reproductive sphere is based on a logic of contentment, of sustaining relationships, and of ensuring well-being. We have no interest in increasing the time spent electing a new government every four years or the number of tomato plants in my garden. The keyword in the reproductive logic is *sufficiency*: just enough to meet needs. It is a qualitative logic aimed at sustaining an activity in the long run. By contrast, the growth of monetary aggregates like revenue, profit, and GDP knows no bounds: it follows a quantitative logic aimed at accumulation. With limited total resources, sooner or later accumulative activities end up monopolizing the resources of stationary activities.

It's a vicious cycle. Past a certain point, the more time and effort we devote to the production of commodities, the less we devote to well-being, family, and community. The more the social fabric deteriorates, the more difficult it becomes to reproduce the labor force. Philosopher Nancy Fraser calls this mechanism the "social-reproductive contradiction."[20] On the one hand, social reproduction is necessary for capital accumulation (the baker has to be in good shape to produce); on the other hand, capitalism's drive for unlimited accumulation tends to destabilize the reproductive processes on which it relies (a baker who works too hard risks a workplace accident or burnout).

The problem is that a depressed baker not only stops making bread (a decrease in production—and so GDP), but also stops tending to their garden, participating in local association meetings, chatting with neighbors, raising children, engaging in political debates, etc. When reproduction stops, everything stops.

This offers an interesting hypothesis for why our high-GDP societies are currently facing an economic slowdown (the infamous "secular stagnation"). We have overexploited reproductive labor. In a situation where *real* technical progress (not just the substitution between factors of production) is slow, we can only continue expanding the market economy by degrading our reproductive capacities, and so ultimately our potential growth—a classic case of the snake eating its own tail.

Bad Growth

The expansion of market activity isn't always synonymous with progress. A country like the United States, which often experiences both economic booms and "social recessions," is a perfect example.[21] People buy more, but often for the wrong reasons, and always at the expense of the free time they must sacrifice to maintain their purchasing power. It's giving up your life to make a living, some would say. We see the same logic at the macroeconomic level: giving up society to finance it. What looks like vitality in national accounting terms (GDP growth) is in fact only agitation that is counterproductive to our collective well-being.

This was Ezra Mishan's thesis, an English economist at the London School of Economics, in *The Costs of Economic*

Growth (1976).[22] The author was one of the first of his time to suggest that economic growth wasn't purely beneficial. A rise in commercial activity brought on psychological distress, workplace burnout, the erosion of community life, and pollution. Even more groundbreaking, Mishan argued that, in the context of developed countries, the costs of growth often outweighed its benefits.

This idea was later revisited by Herman Daly, who spoke of "anti-economic growth," by Jan Drewnowski with the image of an "affluence line" not to cross, and by Manfred Max-Neef with his "threshold hypothesis," for whom striving for growth became counterproductive as a development strategy.[23] According to these thinkers, prosperity is not a matter of infinite growth (accumulation), but rather of optimal size (sufficiency). It is curious, in fact, that economists define their science as one of *optimality*, while never applying this principle to the size of the economy itself. If economists are concerned with well-being, and if well-being is about sufficiency, it's high time we ask ourselves what an economy's optimal size is.

Prosperity is not only a matter of quantity, but also of quality. Some forms of monetary growth are achieved at the expense of something else. Personal data, for example. Its global market is worth around 300 billion euros, with an average price of around 600 euros for a consumer's profile.[24] The more data is sold, the richer we get in terms of GDP, but is that really progress? This growth is celebrated by companies using it to improve their advertising (and so to incentivize the purchase of nonessential items), but lamented by users who are gradually losing control of their privacy. Once again: GDP is on the rise, but society is in decline.

This is the problem with an economic system organized around the indiscriminate maximization of monetary value. As I have already pointed out, GDP does not distinguish between desirable and undesirable activities, those that satisfy real needs and those that simply create new ones through advertising, planned obsolescence, and dependence on existing infrastructure.

How many things do we produce and consume today that we don't really need? We produce junk food *and* pay doctors to treat obesity; SUVs, oil boilers, airplane trips, *and* air conditioners to deal with increasingly frequent heatwaves. GDP is largely an impartial agitation, stimulated just as much by a boom in essential goods as by the hoarding of useless ones.

What Is Commodification?

One could think that the dismantling of social infrastructure may not be a problem if it can be replaced by commercial alternatives. After all, whether it's self-managed, public, managed by a cooperative, or a for-profit business, a daycare is still a daycare. The problem: capitalism speaks only one language, that of money (and as we have seen, of the fastest possible accumulation of it). This imperative requires a specific organization of the economy that transforms everything into commodities. But this mode of economic organization is ill-suited to certain goods and services.

Commodities are products that are exchanged in a market, like a zucchini in a store, an hour of work by a freelancer, or an apartment you are trying to sell. But before being a commodity, the zucchini was just a vegetable, the hour of work was just time in a person's life, and the apartment just the home of someone who had no intention of selling it. In other words, these things existed outside the market's domain.

Commodification is a social protocol—shared rules that allow us to manage the allocation of certain resources. Concretely, it involves transforming something into a product that can be traded in a market. *Commodifying* zucchinis means setting up an entire social infrastructure that enables the exchange of zucchinis in a market: a marketplace, prices, rules of trade, quality standards, etc.

To simplify, we can break this process down into four steps: standardization, quantification, monetization, and privatization. Take a rabbit, for example. For it to become a commodity, it must be *standardized*, that is, rendered comparable to other rabbits. We could designate it as a Norman rabbit, making it comparable to all other members of its species. Next, it needs to be *quantified*, either as a single unit (one individual rabbit) or as 5 kg of rabbit meat. Finally, it is *monetized* (the rabbit becomes rabbit meat priced at 19 euros per kilo) and *privatized*, so that its ownership is attributed to someone who can then transfer that property right to someone else (the rabbit becomes *my* rabbit).

Something that is not *comparable*, *measurable*, *commensurable*, and *appropriable* cannot be traded in a market. For the rabbit to become a commodity, it has to become *my 5 kg of Norman rabbit* meat that you can buy for *19 €/kg*. The word "commodity" itself is indicative. Commodities are such in the sense that their existence is simplified in order to make economic exchange more *commode*, the French word for convenient. That is why the butcher's counter will not say "rabbit" but "Norman rabbit, 19 €/kg." This is an important point to remember: commodification is the simplification of complex socio-ecological characteristics to facilitate trade.

In theory, anything can be commodified. In practice, however, some things are harder to commodify than others. Jack P. Manno evaluates a thing's "commodity potential" by considering sixteen attributes.[25] Goods and services with high commodity potential are "alienable, excludable, standardized, uniform, adaptable, depersonalized, anonymous, mobile, transferable, universal, and context independent." And those with low commodity potential are "openly accessible or difficult to charge for, context dependent, integrated, personalized, and localized." It would be easier to commodify a kilo of carrots or a barrel of oil than a coral reef or a romantic relationship.

It is important to understand that commodification does not transform products materially. Whether we grow it to sell it or eat it, a zucchini remains the same. But commodification is not neutral either (this will be the focus of the next section): growing zucchinis to sell them imposes different constraints than growing them for one's own consumption (misshapen fruits and vegetables—so-called "ugly produce"—will not be sold in supermarkets, even if they are perfectly edible). Same thing for labor. Once commodified, certain previously useful tasks will no longer be recognized as such if the market does not accord them any value, and so the economy as a whole will move toward tasks with high commercial value (hence the proliferation of business schools).

The perimeter of commodification is, therefore, a political choice. In France, you can sell zucchinis but not organs. As a social protocol, commodification is more or less regulated. You can sell zucchinis on Saturday mornings at the market but not in the subway. You can rent out your apartment in Paris but not above a set rent ceiling. You can buy hours of labor, but not below the minimum wage. One of the fundamental tasks of economic governance is to determine the limits of the market's domain and to regulate its functioning.

The Corruption of Commodities

This protocol may seem trivial. Market, semi-market, non-market—what does it matter? Well, we often summarize economic history as a progressive march toward commodification, which we implicitly associate with progress. But what seems like a detail of national accounting is actually a fundamental question of economic policy, because the choice to commodify or decommodify something changes our relationship with the world around us. Commodification affects not only the management of a product but also its users, the conditions of access to the product, and ultimately the very essence of the activity in question.

In *Social Limits to Growth* (1976), Fred Hirsch talks about a "commercialization effect": commodifying something can degrade the satisfaction we derive from it. Hiring an actor to pretend to be your friend for an afternoon surely does not have the same appeal as an authentic friendship. Friendship is a service that is hard to commodify. Hiring someone to help you move will not have the same social value (nor the same long-term consequences) as inviting a group of friends over to do it together.

For philosopher Michael Sandel, commodification will even "corrupt" an activity if it leads us to treat it according to an inferior norm than would otherwise be appropriate.[26] "Having children for the purpose of selling them to make money is a corruption of parenthood, for it treats children as things to sell rather than as beings to love."[27] Making friends to get money out of them would be a corruption of friendship which, by definition, is indifferent to any material or financial advantage. We would find it morally suspect if a doctor, judge, or minister were motivated only by profit.

Some might see Airbnb as a corruption of the hospitality found on CouchSurfing. Indeed, paying for something can radically change our experience of a service. We do not behave in the same way with a host who generously puts us up as we do with someone who does it for money. Commodification risks replacing instincts for sharing and reciprocity—based on trust and sympathy—with the cold, impersonal, and calculated logic of market exchange.

Thinking in terms of "financial incentives," as microeconomists call them, can quickly make us forget other kinds of incentives. If a friend makes you a birthday cake, few will dare complain that the cake is not to their taste. But if we pay for that same cake, it better be good, or else we will complain because we "didn't get our money's worth." The cake is exactly the same, but the social relationship is different: now you interact with the person who made the cake through the medium of price. And in certain situations, this price can take precedence over social and moral instincts of politeness and graciousness.

Take blood donation. You might think that offering a monetary reward would incentivize people to donate more. Yet studies show that the opposite is true: financial logic corrupts the spirit of charity, discouraging people from giving.[28]

The same pattern was observed in daycares in Israel.[29] People were more susceptible to being late picking up their kids from daycares that imposed a fine for lateness than from those that did not. As the article's title puts it, "a fine is a price": parents started seeing the fine as the price of a service—in this case the extended care covering their delay. Before the fine, courtesy motivated them to arrive on time. After the fine, the economic incentive had corrupted the social incentive.

We could also mention "carbon offsets." For a few extra euros, we grant ourselves the right to pollute and relieve ourselves of all responsibility for the impact of our actions on the climate.

Commodification As Social Dissolution

This corruption multiplies into a systemic effect when commodification becomes important to our social structure. Economic growth both feeds on and erodes our social fabric, a phenomenon that Jacques Généreux calls "dissociety," "that centrifugal force that splits into rival elements the once-interdependent components of human society."[30]

There is a difference between buying vegetables at the town

market on a Saturday morning, haggling over a trinket at the flea market, or paying a neighbor for piano lessons, and a society where most social relations occur through market transactions. When commodification reaches a critical mass, it becomes impossible to satisfy one's needs outside of the market sphere. This reflects the idea of the natural selection of commodities mentioned earlier: if you want to go away for the weekend but all available apartments are on Airbnb, you will have no choice but to list yours on Airbnb too, to earn the money needed to rent the one you want. It's the same for sales: if real estate prices become exorbitant, we cannot individually decide to sell at a fair price without taking on the risk of not being able to afford new housing.

The more markets there are, the more we see markets everywhere. Commodification brings with it a dependence on commodities and their internal logic. We become capitalists despite ourselves, greed becoming the hegemonic drive of social interactions. Karl Polanyi, in *The Grand Transformation*, wrote as early as 1944 that "to allow the market mechanism to be sole director of the fate of human beings and their natural environment would result in the demolition of society."[31] Notably, before he renamed it *The Great Transformation*, the original title of Polanyi's book was *Freedom from Economics*.[32] Here, we encounter the flipside of commodification: its strength—commodities—is also a weakness, for certain things are difficult to simplify. That's why Polanyi uses "fictitious commodities" to designate things that are treated as commodities but should not be, like labor, land, and money.

The prevalence of market exchange as a mode of allocation reduces the possibility for three other forms of allocation to develop: *donation*, *reciprocity*, and *redistribution*. In a world where markets are omnipresent, attitudes like hospitality, generous assistance, and charity become services requiring payment. The plot of land where I used to go fishing with my grandfather becomes real estate and the scientific article that I was excited to share becomes a product to be sold to the highest bidder.

This obsession becomes collective in a society where everything is for sale. If my colleagues start selling the books they used to share for free, I will have no choice but to sell mine in order to access theirs. If we organize this sale through for-profit publishers, we will receive only a small portion of the book's sale price (between 9% and 13% in the present case), and so we will need to publish more—just to earn enough to access things we could have accessed for free in a non-market system of reciprocity.

If, as anthropologist David Graeber argues, it is non-market relations that maintain cohesion in a society, commodification is problematic because it erodes this social glue.[33] The diversity of reciprocal relationships (between a guest and their host, a student and their professor, a passenger and driver, or an artist and their audience) is reduced, eliminated even, by market exchange. If I can rent on Airbnb, pay for private lessons on an online platform, buy a concert ticket, and call an Uber, the act of payment replaces an unquantifiable and personal social debt with an exact and impersonal monetary debt.

The danger comes from exactitude. I give you A, you give me B—we're even. In the logic of the gift (giving, receiving, giving back) that Marcel Mauss describes in his essay *The Gift* (1925), it's the impossibility of immediately paying back exactly what we owe that keeps social bonds alive. The market's monetary logic simplifies these relationships to make trade more practical, but it does so by sacrificing the sociality of economic interactions. *Paying* becomes a substitute for other social interactions, like *thanking* or *reciprocating*. It's an interesting paradox that we experience every day at the supermarket. If it were to close, I would starve in a few days. And yet, I express no gratitude toward all the people that keep me fed. I pay them, and I consider that enough.

The impact of the omnipresent commodification of social life sometimes goes even further, justifying behaviors that would otherwise be considered socially unacceptable. I do not need to pick up after my dog, I pay taxes for that. I can fly as much as I want during a climate crisis because I offset my emissions. I know that these consumer loans are basically fraud, but I have revenue targets to meet. These people may have waited hours for this ride, but my premium pass gives me the right to skip the line. Like an invisible matrix, economic logic suffocates our social instincts, our *savoir-vivre*.

The Economization of Mindsets

Commodification has sociological but also psychological effects. We might not be the cold and rational calculators some economists describe in their models (the *Homo economicus* theory), but we certainly could become them.

The market economy is sort of like a real-life video game—a simplified simulation of social life. I go to the supermarket and choose products based on their price; I decide which job I want based on the salary; I select my projects based on their potential profitability. Dissociated from their cultural and ecological context, we approach commodities with a purely economic mindset. When I buy, I must always minimize the price, and when I sell, I must always maximize it. Regardless of what is sold and to whom, the range of social and moral incentives is reduced to a purely rational, monetary calculation.

The more time we spend playing the market economy game (we could say the capitalism game), the more this mindset of maximizing monetary gain becomes common sense. After getting used to collecting rent on an apartment, it's hard to go back to a relationship of disinterested giving—the "opportunity cost" of not being able to rent it out for money will always be in the back of our minds. We develop what Marx denounced as "commodity fetishism,"[34] an obsession with the financial potential of things.

This commodification even transforms our relationship with time. If I am paid the minimum wage in France, an hour of my time is worth €8.59 and I can now easily monetize various activities, like brushing my teeth (€0.43), taking a 20-minute nap (€2.86), or waiting in line for 45 minutes to vote in a presidential election (€6.44). It's economic utilitarianism pushed to paroxysm: every choice becomes comparable to every other one through the medium of money. Time becomes capital that we must save, invest, or lose. And in societies with high inequality, the time of the poor is worth far less than that of the rich—hence the explosion of platforms like TaskRabbit, which allow those with high purchasing power to pay other less fortunate people to do their laundry, watch their kids, and wait in line for them.[35]

To conclude this chapter, let's return to Adam Smith. All production depends on a reproductive infrastructure that is limited by the time devoted to it. Just as infinite growth is impossible on a finite planet, infinite growth is also impossible in a community whose capacity to reproduce itself is finite. Once again, it is a matter of proportion. In the same way that a branch cannot become heavier than the trunk that supports it, the market economy will never truly be able to emancipate itself from the social fabric that sustains it. This is the first social limit to growth.

So, GDP growth is no magical surplus. Increasing market production is always a bit like making a new sweater with the wool from an old one. First of all, there will never be more sweaters than there is wool (the ecological limits from Chapter 2). Next, knitting takes time, time that will not be spent doing something else (the social limits from this chapter). In certain contexts, and under certain thresholds, it makes sense to produce more and to develop new markets. But let's not forget that this expansion must remain proportional to the infrastructure that sustains it. Market growth too intense will act as a force of social dissolution.

The exponential commodification of the social sphere is not only unsustainable in the long run (because this social sphere is limited), but it is also sometimes undesirable. Here is the second social limit to growth: some things cannot be commodified without deteriorating. Quantifiable wealth and "relational poverty"[36] can very well co-exist. Beyond a certain point, obstinately striving to grow the economy means extending a market logic to social spheres that are not suited to it.

4
FALSE PROMISES
The Political Limits to Growth

Sure, economic growth encounters ecological limits. Okay, it is hard to sustain in the long term from a social perspective. But, its proponents argue, isn't it a necessary evil? Aren't these nuisances simply the "price to pay" to reap growth's benefits: eradicating poverty, reducing inequality, lowering unemployment, financing public spending, and even improving our quality of life?

The GDP genie grants us these five wishes, according to growth apologists. Let's produce and consume more, keep the economy going, and the rest will follow. But does growth actually deliver on these promises? As we will see, no. Can we solve these problems *without* growth? As we will see, yes.

POVERTY

The logic seems foolproof: if growth equals abundance, then degrowth will cause scarcity. "Degrowth means impoverishing the French people," says Bruno Le Maire: "if you have degrowth, you will have less wealth, and you will have more poverty."[1] To abandon growth would thus be "the road to poverty," to borrow Jean-Philippe Delsol's words.[2]

And indeed, at first glance, we might believe there is a lack of resources. In 2018, 5.3 million people in France lived on less than 885 euros per month, 6.7 million faced energy insecurity, and 5 million relied on food assistance.[3] Broadening the focus, INSEE estimates that there are 10 million poor people in Metropolitan France.[4] This poverty is real, but does its cause lie in too small an economy? Put another way, are there unhoused people because of a lack of housing, energy-insecure people because of a lack of energy, malnourished people because of a lack of food, and low incomes because of a lack of wealth?

To answer this question, let's start by taking stock of what we need in order to put an end to poverty in France. One way to do this is by calculating "reference budgets," under the procedure developed by the National Observatory on Poverty and Social Exclusion.[5] To set them, groups of citizens are asked about the goods and services necessary to live decently. These "reference baskets" are then valued based on their cost, to ultimately obtain a reference budget that will vary according to family configuration and location (between 1,424 euros for an active single person and 3,284 euros for a couple with children, with adjustments made according to the city).

By multiplying these different reference budgets by the number of people involved, we can estimate the national income necessary to allow the entire population to satisfy its needs. This is how we set a minimum threshold for national income—a sort of economic floor. Last step: we compare this minimum level to current national income to gauge whether or not a country generates enough wealth.

According to Pierre Concialdi's calculations, an economist at the Institut de Recherches Économiques et Sociales, this macroeconomic surplus was null in the aftermath of World War II, and the quasi-totality of national income would thus have been necessary to meet the needs of the French people.[6] In this situation, any reduction in national income would have plunged part of the population into poverty.

However, starting in the 1960s, the situation radically changed. From the 1960s to the mid-1970s, a macroeconomic surplus emerged, representing nearly half of total income. In 2013, this surplus reached 42% of national income, or about 900 billion euros, and the order of magnitude has varied little since (the surplus was 44% in 2021, according to Pierre Concialdi's latest estimates). This figure is extremely important: it shows that it is theoretically possible for everyone to live decently, we have enough wealth for that. Therefore, economic growth is no longer a necessary condition for eradicating poverty in France.

We have enough income, but it is poorly distributed, and some view redistribution unfavorably. Economic growth is seen as a better solution, because it could boost the incomes of the poor without reducing those of the wealthy, thereby circumventing a thorny political issue. But growth would still have to boost the incomes of the poorest households, which, in reality, is rarely the case.

Between 1938 and 2015, the poorest 50% of French people captured only 20% of total growth—a share equivalent to that of the richest 1%.[7] This trend reflects a more general increase in inequality, which we will explore in the next section. As for the bottom of the pyramid, the result is clear: poverty (measured at 60% of the median income) has increased in France over the last decade, going from 13.8% in 2013 (8.5 million people) to 14.8% in 2018 (9.3 million people), and that despite the growth of GDP.[8]

Not only does growth fail to reduce poverty, but it is also possible to end poverty *without* growth. As Denis Colombi reminds us in *Où va l'argent des pauvres* (*Where Does Poor People's Money Go*), the easiest solution to poverty is to give money to people who don't have any. Today in France, the redistributive benefits aimed at reducing poverty constitute a quarter of all government benefits, and income support programs (27.2 billion euros) represented 1.2% of GDP in 2019.[9] Let's remember the 900 billion macroeconomic surplus: we do not need to grow total GDP to increase these benefits, we only need to reallocate the wealth that already exists.

The options are plenty: transforming the RSA[i] into an unconditional "guaranteed minimum social income," indexed to the median income and accessible starting at eighteen years old; raising the minimum retirement pension to 1,000 euros; increasing the current minimum wage by indexing it to "reference budgets," for example, to ensure it is enough to live on decently (the concept of a *real living wage*)[10]—in France, this would mean an increase of 20% to 30%.[11] There will be disagreements over form, which we will address in Chapter 7, but what is important at this stage is to understand that it is not necessary to increase the total amount of income to put an end to monetary poverty.

Another solution for eradicating poverty without growth is to decommodify part of the economy. In a society where everything is for sale, any loss in purchasing power is a loss in *living power*, meaning our capacity to meet our needs. But that is not the case in a society that guarantees free access to basic services. This is actually already true for certain public services. In 2018, in-kind transfers represented the equivalent of 28% of household disposable income.[12] So-called fixed expenses (those which households cannot avoid, like rent, water, electricity, insurance, etc.) represented a disproportionately large share of low-income budgets. In France, while these expenses increased from 24% in 1979 to 48% in 2005 for the poorest 10% of households, they only went from 20% to 27% for the richest 10%.[13] Investing in public services therefore constitutes a genuine redistribution channel.

Here too, there are plenty of proposals: the establishment of "food social security," with €150 credited on a social security

---

[i] France's *revenu de solidarité active*, or RSA, provides a minimum income to people who are unemployed or have incomes below a certain threshold.

card for purchases in certain food categories; the expansion of the "energy check" program (between €48 and €277 for the poorest households) and of the "Culture Pass" (€300 for eighteen-year-olds) to cover other goods and services (this will be one of the proposals in Chapter 6); a "universal autonomy allowance" of 600 to 1,000 euros for students;[14] no charge for an initial amount of water and electricity; and free local public transportation, as is already the case in Dunkirk and more than sixty other cities in France.

Redistributing is not enough. We must also ensure that the value added of production is distributed more equitably from the start. On the list of the ten worst paid jobs in France, there are 227,001 domestic workers (39% of whom are working poor), 369,574 cleaning professionals (42% working poor), and 465,512 childcare workers (35% of whom are working poor).[15] This is doubly paradoxical, as these professions are essential. Given the choice, would you rather live in a country without a national soccer team (annual cost: 220 million euros) or without garbage collectors (annual cost: 138 million euros)? Redistribution (taxing soccer players to give to garbage collectors) is only a remedial solution. Wouldn't it be better to ensure that all activity is decently remunerated, and that those who are inactive receive a guaranteed minimum income, so that nobody falls into poverty?

Let's say it again: poverty in France is not a question of production (the wealth is already there and overabundant) but simply of allocation—that is, of sharing. Attempting to eradicate poverty by stimulating GDP growth is like trying to change a car's direction by adding gas to a full tank.

To eradicate poverty in France, no need to "make the cake bigger," just change the way it's sliced (one should also consider what ingredients it is made of, a subject that will preoccupy us throughout this book). But careful: *sharing* does not mean *charity*. Taxing the soccer players to increase the wages of garbage collectors is not an act of generosity by the former toward the latter: it is the return to reason of a system that, eyes fixed on exchange values, gradually forgot where the wealth of nations came from.

Inequality

There was a time when economists swore only by the "Kuznets curve." In 1955, economist Simon Kuznets published an empirical study on the relationship between economic growth and income inequality. Using statistical data for the United States, England, and Germany from 1913 to 1948, Kuznets discovered the bell-shaped curve we now call a "Kuznets curve." When a country industrializes, the author explained, only a minority of the population has access to the new industrial sectors. As the income per worker is lower in the traditional sector than in these new sectors, income inequality increases. But as industrialization continues, the other workers migrate toward the new sectors, and past a certain threshold, overall income inequality falls.

This theory suggests that, in the long term, the growth of high incomes ends up "trickling down" to the bottom, to use an expression from the 1980s. Today, we see this same idea in the "lead climber" analogy, those we should prioritize in order to pull the whole of society up. We also talk about "inclusive growth" to describe an increase in GDP that would benefit the poorest households. Growth in the total size of the economy would lead to the harmonization of incomes *from the top*, allowing the poor to make money faster than the wealthy, thus reducing inequality. "So long as there is growth, there is hope, and that makes large income differentials tolerable," a member of the United States Federal Reserve Board used to say.

There's a problem: the trickle-down theory is a myth with

no theoretical or empirical basis. To understand why, let's break down national income. In Chapter 1, we saw that GDP adds up different types of income which are aggregated into a synthetic figure: *per capita* GDP. The growth of this figure does not tell us whether it is wages (the only source of income for the poorest households) or income from capital in the form of dividends, rental income, interest, profits, capital gains, royalties, etc. (collected only by affluent households) that yields the growth. And yet, this is essential information, for it marks the difference between an increase in GDP that reduces inequalities (*inclusive* growth, where wages rise faster than capital income) and an increase that worsens them (*exclusive* growth, where the owners of capital get richer faster than wage earners).

The growth of a capitalist economy is exclusive by default. Thomas Piketty proves it in *Capital in the Twenty-First Century*. Only government interventions (which redistribute wealth) as well as wars and recessions (which destroy a portion of rentiers' assets) have managed to reverse the trend. Economic growth is not the general growth of incomes, but rather growth at various speeds: a tortoise for the poorest, whose only income is their wages, and a hare for the wealthiest, who reap returns on their capital (in addition to their wages).

These disparities are glaring when we compare the difference between wage inequality, income inequality (wages plus capital income), and wealth inequality. In 2018, the lowest-paid 10% of workers earned less than 1,282 euros per month (net monthly wages in full-time equivalent), whereas to belong to the top 10% of earners, you had to make at least 2.9 times more, or over €3,776 (the wealth threshold according to the French Inequality Observatory).[16] In other words, if you make €3,776 or more per month, at least 89% of workers in France make less than you do.[17]

Income inequality, however, is more than double wage inequality: the top decile's annual average income is as high as

€61,100, or 7.1 times the average income of the poorest 10% (€8,600), even after taxes and government benefits. When it comes to wealth, inequality rates skyrocket. The bottom 10% possess less than 3,800 euros (gross assets, without subtracting liabilities) and the top 10% hoard an average 1,280,000 euros, meaning 336 times more.[18]

GDP is a flow and growth is the intensification of that flow (Chapter 1). Thus growth is like a swollen river, the flow of water representing GDP as a whole. This flow moves according to the rocks that litter the riverbed. It is the rocks (wealth) that determine the direction of the water flow (income). Today, wealth inequality is such that the assets owned by the upper classes form a dam that redirects the vast majority of the water flow toward their own bank accounts, and lets a tiny trickle through for the rest of the population.

This dam is colossal: the wealthiest 10% in France (between 3 and 6.5 million people) own more than half of the nation's wealth, which allows them to capture a third of total income—about the same amount of income as the poorest 40%.[ii] The top 1% (630,000 people) receive 7.2% of all income, or 7.2 times more than what they would receive if income were shared equally, and the top 0.1% (63,000 people) receive 2.2% of all income, or 22 times more than under an equal division of income.[19] By comparison, the poorer half of the French population owns only 4.9% of total wealth and collects 23% of the national income (primarily through their wages).

[ii] The wealthiest 10% (average annual income: €116,900; average net worth: €1,355,800) own 59.5% of the net assets of all households, which allows them to capture 32.2% of all income according to the World Inequality Lab's "World Inequality Report" (2022, p. 193). According to the Inequality Observatory's *Rapport sur les riches en France* (2022, pp. 12-13), the wealthiest 10% (minimum monthly income: €3,673; minimum net worth: €607,700; average net worth: €1,280,000) own 46% of national wealth, which allows them to capture 28% of all pre-tax income. The "Palma ratio" in 2019 is 1.06, which means that the wealthiest 10% receive 1.06 times what the poorest 40% receive (*Rapport sur les riches en France*, 2022, p. 49).

Inequalities self-amplify. The more the rich enrich themselves, the more they can invest their savings or buy stock and real estate, and the more they increase their income with interest, dividends, rental income, and capital gains. Wealth inequality generates income inequality, which reinforces wealth inequality. Over time, the dam gets higher and higher, and a greater and greater portion of value added flows to those who are already rich.

It's a virtuous cycle for the rentiers and a vicious cycle for the wage earners who, meanwhile, see the volume of water gradually dwindle. Between 1983 and 2015, the richest 1% alone captured 21% of total growth, compared to 20% for the poorest 50%.[20] Since 1999, the top decile's average annual standard of living has risen by 9,100 euros, an increase three times greater than that of the middle class (only 3,300 euros).[21] Given that inequalities harm everyone (even the rich, studies tell us,[22] because they cause a variety of public health issues that reverberate across society as a whole), and that wealth does not trickle down, we could very well have done without 21% of the growth since the 1980s—the portion of income growth that was captured by those who were already rich.

Theoretically, we could indeed reduce inequality *without* growth. With a constant GDP, it would suffice to shrink the rents portion (returns, rental income, dividends, capital gains, etc.) and expand the wages portion of national income. The question here is not how best to do so (we will return to that in Chapter 7), but simply to demystify the idea that growth is necessary to combat inequality. Nevertheless, before we get into more detail, let's go over a few possible strategies.

To increase the wages portion, we need to promote labor-intensive activities. A happy coincidence, because it is precisely these activities that will be likely to grow with the ecological transition. Today, agriculture is highly intensive, industrialized, mechanized, and dependent on imports. When we replace labor with capital (through automation, for example), the wages portion of total income shrinks, and vice versa. The same job-destroying effect occurs when we export labor-intensive tasks overseas. In this sense, the relocalization of production would re-enrich production with labor, and doubly so if it is done (to stick to the agriculture example) under the agroecological model—meaning production that is low in machinery and inputs, and high in labor.

But even this strategy immediately hits an obstacle. Today, a farmer's work yields an annual net income of 17,700 euros, and 18% of farmers in France live below the poverty line (versus 13% for all households).[23] They cannot make a living off their labor, and they are not the only ones. In 2017, there were 1.2 million "working poor" in France, living on less than 885 euros per month (representing 4.7% of all workers).[24] If we zoom out to the monetary poverty line, set at 60% of the median standard of living (1,041 euros in 2017), we find more than 2.1 million workers, including 1.6 million wage earners.[25]

To reduce inequality without growth, we need to revalorize wages, meaning redefine how value added is distributed. In 2014, only 6.50 euros out of every 100 euros spent on food reached farmers, 30% less than in 1999.[26] Instead of increasing the total volume of agricultural products, we should reduce the role of mass distribution and intermediaries to distribute the value added more equitably. There are many ways to achieve this. We could start by establishing a maximum wage, as suggested in the proposed law "for a decent limit to income disparities,"[27] and cap high salaries to twelve times the average salary of the lowest-paid decile of workers, or we could go even further and limit the wage gap to a ratio of 1 to 4, as proposed by the Appalled Economists.[28]

If wealth and income inequality are higher than wage inequality (which is the case), redistributing wealth and income is a far more effective way to reduce inequality. To deconcentrate capital, we will need to reinforce the taxation of wealth. Here too, there are many options. We could reinstate the progressive wealth tax (the *impôt sur la fortune* or ISF), which was replaced by the lighter and less progressive property tax (the *impôt sur la fortune immobilière* or IFI).[29] We could overhaul inheritance taxation to remove the many deductions, exemptions, and loopholes that benefit the richest households. We could also regulate property ownership (today, 24% of all households own 68% of all housing),[30] by taxing property accumulation and capping rental income and capital gains. Another option is a one-time, progressive tax on large estates, which could be collected, for instance, to finance the fight against climate change.[31] All of this must of course be paired with a fight against tax fraud and tax evasion.

As for incomes, we could cap them with a highly progressive tax system. This is Thomas Piketty's proposal: seven brackets ranging from 10% to 90%, defined in relation to the average income. For example, all income greater than 10 times the average income would be taxed at 60%, and all income greater than 10,000 times the average income would be taxed at 90%. By the same logic, it is possible to limit inequality even more drastically by lowering these ratios.[32] (As a reminder, today the maximum tax rate on income in France is 45%).

The objective here is not to lay out a perfect plan for reducing economic inequality. My thesis is much simpler: to reduce inequality, there is no need to grow the economy as a whole, we simply need to share.[iii] Share existing wealth first through the redistribution of existing capital; but also better distribute future wealth by increasing the wages portion (and especially that

---

[iii] Note that here we have only been discussing economic inequalities (of wages, income, or wealth) and that many other forms exist, namely intergenerational inequality, environmental inequality, and inequalities among living beings. Given what I laid out in Chapter 2, it is clear that growth (in a country already as rich as France) exacerbates these ecological and zoological inequalities.

of the lowest wages) and by reducing the rents portion in the division of value added—this will be one of the central questions in Chapter 7.

Employment

On the Europe 1 radio station in October 2020, entrepreneur Denis Payre freaked out: "Degrowth environmentalism forgets that, crucially, under a 1% growth rate, unemployment rises very quickly."[33] Godwin's law: if we start questioning growth, sooner or later we face the specter of mass unemployment. The link between employment and growth is so ingrained in the collective imagination that the two are fused in one of the United Nations' sustainable development goals: "decent work and sustainable growth."

But the relationship between growth and unemployment is more complex than it seems, and the issue of work goes far beyond GDP or employment. "Okun's law" asserts that employment always moves in the same direction as growth.[iv] But it's not that simple. Employment depends on production, labor productivity, and working hours. If we produce 1% more, but the hourly productivity of work also goes up by 1%, the employment rate will not change. If we produce 1% less, but labor productivity falls by more than 1% or the hours worked per worker fall by more than 1%, the same volume of output will require *more* hours of work, and so potentially more jobs.

There are therefore at least three ways to create jobs: producing more, working more slowly, and working for less time. The *producing more* option is well suited to sectors that we

---

[iv] Okun's law comes from a 1962 empirical study by American economist Arthur M. Okun ("Potential GNP: Its measurement and significance"), where he observed that a 3% increase in real GDP corresponded to a 1% reduction in unemployment.

would like to see develop, but not to those we would like to see decline. The second strategy (*working more slowly*) can prove useful in sectors where slowing down would mean improved working conditions (particularly when shifting from industrial to artisanal production). And *working for less time* would be better appreciated in sectors where workers suffer through their job or in those set to downsize and/or disappear.

As for the interaction between these factors, we could fill pages describing the debate among economists on the subject, but that wouldn't take us very far. Some think it is production that drives demand, and so growth that generates employment; others argue it is employment that drives demand, and so employment that generates growth. The debates on working hours and labor productivity are at least as lively and polarized. Some will point to periods where job creation coincided with GDP growth, and others will point to periods where you see the opposite. Ultimately, the question is poorly framed, and the debate is quickly bogged down in abstraction, limited by too narrow a definition of wealth (GDP) and work (paid employment).[34]

Let's suggest a different starting point: what activities do we need? Or more generally, broadening the concept of work, what do we want to produce, and how? In the same way that we define a recession as negative growth, unemployment is often reduced to the absence of employment—a sort of *negative employment*. But what absence is unemployment the expression of?

The goal of *full employment* is meaningless if it is not related to the needs satisfied at work (like social participation and the opportunity for personal development) and by work (as a method of production for useful goods and services). As Chapter 1 defined it, the purpose of an economy is the parsimonious organization of contentment. Therefore, like many other issues in economics, the issue of work is one of sufficiency and autonomy: just enough work to produce what we need, and work under comfortable conditions.

Let's begin with what work produces. Not all job creation is desirable because a job does not necessarily perform useful work. At the extreme end of the spectrum, we find what British anthropologist David Graeber calls "bullshit jobs": "a form of paid employment that is so completely pointless, unnecessary, or pernicious that even the employee cannot justify its existence."[35] Based on numerous testimonies, the author develops a typology of these "full-time imposters":[36] analysts paid to write reports that no one reads, corporate lawyers who only exist because of other corporate lawyers (same logic in the advertising industry), assistants of assistants of assistants, etc., as well as a whole managerial class that could disappear tomorrow without any notable change to society.

This is, after all, the ultimate test of a job's social utility: what would happen if I stopped working tomorrow? The garbage collector would see trash cans fill with vermin and the nurse's patients would grow impatient; but what would happen to the telemarketer, or the click booster developer, or the Search Engine Optimization specialist?

This is one of the most important lessons from the pandemic: job utility is not proportional to wage, contrary to what some economists may think. It is actually often the opposite: the most useful jobs from a needs perspective—nursing assistants (gross monthly salary: €2,292), police officers (€1,921), teachers (€2,075), and garbage collectors (€2,433)—are less well paid than real estate agents (€5,282), brokers (€9,375), consultants (€4,999), and investment bankers (€5,834).[37] It is obvious that the latter group's remuneration does not stem from any greater utility than that of the former, but is only the result of a "labor market" that assigns wages according to lucrative potential and perverts our perceptions of what truly matters.

More than just useless, some jobs can be macroeconomically counterproductive. Creating positions in the automobile industry, for example, encourages car production and the associated ecological degradation. It generates income today, but it also engenders a lot of work in the anthropological sense of the term, meaning activities that, in the future, will demand time and effort. I am thinking specifically of all the extra effort required to adapt to the effects of climate change and biodiversity collapse. Same thing if a job is performed under such precarious conditions that it degrades individuals (work accidents, musculoskeletal disorders, social exclusion, workplace burnout, etc.), what we have previously called the *depreciation of labor*. What is the use in creating food delivery jobs under conditions where workers sacrifice their health for meagre pay, and for a service that is, most often, not essential?

Some will say that these useless or counterproductive jobs allow people to "make a living." And so we realize that the question of employment is never separate from that of poverty and inequality. In a society where everything is for sale (and where we are constantly encouraged to buy more), those who do not have access to property and the rents it yields are dependent on wages, hence the fear of unemployment.

A job allows us to pay our bills, but is this fact alone a necessary condition to demonstrate that we need one? If we pushed this absurd logic a bit further, we would find ourselves—as John Maynard Keynes put it in the 1930s, during a period of full-employment-obsessed recovery—paying half the population to dig holes and the other half to fill them up. Today, we encounter the same logic in our approach to the ecological transition: pay part of the population to build SUVs, design advertisements, and extract oil, and another to treat the illnesses linked to air pollution, treat malaise, and construct water bomber planes to fight forest fires.

An individual or a company may worry about not having enough to make it through the end of the month, but that is not the case for an economy. At the macroeconomic level, there is always enough income to buy what is produced because incomes flow directly from production; that is why GDP measured as the sum of final product prices is the same as GDP measured as the sum of all incomes. This does not mean that supply automatically creates demand, but that in a country like France poverty is a distribution issue. The dependence on paid employment (often reluctantly endured), along with the obligation to work full-time for life, stems from a specific choice of economic organization: the commodification of employment in a capitalist system under neoliberal governance.

But this dependence is not inevitable. In an economy with a more balanced distribution of value added, democratic control over prices, and a culture of sufficiency, we could all become "rentiers," with wages representing only a small part of our wealth. Guaranteed minimum income, free public services, food benefits, social housing, price caps, the redistribution of inheritance—there, a whole program that would permit the decoupling of living power from purchasing power, and thus, for many, from paid employment.

Let's now discuss the quality of work as a social activity. Unemployment is a hardship, not just because of the precarity it entails, but also because it is a factor of exclusion, especially in a society whose code of ethics glorifies work. Unemployment is traumatic because it isolates us, withholding our right to participate in social life. This right is fundamental; it is beyond risky to entrust it to a "labor market" (as we saw in the previous chapter, labor is one of those things whose essence can be degraded by commodification). We do not entrust justice to a "justice market," or transplants to an "organ market." For a simple reason: these goods and services are too important for their governance to be left to volatile markets. The same goes for work: it is far too vital an activity to be commodified.

What if the solution to mass unemployment were not to create mass employment, but rather to reorganize how we all contribute to economic activity? These contributions are many, and lots of useful activities are not currently recognized as work deserving remuneration. Raising children, running a sports association, giving free language lessons, writing an economics book on degrowth, and all the informal daily acts of solidarity; these activities produce utility (use value) without being counted as a source of exchange value, and thus without being recognized as wealth.

Instead of creating employment for the sake of creating employment, let's start by recognizing certain forms of work as deserving remuneration. Some call for a "care income" to remunerate unpaid reproductive labor, which today is largely taken on by women.[38] Others advocate for an "ecological transition income" to support people and initiatives already active or emerging in fields related to the transition;[39] a "wage for life"[40] that would remunerate a person according to their level of qualification and irrespective of actual output; an "unconditional autonomy allowance"[41] that would recognize non-market labor and everyone's contribution to a society's pluralistic wealth; and "zero long-term unemployment zones,"[42] which would operationalize the idea of guaranteed employment.[43]

And let's not forget that the goal of an economy is to economize the resources at its disposal, starting with human labor. As we saw in the previous chapter, we too are finite resources with limits that cannot be exceeded. A well-performing economy should logically *reduce* working hours (at least those that no one takes pleasure in) to increase free time. Maximizing GDP to "create employment" is as absurd as maximizing the fuss in a kitchen to "create kitchen time." The aim of an economy is not activity for its own sake, but optimizing the satisfaction of needs. The complex question of unemployment (like that of poverty and inequality) is not solved by simply boosting GDP, but rather by thoroughly reforming the social organization of work.

The Public Budget

At the 2020 World Economic Forum in Davos, Austrian Chancellor Sebastian Kurz declared, in response to criticisms of growth, that "happiness does not finance retirement." Emmanuel Macron echoed the same idea, arguing against degrowth because it would cripple the welfare state.[v] This is yet another of growth's promises: when the state's coffers are empty, only GDP growth can save us from austerity.

And indeed, the public budget depends on a number of taxes, including some on market activity. In 2019, gross tax revenue in France was as high as 414.6 billion euros: 45% from the tax on value added (186 bn), 21% from the income tax (87 bn), 16% from the corporate tax (67 bn), 4% from the domestic consumption tax on energy products (17 bn), and the remaining 14% from various taxes like those on property or inheritance. All else being equal, a contraction of the market economy would constrict revenues from these taxes, and so the state's budget, which could no longer guarantee the quality of public services.

The first flaw in this reasoning is that it sees public services as unproductive luxuries made possible by levies on private activity. This is wrong.[44] Public services are a form of production in their own right. A private company borrows funds—most often created ex nihilo by the banks—to cover the costs of an output it will later sell at a higher cost. The state does exactly the same when it produces health or education services. Yet these services are distributed to citizens more or less free of charge and funded collectively through taxation.

Some countries finance services collectively and others do so

---

[v] "We produce to finance a social model and a welfare state. And so, to those who say there is a climate emergency and that we must stop everything that pollutes . . . I say, fine, what is your social plan? Who will fund retirement? Who will fund healthcare? Who will fund education? Nobody. Because production is necessary." (Emmanual Macron in Pau before a panel selected by the newspaper *Sud Ouest*, March 18, 2022).

privately, but in both cases value added is created. Put another way, the funding of public activities is no more dependent on growth than the funding of private activities. We might even argue that public production is more efficient because its costs are low compared to the private sector—no shareholder dividends, advertising, sales commissions, etc.

Let's take a specific example: pensions. In a pay-as-you-go system like France's, we make contributions during our economically active life (thus funding present-day pensions) in order to collect a pension later (funded by future workers' contributions). An economy does not need to grow to finance these pensions: it just needs to ensure intergenerational equilibrium and a sufficient contribution rate.[45] These contributions primarily depend on wages, which represent only part of economic growth. Increasing shareholder dividends does not increase contributions to the pension system. Once again, determining the minimum pension amount is not a matter of production, but of how value added is distributed. The latest report from the Conseil d'Orientation des Retraites includes a section titled "a reduced dependence on economic growth," which estimates the variation in pension payments through 2070 under different growth scenarios.[46] The difference between the two extreme scenarios (a growth forecast of 1% versus 1.8%) represents only a two point variation (from 12% of GDP devoted to pension payments to 14% for the lower growth rate).

The second limitation of this reasoning concerns the net taxation of growth. As we saw in earlier chapters, market growth also generates social and environmental costs. Every year, the medical expenses reimbursed by health insurance in France to cover pathologies attributable to air pollution are as high as 3 billion euros.[47] According to the French Institute for Public Health Surveillance, the cost of handling the 30,000 cases of workplace burnout each year in France is roughly the same.[48] Producing *more* cars is no guarantee of net revenue for the state if this activity creates more costs than benefits. If that's the case, a decrease in car production would therefore alleviate the burden on the public budget.

Let's add that some public spending is linked not to economic activity itself, but to the way in which that activity is organized. Take scientific research, for example. A portion of public funding earmarked for research remunerates the companies responsible for the publication of academic journals. "Responsible for" is a generous way to put it, as almost all these journals' activities—research, peer review, and editorial work—are done for no pay by researchers, hence the extraordinary profit margin of a company like Elsevier: 40%, or almost four times the average margin of a traditional journal.[49]

If, starting tomorrow, French universities refused to pay Elsevier's subscription fees and instead found ways for researchers to publish in open-access journals, the cost of research in France would shrink. Nothing would change in terms of the volume of research, but the public budget would shed an unnecessary cost. Instead of straining to increase the public budget to be able to publish more, it would suffice to expropriate the private companies that profit unfairly from a monopolistic situation. Healthcare is a similar case, with drug prices almost always exceeding their production costs,[50] and even wind turbine manufacturing, which would cost up to 65% less if wind turbines were produced by not-for-profit cooperatives.[51]

Some may argue that, even after partial de-commodification, a rise in the production of scientific articles (or medications) will generate additional costs that will need to be covered. This brings us back to the first error in reasoning: the idea that public services depend on a windfall of private money. This is not the case. Production, whether private or public, is limited by two fundamental factors of production: available time and natural resources.

If we want *more* research (or more of anything, for that

matter), we will have to mobilize more work hours and more energy and materials. Money is only an intermediary for value, and the argument that we are limited because there is not enough money is a myth. As long as real production capabilities exist and can be mobilized, production is possible. There are many ways to mobilize these capabilities—through market or non-market relations, with or without using money, and under various institutional arrangements.

What about debt? Isn't economic growth the only way to pay down the public debt? Once again, an error in reasoning. We often measure public debt as a public debt/GDP ratio—118% of GDP at the end of the first quarter of 2021, for example—which creates the impression that increasing GDP is necessary to lowering the debt.

This is misleading for a number of reasons. Let's start by noting that public debt never has to be paid back in full. The state is not an economic agent like the others, because it can "roll over" its debt—meaning that it can issue new debt instruments to repay the old. Once a debt instrument reaches maturity (that is, when it must be repaid), the state can just repay it by issuing a new debt instrument. The real cost of public debt is the interest payments the state must make during the period of the loan—what we call the "debt burden."

GDP is a flow and debt is a stock. To measure the debt's weight, we compare the *public debt burden* (the annual monetary flow devoted to debt payments) to GDP (the total monetary flow) or to the total amount of public revenue.[52] In this way, we can identify the share of GDP that must be allocated to the debt burden (the logic is the same for a business assessing its debt burden by estimating the annual cost of its repayment). The cost of France's public debt neared 33.2 billion euros in 2020, which is 2.5% of all public revenue or 1.5% of GDP. Ultimately, this cost is a public expenditure like any other, a cost that depends on the interest rates at which the state borrows, and more generally on the way the monetary system is structured.

Currently, the state is financed by affluent households through financial intermediaries. Even if it is hard to determine exactly who holds France's public debt, we know that the majority of financial assets (including public debt instruments) are held by the richest households, whose total wealth is 50% to 90% composed of financial assets.[53] This method of financing bears a cost—the income collected by those who lend to the state. The same money that was not taxed (after the wealth tax was suppressed or after the income tax's progressivity was reduced, for example) will thus be saved and invested in the public debt, demanding interest payments from then on. It becomes clear that the imperative of debt repayment is not some inescapable technical mechanism, but the result of a taxation decision and, thus, of a redistribution policy.

According to a 2014 calculation by the French Collective for a Citizens' Audit of Public Debt, the current public debt would be 29 GDP points lower if the state had borrowed directly from households and banks at a real interest rate of 2% (equivalent to the long-term growth rate and interest rate) instead of financing itself on the financial markets.[54] Why struggle to grow at all costs when we could simply structure state financing differently? At the risk of repeating ourselves, the argument remains the same: public debt sustainability, and the issue of public budgets more broadly, is not a question of GDP size but rather of the distribution of value added.

Quality of Life

Growth is "absolutely necessary for living standards to rise," says Anne-Laure Delatte, deputy director of the Center for Prospective Studies and International Information.[55] For while money can't buy happiness, it does buy all the things that contribute to it: a good education, decent housing, access to healthcare, a healthy diet, the opportunity to travel, etc. We don't call it "purchasing power" for nothing—in an economy where we satisfy our needs by buying things, to be rich is to be free of need.

Under this theory, we should see a strong correlation between GDP and happiness, but in reality that is not the case. This observation is not new. We see it across a vast body of literature dating back to the work of American economist Richard Easterlin in the 1970s. In a 1974 article, Easterlin presented over thirty studies conducted in nineteen different countries on the link between GDP and happiness.[56] The result: while there is a positive correlation between the two variables, the link loosens beyond a certain level of per capita income. Hence the modern references to "Easterlin's paradox," that situation where societies continue to "grow richer" without improving their well-being.

Studies have evolved a lot since, considering not only subjective indicators of well-being like happiness, but also objective indicators like life expectancy, education levels, access to energy, and the quality of democracy. One of the key studies on the subject, published in the prestigious *Nature Sustainability* journal in November 2021, compares social outcomes in more than 140 countries relative to their ecological footprint.[57]

We learn that Costa Rica (with a per capita GDP of €12,140), France (€39,030), Finland (€48,773), and the United States (€63,413) have a similar quality of life with GDP levels that vary by a factor of 1 to 5. The latest ranking in the "World Happiness Report" reveals the same pattern: Finland and Denmark are at the top of the list with a GDP per capita well below that of countries ranked much lower.[58]

Over the last fifteen years, and for the 149 countries ranked, non-economic variables account for 74% of the level of happiness, compared with only 26% for per capita GDP.[59] These findings align with Easterlin's saturation theory: past a certain level of monetary wealth, the production of commodities (measured in money) no longer matters.

This result resonates with what social scientists tell us about happiness. A study that tracked 724 Americans from the 1930s throughout their life to better understand the determinants of health and happiness concluded that what matters most are human relationships: love, friendship, and family.[60] An Australian nurse in palliative care cataloged the five most common regrets of the dying: not having followed their dreams, having worked too much, not having had the courage to express their feelings, not having spent enough time with their friends, and not having given themselves the opportunity to truly be happy.[61] No one, on their deathbed, regrets not having contributed enough to GDP.

Take health. In 1975, economist Samuel Preston unveiled another paradox, this time between GDP and life expectancy.[62] Growth in a poor country was accompanied by a significant rise in life expectancy, while the change was minimal or nonexistent for a rich country. Some might argue that life expectancy naturally levels off because of biological limits, but GDP ceases to affect health long before reaching this ceiling. Portugal, for example, has a life expectancy of 81.1 years, which is 2.4 years longer than the American average, and that with 65% less income per capita.[63] U.S. GDP is eight times that of France and has been growing faster for almost forty years,[64] yet health outcomes are much better in France.

It would be wrong to think that we need to increase GDP to improve health. Considering that in France the richest 5% of men (with an average monthly income of 5,800 euros) live 13 years longer than the poorest 5% (470 euros),[65] reducing inequality would be a much more effective strategy for improving life expectancy than increasing GDP.

This trend holds true for most indicators of health and

social well-being. As shown by British epidemiologist Richard Wilkinson,[66] residents of egalitarian countries live longer and in better health, have fewer unwanted pregnancies and lower infant mortality, and have more trust in one another. They have lower crime and incarceration rates, consume fewer drugs and less alcohol, and show higher rates of academic success and greater social mobility. According to Wilkinson,[67] if the United Kingdom were to reduce its income inequality by half, the country could halve its crime and obesity rates, reduce mental illness by two thirds, cut incarceration and teen pregnancies by 80%, and increase the level of trust by 85%—and all without any increase in national income.

It's not money that determines well-being but what it enables us to buy, we're often told. First, let's note that growth does not create purchasing power: that depends more on the distribution of value added than on the level of production (see the section on inequality). A single figure illustrates this: between 1967 and 2013, U.S. GDP grew from 4 to 16 trillion dollars, while over the same period, American real median household income only increased by 19% until 1999 and has stagnated since.[68] GDP *per capita* increases but it is only a statistical illusion, as median household income stays flat.

Moreover, purchasing power (or standard of living) is only one way to increase "living power"[69] (that is, quality of life), or what Indian economist Amartya Sen calls "capabilities."[70] I meet my need for knowledge by reading a book that I bought at a bookstore, but others could do the same by borrowing it from a library.

The city of London provides for its residents' housing needs through a mostly private real estate market, while the city of Vienna does so through a market that is mostly public and co-operative. Housing in London is more dependent on income than in Vienna, because its cost incorporates the rent owed to property owners, which is not the case for the social housing system prevalent in Vienna (the same logic applies to public transportation, healthcare, education, energy, telecommunications, etc.). This has nothing to do with housing quality or quality of life, which, according to the latest *Mercer Quality of Living* ranking, is much higher in Vienna (ranked first) than in London (ranked 41st). The needs are the same, but the economic organization of their satisfaction differs. Land inequality in London creates a dependency on income growth, while Vienna's social model fosters independence from growth.

The real question is: is it wise to treat the satisfaction of needs as something that should grow indefinitely? This would conflate hoarding with abundance. Need satisfaction does not answer to the logic of infinity. Fundamental needs like subsistence, protection, and freedom meet *sufficiency thresholds*: enough food to be in good health, enough living space to feel comfortable at home, enough ways of getting around to feel free, etc. No one needs an infinite increase in medications or doctors; we just need access to the quantity and quality of care necessary to stay healthy. People without a bike need *one* bike, not an annual (and perpetual) 3% increase in bike production. And once that bike is produced, mobility needs depend on our capacity to maintain and repair it, needs we can either commodify (adding to GDP), or organize collectively through non-market networks of reciprocity like self-managed bike shops (no GDP increase).

Part of our material comfort depends on things that we already have. I do not need to *buy* a washing machine—I need to *have access* to a washing machine when I want to do my laundry. In Sweden, most buildings have a "*tvättstuga*" (common laundry room), while in France, more than 96% of households are equipped with an individual washer. By pooling the ownership of washing machines, we buy fewer of them, which reduces GDP and our dependence on purchasing power, all while increasing living power (here, the ability to do laundry at a lower cost). The production necessary becomes stationary, just enough to replace and repair existing machines, with minor fluctuations up and down depending on the evolution of needs.

Another part of our comfort depends on things that are not counted in GDP. Spending time in nature is crucial for well-being. But for that, you need time and nature, two factors of well-being that are often undermined by economic growth. What's the point of producing more (washers, for example) and polluting more when we could produce less for the same final service, through shared use? This would allow us to work less, thus freeing up time that could be enjoyed in a natural environment not devastated by our productive activities.

According to sociologists, it is neither work nor shopping that makes us happy. If we rank all our daily activities according to the degree of satisfaction they provide, work comes in 21st place, just after grocery shopping.[71] At the top of the list are activities that are more qualitative than quantitative: going to the movies, the library, and the museum, taking a walk, spending time with loved ones, playing sports, reading, and taking a nap.

There is another reason why growing the total size of the economy will not improve the well-being of everyone. A small detour through theory: in *The Theory of the Leisure Class*, Thorstein Veblen (1857-1929), the founding father of institutional economics, asserted something that now seems obvious: we consume not only to satisfy our direct needs (housing, food, transportation, etc.), but also to display social status, to distinguish ourselves.

There was a time when this distinction was achieved through ownership: some people owned a car, a television set, or went on vacation, while others did not have such access. Today, access to these goods is democratized, and the hierarchies between consumer classes have become more subtle. Some drive a Renault and others own a Porsche, some wear H&M and others wear Lacoste, some vacation in Lozère, others in Tahiti. Status is no longer defined only by ownership (having or not having something), but by comparison (the prestige of that thing compared to other things).

The allure of these products does not derive primarily from their intrinsic quality (or at least that is not the most determining factor), but rather from the prestige they procure. The Nobel Prize is only a source of prestige because it is awarded to very few people, allowing recipients to elevate themselves above others. If everyone had one, it would have no value. Same thing for a Rolex or a Prada bag. James Duesenberry calls this a "demonstration effect": we consume in a certain way to display our social status.[72]

There is a collective dynamic to consumption. If the people I admire increase their consumption, I will feel compelled to increase my own so as not to feel inferior. This is the "bandwagon effect." We could also want to consume more (or differently) to differentiate ourselves from a class we consider inferior—we'll call that the "snob effect." The greater the disparities, the stronger these effects, triggering what Robert H. Frank calls "expenditure cascades": the increase in consumption by a given class provokes a rise in consumption by the class below, which is in turn imitated by the next class.[73] In a materialistic society, these phenomena drive people to buy more, but we can see how the underlying logic of the race for prestige could have the opposite effect. In a society where minimalism signified prestige, there would be pressure to consume less.

The key point here is that if everyone increases their consumption, no one truly advances. This is Austrian economist Fred Hirsch's thesis in *Social Limits to Growth* (1976). The satisfaction someone derives from a "positional" good does not depend on their own level of consumption but on that of other people. It's a zero-sum game, where each individual strives to have more, but because everyone is doing the same, they all remain in the same relative position—hence the "positional treadmill"[74] metaphor. As Hirsch puts it, "if everyone stands on tiptoe, no one sees better." What's the use in doubling our working hours to be able to afford a Ferrari, if the only point of having a Ferrari is to impress other people (who will not be impressed because they will have one too). To stand out, you will now have to own two Ferraris, and so on. Ultimately, the increase in Ferraris will not increase well-being.

Growth's promise as a source of happiness is empty. To think that GDP increases well-being is to look at the finger that points to the moon. For a well-being economy, let's stop talking about quantitative standards of living and concentrate on quality of life—on living power, meaningfulness, and community rather than on purchasing power. If needs are unmet, let us produce what is necessary to satisfy them and then let's stop. Growth should be reimagined as a temporary strategy to adjust to a situation of deficiency, and not as the default mode of operation for a developed economy.

Growth is a bogus cure, "the magic elixir of impossible dreams."[75] Hoping to resolve complex problems like unemployment, poverty, inequality, austerity, and malaise by pushing the GDP button is kind of like trying to fix a computer by hitting it with a hammer. The eradication of poverty, the reduction of inequalities, employment, public services, and well-being do not flow from the quantifiable upticks of an abstract indicator. *How to increase GDP* is a poor substitute for a much more fundamental question: what do we really need? How do we want to live? And what do we want to produce?

Some might qualify this argument: if growth is not sufficient to resolve all problems, it is still at least necessary—this is the "theorem of growth as prerequisite" that economist Jean Gadrey critiqued over a decade ago.[76] If they concede that growth does not reduce inequality, they will say that at least it raises the income spectrum, thereby reducing poverty. And if they accept that growth is not necessary for creating jobs, they will argue that the challenge lies in our capacity to remunerate these new jobs. And if they concede that it is possible to finance activities without growth, then the lack of jobs becomes the obstacle. These lines of reasoning are perfectly circular and, within the framework of dominant economic theories, insoluble.

The last line of defense will be to say that all these things are possible in theory, but politically unfeasible. Yes, we could make poverty disappear and reduce inequality by redistributing existing wealth; yes, it is possible to find work for every job seeker without necessarily increasing material production, and so on, but politicians will not do it. If the debate gets this far, this chapter will have achieved its aim: to demonstrate that the barriers to action are not economic, but political, moral, and cultural.

5
A Brief History of Degrowth
From Objection to Growth to Post-Growth

Degrowth is more complex a subject than we might think, the culmination of several generations of ideas going back at least to the 1960s. Starting as a simple *objection to growth* in the 1970s, the term evolved to become *degrowth* and *post-growth* in the 2000s.

The history I will retrace here is the one of these terms, much shorter and more recent than an archeology of the ideas that contributed to their formation.[i] To simplify things, I will proceed in three phases: prehistory, genesis, and effervescence. In the 1970s, a few isolated intellectuals laid out the conceptual premises in developing an *objection to growth*. Beginning in 2002, the term *décroissance* emerged in France and started gaining popularity in Europe and in Quebec. After the first international conference on the topic in 2008, *décroissance* becomes *degrowth* and takes over the Anglosphere and the rest of the world, a phase that takes us all the way to the present day.

---

[i] Since the early 2010s, Serge Latouche, one of the first degrowth theorists in France, has taken on this herculean task through a series of books titled *Les précurseurs de la décroissance*. The collection includes 32 volumes and encompasses a variety of ideas and characters, like Françoise d'Eaubonne's ecofeminism, Murray Bookchin's libertarian municipalism, Ivan Illich's tools for conviviality, Theodore Roszak's ecopsychology, and Cornelius Castoriadis's radical autonomy.

The Prehistory of Degrowth

The term "*décroissance*" did not appear in 2002 as if by magic. Its emergence was the result of a long fermentation that began in the 1960s. In line with hippie counterculture and following the so-called "Trente Glorieuses," the May 1968 revolution popularized a critique of the system steeped in political ecology, feminism, third-worldism, anarchism, and anticapitalism. The graffiti of the time speaks volumes: "down with the consumption society," "the economy is wounded—I hope she dies!", or better yet, "you don't fall in love with a growth rate." Society was in turmoil, and it is to these first sparks that we owe the premises of degrowth. I will retrace three notable uses of the term.

The word "*décroissance*" makes one of its first notable appearances at a public debate on June 13, 1972, through the lips of André Gorz,[1] cofounder of the *Nouvel Observateur* and one of the founding fathers of political ecology. Commenting on the Meadows report's conclusions, Gorz posed the following question: "Is the global equilibrium, of which the non-growth—or even degrowth—of material production is a condition, compatible with the survival of the [capitalist] system?" At the time, and in this specific context, degrowth refers only to the phenomenon of reducing production as such, a "productive contraction" as André Gorz sometimes put it in his writing.[2]

To understand this first reference to degrowth, we must turn back to two works that set the terms of debate at the time. We owe the first to Nicholas Georgescu-Roegen[3] (1906-1994), a Romanian and naturalized American mathematician and economist. In *The Entropy Law and the Economic Process* (1971), he was one of the first to link the natural sciences with economics, proposing a new approach he called *bioeconomics*, which would later contribute to the emergence of *ecological economics*. In his view, economic production must be seen as an extension of the biological process and, as such, should conform to the principles of thermodynamics and evolution. Thus, the economic process can be understood as a metabolism that feeds on energy and good-quality material drawn from nature, while it ejects these same resources in the form of waste. Production comes with an irreversible dissipation of energy and matter. Nothing is lost, nothing is created, and everything is transformed (the first law of thermodynamics), and if this transformation degrades the resources it uses (second law, that of entropy), it means that there can be no infinite material growth in a finite world.

The Limits to Growth is the second work without which we would never have talked about degrowth. A true best-seller (over 12 million copies sold, translated into 37 languages), it is the fruit of many years of labor by a small group of model developers at the Massachusetts Institute of Technology (MIT) led by Dennis and Donella Meadows.[4] Applying a new modeling technique (system dynamics), they built "World3," a computer model they used to simulate twelve prospective scenarios studying the evolution of industrial production, population growth, food production, resource depletion, and pollution. Their conclusions were unequivocal: sooner or later, any exponential growth in production and population will end up outstripping the planet's ecological limits. By consequence, the planet's health demands that human societies respect a "global equilibrium."

Nicholas Georgescu-Roegen gives us a theory (no infinite growth in a finite world), and the Meadows an attempt at empirical demonstration[ii] (if growth continues, it will eventually

---

[ii] Today, the Meadows' fears are more than justified. Since the initial study (1972), the book has been reissued and updated by the authors twice (in 1992 and in 2004). In 2008, Graham Turner, an Australian researcher, published a scientific article confirming the Meadows' "standard run" scenario for the 1970-2000 period ("A comparison of *The Limits to Growth* with 30 years of reality"). More recently, in 2020, Gaya Herrington ran the numbers again, confirming the accuracy of certain scenarios through 2019 ("Update to *Limits to Growth*: Comparing the World3 model with empirical data").

meet ecological obstacles). From the confluence of these two works would emerge a new idea: *the objection to growth*. To be an objector to growth is to be alarmed by growth curves that would soon exhaust natural resources, endanger ecosystems, and degrade collective life. By analogy to *conscientious objectors*, growth objectors are opposed to the continuous increase of production and consumption.

In 1973, the journal *La Nef* used the expression for the first time and dedicated an entire issue to growth objectors—where we find degrowth's second appearance. André Amar, a philosopher who earned his degree at the École Normale Supérieure, wrote in an article titled "La croissance et le problème moral" ("Growth and the Moral Problem"): "If degrowth, at least in certain forms, now seems to be necessary, we cannot, by contrast, treat the economic or political problems it raises superficially." He defined growth not only as a real phenomenon (the industrial production of Gorz and the Meadows), but also as an ideology. For the author, the "growth phenomenon" is rooted in "the spirit of modern Western civilization," leading him to call for "a profound transformation in our thinking"—a similar proposition to what Serge Latouche would later call the *decolonization of the growth imaginary*.

The third mention of the term "*décroissance*" comes from Bernard Charbonneau,[5] another pioneer of political ecology. A year after publishing the book *Le Système et le Chaos. Critique du développement exponentiel*, in March 1974, he wrote a three-page piece in the Protestant journal *Foi & vie* titled "*Coûts de la croissance et gains de la décroissance*" ("Costs of Growth and Benefits of Degrowth").

This short passage is, in my view, the one that best prefigures the idea of degrowth in its contemporary complexity. "It turns out that exponential growth, as much as it solved problems, also created them; that it entailed costs of all kinds: economic, ecological, and social. We discovered that, as all action is ambiguous, production could just as well be called destruction of raw materials: whoever produces wood razes a forest, the same thing put two different ways."[6] Charbonneau continues: "But if growth is an ambiguous phenomenon, so is degrowth, and its costs entail benefits. By producing less oil, the Arab states conserve their reserves and prolong the transition to prepare for the day when they will be depleted. And, if we have to give up the Concorde, the production of clean air and silence, which is expensive per cubic meter, will increase. Instead of a 40-page newspaper, we will have a clearer river; and the environment will be better preserved [...]. If growth begets social mobility, degrowth favors stability, and so social equilibrium, which can also be a source of happiness; and, as much as on production, we will focus on its methods and its distribution."

Unsurprisingly, these few appearances of the term "*décroissance*" were not enough to ignite public debate, with perhaps one exception. In 1972, Sicco Mansholt, vice president of the European Commission, wrote to its president, Franco-Maria Malfatti, to suggest replacing the pursuit of economic growth with that of "gross national profit." We would never have heard of this letter if he had not been named president of the Commission a month later, following Malfatti's resignation. Mansholt, who would only last six months in the role, reiterated his call in an interview with the *Nouvel Observateur*. "The question is: given the long-term limits imposed on the production of energy, food, iron, zinc, copper, water, etc., is it possible to maintain our growth rate without profoundly modifying our society? When we examine the issue rationally, the answer is clearly no. So, it is no longer even a matter of zero growth but of sub-zero growth. To put it bluntly: we must reduce our economic growth, our purely material growth, and replace it with another kind of growth—that of culture, of happiness, of well-being."[7] Here, degrowth is at once a reduction of material production and a societal project centered on new values.

The word was rarely evoked, but the idea developed under other names. Pierre Kende imagined a non-productivist socialism in as early as 1971 in *L'abondance est-elle possible?* In *Small is Beautiful: Economics as If People Mattered* (1973), Ernst Friedrich Schumacher popularized Buddhist wisdom and suggested contracting the economic sphere. In 1974, Richard Easterlin published an empirical article on the relationship between GDP and subjective well-being, showing for the first time that past a certain threshold of per capita GDP, growth no longer brings happiness. Two years later, the relationship between growth and well-being was explored in greater detail by Fred Hirsch in *Social Limits to Growth* and by Timor Scitovsky in *The Joyless Economy*, reaching the same conclusion: money—and its growth—can't buy happiness. Let's also mention *If Women Counted* (1988) by New Zealander Marilyn Waring, one of the first to formulate an anti-capitalist critique of national accounting.

This list could go on for several pages, but let's prioritize and stop at American economist Herman Daly,[8] a student of Nicholas Georgescu-Roegen and a founding figure of ecological economics,[9] a heterodox school of thought that conceptualizes the economy in its interactions with nature. In 1973, Daly published *Toward a Steady-State Economy*, an anthology of writings revisiting the ideas of various pioneers of the critique of growth, including N. Georgescu-Roegen, E. F. Schumacher, the Meadows, and others like economist Kenneth Boulding and theologian John B. Cobb. A few years later, *Steady-State Economics* (1977) was published, where Daly developed a concept we still use today: "the steady-state economy." Following John Stuart Mill's optimistic intuition in one of the chapters of *Principles of Political Economy* ("Of the Stationary State," 1848), Daly maintained that growth should be considered a temporary step toward maturity and sufficiency. Beyond a certain threshold, the pursuit of economic growth becomes counterproductive—what Daly would later call "uneconomic growth."

Daly was not alone. The 1970s are teeming with works that would later be reclaimed by contemporary authors to advocate for the idea of economic degrowth. André Gorz and his critique of work, Ivan Illich on tools for conviviality, Françoise D'Eaubonne and eco-feminism, Cornelius Castoriadis and his dialectic of autonomy and heteronomy, Jacques Ellul and his critique of technology, Murray Bookchin and his libertarian socialist ecology, René Dumont and his radical ecology, Bernard Charbonneau on the critique of development, and François Partant on post-development.[10]

We could also mention the Cocoyoc Declaration, the result of a symposium in Mexico in 1975. Although it did not use the term "degrowth" (the popular term in those circles at the time was "ecodevelopment"), it very clearly defined its contours: "A process of growth that benefits only a very small minority and that maintains or exacerbates the disparities between countries and within countries is not development. It is exploitation [. . .]. The overconsumption that monopolizes resources and accumulates waste must be restrained, while the production of essential goods for the poorest populations must increase."

But let's return to the term "*décroissance*," and more specifically, the first time it appeared in the title of a book in French. In 1979, French philosopher Jacques Grinevald and Belgian-Swiss jurist and historian Ivo Rens translated four essays by Nicholas Georgescu-Roegen and published them in a collection titled *Demain la décroissance*, or "Tomorrow, Degrowth" (the title was chosen in response to *Demain le capitalisme,* or "Tomorrow, Capitalism," a book now associated with neoliberalism, published the year before by economist Henri Lepage). The word was chosen by mutual agreement between the author (who spoke French) and the two editors to translate the concepts of *decline* and *declining state*, which appeared often in

Georgescu-Roegen's writings. More than just a collection, the selected passages breathed life into an idea that had never really been developed in Georgescu-Roegen's work. According to historian Timothée Duverger, it is with this book that the concept of degrowth was truly born.[11]

THE BIRTH OF DEGROWTH

In the 1970s, some worried about hypothetical ecological overshoots. Thirty years later, ecological limits were no longer ahead, but behind us. The IPCC reported on the troubling state of the climate, energy specialists declared that "peak oil"[12] was imminent—ecologists sounded the alarm. Hence the following conceptual development: the *objection to growth* (concern over potentially destructive growth) morphed into *degrowth* (the realization that we must not only halt growth but also contract the size of the economy). Two decades of "sustainable development" had no significant impact on our trajectory and the nightmarish future that the Meadows had predicted was materializing. Talking about "growth limits" was no longer enough of a wake-up call. We needed to go further and find a concept with shock value to awaken consciences: *degrowth*.

After two decades in gestation, two parallel events in 2002 brought forth the concept of degrowth as we know it today. In February 2002, the activist environmentalist magazine *Silence* published a special issue titled "*Décroissance soutenable et conviviale*" ("Sustainable and Inclusive Degrowth"), an issue that gained attention thanks to the publication that same month of an article by Hervé Kempf in *Le Monde*: "Sauver le monde par la 'décroissance soutenable'" ("Saving the World through 'Sustainable Degrowth'"). The opening article of the special issue, written by Bruno Clémentin and Vincent Cheynet, posited "sustainable degrowth," for the first time, as an alternative to the oxymoron of "sustainable development," development that could never be sustainable without moving beyond capitalism and its obsession with growth.

The first article only reprised the definition of degrowth inherited from the 1970s (Gorz's productive contraction), but another piece in the issue written by Mauro Bonaiuti, one of the first Italian intellectuals to use the term, went further. The author called for a "profound transformation of the economic and productive imagination," where "material degrowth" could transform into "relational and spiritual growth." Here we see the origin of what would later become one of the movement's slogans, "*moins de biens, plus de liens*" ("fewer things, more relationships"). Degrowth was no longer just less (production) but also more (social relationships, resonance, happiness, etc.).

Even more groundbreaking, Serge Latouche's article added a radically new dimension: degrowth as "decolonization of the growth imaginary." Titled "À bas le développement durable! Vive la décroissance conviviale!" ("Down with Sustainable Development! Long Live Convivial Degrowth!"), the article called for an "escape from development and economism," linking degrowth to the abandonment of an "economic imaginary"—the belief that *more* always means *better*. From this point on, Serge Latouche started to conceptualize degrowth as an "exit from economics," meaning the abandonment of a utilitarian worldview, characterized by an extractive relationship with nature, blind productivism, the omnipresent commodification of social relations, unlimited consumerist impulses, and an obsession with money and its accumulation.

The *decolonization of the growth imaginary* became one of the most famous phrases in the degrowth corpus. It aptly captures the concept's central idea: to disentangle ourselves from a monomaniacal way of thinking obsessed with monetary value and its accumulation. The word may deter some, but it undeniably constitutes a counterculture slogan, a critique of capitalism as an ideology. Hence Serge Latouche's phonetic quip: before we can *degrow* ("*décroître*"), we must first *disbelieve* ("*décroire*"), rid ourselves of the religion of growth.[iii]

If the keyword of the 1970s objection to growth was "reduction," that of 2000s degrowth was "emancipation." The new project of degrowth aimed to deconstruct the grand narrative of growth, as well as the sub-ideologies that feed into it: *economism*, which sacrifices everything for the economy; *neoliberalism* and its governance through markets; *extractivism* and the endless exploitation of nature; *utilitarianism* as a cult of maximization, *capitalism* and its devotion to the accumulation of capital, *commercialism* as the transformation of the world into commodities; *consumerism* and its limitless needs; *techno-scientism* as the denial of limits. At the time, degrowth was above all a critical theory, the rejection of a specific development model and a strategy to uproot it, but not yet the vision for an ideal society (what I will soon describe as *post-growth*).

After this first text, Serge Latouche[13] was thrust to center stage. Professor emeritus at the Université Paris-Sud, trained in law, political science, and economics, his first works focused on poverty (he wrote a thesis in economics—"La paupérisation à l'échelle mondiale," or "World-Scale Pauperization," 1966—based on fieldwork in the Democratic Republic of Congo), and the epistemology of the field of economics (he wrote another thesis in 1974, this time in philosophy, titled "Essai sur l'épistémologie de l'économie politique," or "Essay on the Epistemology of Political Economy"). Drawing on his experiences in Africa and Laos, Latouche proposed a critique of development and growth as legitimization strategies for the

---

[iii] Serge Latouche likes to remind us that degrowth is above all "a-growth"—that is, atheism with respect to growth, a critique of the economistic ideology that sees in the growth of monetary aggregates a new definition of progress.

exploitation of countries in the Global South. In *La Planète des naufragés* (1991), he made the connection between growth and environmental degradation, laying the foundations for the degrowth theory he would develop a decade later.

A few days after the publication of the special issue of *Silence*, a conference was held in Paris titled "Défaire le développement, refaire le monde" ("Undoing Development, Remaking the World"). Latouche would later consider it the founding act of the degrowth movement; it was indeed the first time a group of people physically gathered around the idea. While the term was not in the conference's title, the subject was on the agenda. In the wake of this event, the "Réseau des objecteurs de croissance pour l'après-développement" ("Network of Growth Objectors for Post-Development") was born, with a manifesto drafted by Latouche advocating for "a society in which economic values will have lost their centrality" and for a "decolonization of our imagination and a de-economization of minds."

This new concept of *sustainable degrowth* inspired a few academics and activists, but the enthusiasm remained limited and major media showed little interest in the concept, confined at the time to activist circles. Pierre Rabhi[14] made it his rallying cry in his pre-presidential campaign for the 2002 elections. A farmer and writer from the Sahara living in Cévennes, he unveiled his political agenda as a *call for a conscience insurrection* ("*Appel pour une insurrection des consciences*") that declared from the outset: "Growth is not the solution: it is the problem [. . .] the time for sustainable degrowth has come." His thinking continued the tradition of *voluntary simplicity*, imbued with a spirituality that combined moderation and non-violence. To exit the "overconsumption society," he urged everyone to *do their part*. From this last idea, the Colibri movement was born in 2007, in reference to the Native American legend of a hummingbird who, drop by drop, did its part to extinguish a massive forest fire. Rabhi continued to use the word "*décroissance*" through 2005, before ditching it for "*la sobriété heureuse*" (or "power of restraint").

The first book on degrowth came out in September 2003: *Objectif décroissance. Vers une société harmonieuse*. Edited by Vincent Cheynet, Michel Bernard, and Bruno Clémentin, the book attained some success. With over 8,000 copies sold, it was reprinted three times and translated into Italian, Spanish, and Catalan. This curious concept caught the attention of *Le Monde diplomatique*, which published for the first time an editorial on the subject: "Pour une société de décroissance" ("For a Degrowth Society"), by Serge Latouche. In it, he wrote: "It is therefore degrowth that we must strive for: for a society founded on quality rather than quantity, on cooperation rather than competition, for a humanity free from economism that sets social justice as its objective." Note that it is no longer just a matter of a society *in* degrowth (Gorz's productive contraction) but a society *of* degrowth, that is, a society animated by specific values. After the inevitable degrowth of the 1970s, the project evolved into *convivial* degrowth, the utopia of a different kind of prosperity.

The monthly magazine *La Décroissance, le journal de la joie de vivre* (*Degrowth: The Joie de Vivre Journal*) was launched in March 2004 under the direction of Vincent Cheynet and Vruno Clémentin, the two creators of the concept of "sustainable degrowth." Here too, let's note the evolution from the 1970s. More than just an environmental strategy, degrowth becomes a philosophy centered on values like autonomy, cooperation, sufficiency, sharing, conviviality, and compassion. Today, after nearly 200 issues, the magazine still exists. Its satirical pieces often spark controversy, even within the degrowth movement—which has, more than once, opposed its editorials.

The *sustainable degrowth* slogan quickly spread to other countries. It arrived in Belgium in 2004, where the Mouvement Politique des Objecteurs de Croissance would form a few years later. Two movements emerged in Italy: the Associazione per la Decrescita, centered on research in 2004, and shortly afterward the Movimento per la Decrescita Felice, more focused on activism and local initiatives. Degrowth appeared in Quebec in 2006 during discussions around Serge Mongeau among voluntary simplicity researchers and activists, leading to the creation of the Mouvement Québécois pour une décroissance conviviale. Also in 2006, the Entesa pel decreixement emerged in Catalonia, the first degrowth movement in the Iberian Peninsula. Germany had had a strong movement critiquing growth since the 1970s, but it was the "Beyond Growth" conference organized by Attac in Berlin in 2011 that really got the ball rolling.

So degrowth was spreading, but it was in France that it gained the most traction. Degrowth expanded into a field of action: conferences; a demonstration against Formula 1; academic François Schneider's year-long tour peddling the idea of degrowth, while traveling by donkey; a "Degrowth March"; lively debates on the website decroissance.info; summits to prepare a campaign strategy for the 2007 presidential election; and a campaign for the 2009 European elections. The degrowth movement revolved around two groups: the Parti pour la Décroissance, a political party with electoral ambitions, and the Mouvement des Objecteurs de Croissance, a movement without an electoral mission.

Degrowth was not only a field of action but also a field of study, dominated at the time by two thinkers, Serge Latouche and Paul Ariès. In 2005, Paul Ariès, a political scientist from Lyon, wrote *Décroissance ou barbarie* (*Degrowth or Barbarism*), in which he described degrowth as a *"mot-obus"*[iv] for "annihilating the ideology of growth,"[15] imbuing it with a more political connotation than the simple productive contraction of the 1970s. After Cheynet and Clémentin's *sustainable degrowth*,

---

[iv] A neologism meaning literally "bombshell word" [Translator's Note].

and Latouche's *convivial degrowth*, Ariès talked about "equitable degrowth," linking ecology to the fight against inequality. He breaks it down into thirteen projects: destroying the ideologies of progress, consumerism, and laborism; relocalizing; making essential goods free; respecting nature; rediscovering an authentic lifestyle, connected to the body, time, and space; guaranteeing autonomy; re-symbolizing society; and developing the movement for degrowth.

In 2006, Serge Latouche published the definitive French-language book on the subject. Titled *Le pari de la décroissance* (*The Degrowth Gamble*), the book describes degrowth as a virtuous cycle composed of eight interdependent transformations: reevaluating, reconceptualizing, restructuring, redistributing, relocalizing, reducing, reusing, and recycling. Everything starts with (1) changing the values associated with growth economics—for example by replacing competition with cooperation, self-interest with altruism, and exploitation with care. Changing values necessarily means (2) calling into question the concepts that help us interpret reality, like wealth, moderation, abundance, and scarcity. Calling these concepts into question entails the transformation of modes of (3) production and consumption, as well as of (4) the distribution of property rights, natural resources, employment, and wealth. An indispensable pillar among the eight transformations, (5) relocalization must be economic, cultural, and political. These changes will result in (6) the reduction of a certain number of undesirable products of neoliberal capitalist society, namely the ecological footprint, overconsumption, waste, and working time. To reduce the ecological footprint, we must (7) reuse things and (8) recycle. While Ariès focused on political strategies, Latouche dismissed the idea of gaining power electorally and betted instead on the transformation of civil society.

In order to support these efforts with theory, the biannual

journal *Entropia: revue d'étude théorique et politique de la décroissance* (*Entropia: Journal of Degrowth Theory and Policy*) was launched that same year. Its ambition: to lay out the concept's theoretical foundations. Up to this point, degrowth had primarily been a slogan for activists, rarely taken seriously by universities and policymakers (it would take until the 2010s for a real scientific literature on the subject to emerge). The journal published sixteen issues on various subjects (work, utopia, collapse, counterpower, the sacred, the role of the state, etc.), engaging 174 authors before it ceased publication in 2014.

In the 2000s, degrowth was growing. Ideas were piling up and it was easy to get lost in them. Fabrice Flipo, a philosopher of science and technology at the Université Paris-Diderot, published an academic article in 2007 titled "Voyage dans la galaxie décroissante," whose purpose was to map out the field of degrowth.[v] According to the author, degrowth sits at the intersection of five schools of thought or "sources." *Ecology* describes the degradations caused by growth; *bioeconomics* demonstrates its biophysical limits; what he calls the *culturalist* source rejects a specific vision of development centered on growth; *democracy* resists an all-pervasive economism; and the *spiritual* source emphasizes the fact that growth does not bring happiness. Degrowth as a concept was honed and refined.

---

[v] There were others. Greek researcher Giorgos Kallis broke degrowth down into nine principles in a 2018 book titled *Degrowth* (the end of exploitation, direct democracy, local production, sharing and reclaiming the commons, relational goods, unproductive expenditures and *dépense*, care, diversity, and decommodification). In 2019, the Quebecer Yves-Marie Abraham summed up the idea with the slogan: produce less, share more, decide together. In 2022, the Maison commune de la décroissance proposed a choice of 16 ways to implement degrowth, like slowing down, rewilding nature, eco-feminization, the reduction of working time, or demobility.

Degrowth Today

After a slow start in the 1970s and a disorderly glow up in the early 2000s, degrowth continued to gain in popularity in France and abroad. While the concept achieved relative success in 2002, it was really starting in 2008 that it expanded to wider circles, namely through a conference circuit, scientific literature, books, journals, courses, manifestos, working groups and action groups, and political agendas. What began as a provocative slogan became a veritable movement. Given such a vast panorama, let's put the chronology of events aside and attempt a mapping of contemporary degrowth.

Degrowth as a Field of Study

Today, there are almost 600 academic articles in English on the subject of degrowth,[16] the first dating from 2007. The topics they analyze are diverse, encompassing at least six major areas of research: the historical origins of the growth ideology, ecological economics and the limits to green growth, the economic implications of degrowth, the study of societies and organizations that prosper without growth, the study of technology, and a final area related to politics and centered on the question of democracy and transition.[17]

More and more researchers—in a widening range of disciplines and subjects—are interested in the question. From economics to anthropology, the study of science and technology, management, tourism, geography, marketing; there are now a dozen special issues in scientific journals. Since January 2022, a new academic journal (the *Degrowth Journal*) even specializes in the question. Launched by an international group of seven researchers (including the author of this book), its mission is to pursue the study of degrowth practices and ideas while creating an academic publishing counterculture guided by the principles of "slow science"[18] and open-access.

This literature would not have been so abundant without the organization of a series of international conferences. The first, titled "International Conference on Economic De-Growth for Ecological Sustainability and Social Equity," brought together about a hundred researchers at Telecom SudParis in April 2008. To this gathering we owe the first official definition of the term degrowth: a "voluntary transition toward a just, participatory, and ecologically sustainable economy." Since then, there have been a dozen events[vi] in various countries and on different themes.

In addition to the conferences, courses on degrowth are starting to emerge. The very first, "Théories et politiques de la décroissance," was offered at Sciences Po Paris in 2011, in the Environmental Sciences and Politics master's program, organized by Luc Semal, a political scientist, and Agnès Sinaï, an environmental journalist, cofounder in 2011 of the Institut Momentum. We could also mention, among many others,[19] Yves-Marie Abraham's course at HEC Montréal on "Sustainable Degrowth: Theory and Practice," which has been offered every fall since 2013, as well as the summer school on degrowth hosted at the Autonomous University of Barcelona since 2014 (where I personally discovered the concept), the first university to award (since 2018) a master's program in the subject.

With courses come dissertations and theses. I have cataloged 112 in English and French: 79 dissertations and 33 doctoral theses. The subjects are rich and varied. Luc Semal's on degrowth activism (the first in France on the subject), Dan O'Neill's on a steady-state economy, Iana Nesterova's on the business models compatible with degrowth, Inês Cosme's thesis and her inventory of degrowth proposals, Matthias Schmelzer's history of "the hegemony of growth," Steffen Lange, François

---

[vi] Paris (2008), Barcelona (2010), Montreal (2012), Venice (2012), Leipzig (2014), Budapest (2016), Malmö (2018), Brussels (2018), Mexico City (2018), Vienna (2020), Manchester (2021), and the Hague (2021).

Briens, and Antoine Monserand on the macroeconomics of degrowth, Viviana Asara on democracy, Jennifer Hinton on the role of for-profit business, Aaron Vansintjan on land ownership, Kristofer Dittmer on currencies, Jonas Van der Slycken on national accounting, Samuel Alexander on property.[20] And of course my own in 2019: "The political economy of degrowth," to my knowledge the first thesis on the subject defended in an economics department in France.

Today, there are many books on the subject. Too many to give a full tour, but let's mention a few, starting with the first book in English, published in 2008: *Managing without Growth* by Canadian economist Peter Victor. The author developed a dynamic macroeconomic model (the same method the Meadows used in 1972), which he used to study a degrowth scenario in Canada.

Across the Atlantic, in January 2009, British economist Tim Jackson published *Prosperity without Growth*, the book adaptation of a report[21] by the United Kingdom's Sustainable Development Commission. The book quickly became a bestseller; it was reissued in 2016, translated into 17 languages, and named book of the year by the *Financial Times* in 2010.

Back in France: *Adieu à la croissance: bien vivre dans un monde solidaire* (2010) by Jean Gadrey, professor of economics at the University of Science and Technology in Lille. The book introduces the novel concept of a "post-growth society," "a sustainable society of moderation and full employment, free from the obligation to grow and involving the significant reduction of inequalities." For Gadrey, who does not use the term "degrowth,"[vii] this society would be characterized by more qual-

---

[vii] "I do not use the term 'degrowth' because for the average person, degrowing is the opposite of growing. It is therefore difficult to understand that degrowth is not, for its proponents, negative growth. [. . .] We could say 'a-growth,' 'post-growth,' or 'anti-growth,' as we say atheism, anti-advertising, or post-capitalism. The choice of 'degrowth' as a slogan seems to me like an obstacle to the popularization of the powerful ideas it contains." (pp.120-121)

ity social housing, goods with more durability, more free time, more meaningful work, more solidarity and social connection, more democracy, etc.

In the same vein, in 2013, sociologist Dominique Méda published *La Mystique de la croissance* (*The Mystique of Growth*), a critique of the "pathology of the unlimited,"[22] that growth without moderation achieved at the expense of nature, with GDP obscuring its social and environmental costs. Since *Qu'est-ce que la richesse?* in 1999, Dominique Méda had actively criticized the paradigm of growth and, in parallel to the literature on degrowth, developed a theory of "post-growth" aimed at abandoning any reference to GDP as a metric.[23]

In 2014, *Degrowth: A Vocabulary for a New Era* was published, which became one of the most popular books on the subject. Edited by three researchers from the Barcelona-based Research & Degrowth group, the book is structured as an encyclopedia of 51 concepts, each explored by different authors. Its readers can discover the elements of the degrowth corpus: anti-utilitarianism, bioeconomics, commodification, the Jevons paradox, the social limits to growth, basic income, guaranteed employment, shared working hours, feminist economics, and more. Often used as a textbook for degrowth courses, it has been translated into ten languages.

Works on degrowth are multiplying. Serge Latouche authored *La Décroissance* in the collection "Que sais-je?" ("What Do I Know?") in 2019. In Quebec, sociologist Yves-Marie Abraham, a professor at HEC Montreal, offered an elegant synopsis in *Guérir du mal de l'infini* (2019) (*Healing from the Malady of the Infinite*): produce less, share more, decide together. Giorgos Kallis and several of his colleagues synthesized degrowth in a book that remains the go-to introductory work: *The Case for Degrowth*, 2020. That same year, anthropologist Jason Hickel released the best-seller *Less is More: How Degrowth Will Save the World*, one of my favorite books.

I conclude with my top pick, *The Future is Degrowth: A Guide to a World beyond Capitalism* (2022) by Matthias Schmelzer, Andrea Vetter, and Aaron Vansintjan. The book is a true encyclopedia of degrowth, encompassing the totality of the literature on the subject (nearly a hundred concepts), carefully organized into typologies: seven critiques of economic growth (ecological, socio-economic, cultural, anti-capitalist, feminist, anti-industrialist, and internationalist), five strands of degrowth focusing on different perspectives (institutions, sufficiency, alternative economies, feminism, post-capitalism, and alter-globalization), three principles of degrowth (ecological justice; social justice, self-determination, and the good life; independence from growth imperatives), and six groupings of proposals (democratization, solidarity economy, and the commons; social security, redistribution, and limits on wealth accumulation; convivial and democratic technologies; revalorizing and redistributing labor; democratizing the social metabolism; international solidarity). This book alone perfectly summarizes the vast field of study that degrowth has become.

Degrowth as a Field of Action

Degrowth is more than an academic concept; it has become a vast field of action. This "action" is of course still largely theoretical and mainly limited to the realm of communication. But it is nevertheless an important development: degrowth is spreading beyond the scientific and activist circles of those who are already convinced, igniting new debates, some of which are giving rise to new practices.

We can divide these debates into three tiers of radicality. Many discuss the *objection to growth* (the first and least radical tier), more and more discuss *post-growth* (which often goes further than the simple objection), and a growing minority talk about *degrowth* (the most subversive debates on the subject).

Let's begin with the first tier. The objection to growth is no longer as fringe as it was in the 1970s. Even if the orthodoxy of green growth remains omnipresent, more and more people have stopped believing in "fairy tales of eternal economic growth,"[viii] a famous expression from Swedish activist Greta Thunberg. António Guterres, Secretary General of the United Nations, declared on X that "the current model of infinite growth in a world of finite physical resources will deliver inflation, climate chaos, and conflict."[24] In 2016, a group on "Limits to Growth" was formed in the British Parliament, and in April 2022, Spanish Minister of Consumer Affairs Albert Garzón published an article called "The Limits to Growth: Eco-socialism or Barbarism,"[25] in which he went so far as to endorse the term "degrowth." Even some business figures are waking up. For Bouygues's Director of Sustainable Development Fabrice Bonnifet, "there is no equilibrium between the three pillars of sustainable development."[26]

Reflecting this progressive move away from the decoupling theory, a February 2022 study showed that only 1% of experts working in Germany's Federal Environment Agency still believe in green growth.[27] This disavowal is confirmed by the latest IPCC report, which, in my interpretation, buries once and for all the myth of sufficiently decoupling GDP and ecological burden.[28] Global experts on the subject describe decoupling as "insufficient" with reduction rates that are "far too low," and green growth as a "misleading" and "misguided" strategy that "rests partly on faith." It is harder and harder to deny the truth: economic growth makes it difficult, if not impossible, to reduce emissions, while this reduction is much easier to realize in a

---

[viii] This is from a speech delivered by Swedish activist Greta Thunberg at the United Nations Climate Action Summit in New York in September 2019: "You have stolen my dreams and my childhood with your empty words. And yet I'm one of the lucky ones. People are suffering. People are dying. Entire ecosystems are collapsing. We are at the beginning of a mass extinction, and all you can talk about is money and fairy tales of eternal economic growth. How dare you!"

degrowth scenario where the volume of production and consumption decreases.[29]

The year 2022 marked the fiftieth anniversary of the Meadows report. Extremely controversial at the time, its ideas find almost universal agreement today. No, we cannot produce indefinitely using resources that are finite. *The Limits to Growth* is "the most important book of the last few decades" according to economist Gilles Raveaud.[30] In June 2022, Dennis Meadows was invited to speak before the European Parliament alongside Kate Raworth, Tim Jackson, Ida Kubiszewski, and Robert Costanza. He repeated the same message he delivered in 1972: the growth of production is destroying the planet, adding that he is not a fan of the term "degrowth," which he finds too negative—he prefers to talk about a "mature society."

Others go beyond the objection to growth and talk about *post-growth*. This is the case with important figures like Kate Raworth, Tim Jackson, Isabelle Cassiers in Belgium, and Dominique Méda in France. *Post-growth* is a more vague and therefore less demanding term—which is its advantage. We can use it to criticize the limitations of GDP (without calling capitalism into question) or to talk about an alternative economy (without broaching the difficult topic of transition).

In 2013, a research laboratory at Sciences Po published a report led by Lucas Chancel titled "A post-growth society for the 21st century: Does prosperity have to wait for the return of economic growth?" (the authors answered in the negative). The European Parliament organized conferences on post-growth in September 2018 and in May 2023. In February 2022, Luca Cigna, a doctoral student at the European University Institute, published an article on the London School of Economics' blog in which he asserts that "comparative political economy should take the post-growth debate seriously."[31] The mission-oriented company Prophil published an extensive report on "business and post-growth,"[32] while Agnès Sinaï and Mathilde Szuba teamed up to release a collection of three books, including one on "Post-Growth Economics."

In 2017, a motion was put forward to create a "Post-Growth Society" commission within the Europe Écologie Les Verts (EELV) party, whose goal was to study "a society that no longer seeks GDP growth, but a dynamic equilibrium between human activity and the rhythms of nature."[33] One of the pillars of the 2017 EELV agenda (*"Bien Vivre"*) was titled "Toward a post-growth society," where they stated that "to the dogma of infinite growth," environmentalists counter with "the degrowth of excess"—the only reference to the term in the agenda.[ix]

There is no real theoretical difference between the two concepts. "Post-growth" is used much less frequently than "degrowth" (few academics use the concept of *post-growth*), and often describes basically the same ideas. Across the texts on the subject, the "degrowth society" is similar in terms of values and institutions to the "post-growth society" described by other authors.

Despite the continuity between the two concepts, those who talk about "degrowth" are by far considered more radical. Nevertheless, their number is growing. The title of a *Télérama* op-ed in late 2021 captures the trend: "Degrowth, an idea on the rise."[34] In 2010, the *Larousse* dictionary even offered a definition: "a policy advocating for the deceleration of growth rates from the perspective of sustainable development." A few years later, *Le Robert* dictionary followed suit and proposed another definition: "A political project calling economic growth into question." While these definitions are rather simplistic,[x] they

---

[ix] No mention of "degrowth" or "post-growth" in their 2022 agenda ("Vivant"), even if the objection to growth is present: "We can no longer consider our economic model to be one of growth at all costs" (*Vivant: liberté, égalité, fraternité, biodiversité*, Les Écologistes, 2022, p. 9).

[x] The Larousse definition links two antagonistic concepts (degrowth and sustainable development) and the Robert definition limits itself to the objection to growth without referencing a reduction in the size of the economy.

show that degrowth is not just a transition or even a phenomenon, but rather a more comprehensive paradigm, at once a transition strategy and a *political project*.[35]

And that is surely why it arouses such curiosity. TV24 devoted a short segment to the topic whose title was: "Degrowth: the yoga of economics." The news portal *Blast* hosted Vincent Liegey to "dispel received ideas about degrowth." The television channel Public Sénat held a debate called "Degrowth: the only solution to the environmental crisis?" For its part, *Franceinfo* published "the article you need to read to understand everything about degrowth," *Le Nouvel Obs* wondered if "we should be afraid of degrowth," and *Le Monde* asked, amid the EELV party's primary elections, "where does this concept at the center of the primary debate come from?"[36] The media is waking up and realizing that, in the shadow of a supposedly green but actually ungreenable capitalism, academics and activists have spent two decades developing a plan B.

This excitement is only relative: the concept's popularity in France is nothing compared to the interest it has received abroad, namely in the English-speaking press (206 articles in English in 2020, 182 in 2021, and over a hundred in the first half of 2022).[37] In general, English-language media is less hostile to the concept: lazy critiques are mostly confined to small outlets while articles in major newspapers are usually fairly balanced. That is not the case in France, where certain media continue to indulge in a lively intellectual bashing,[38] giving voice to columnists and pseudo-experts who elbow their way to the front only to display their total ignorance of the subject (and who have read none of the 600 academic articles on degrowth). It's paradoxical: the country that gave birth to the concept—and where we might expect to benefit from the most in-depth discussions—is still to this day bogged down in the same silly clichés that have plagued the debate since the early 2000s.

Even the IPCC has started using the term.[39] It appears fifteen times in the Working Group II report on adapting to climate change. Degrowth/post-growth is presented not only as an alternative to green growth but as a new paradigm for development. "Degrowth goes beyond criticizing economic growth; it explores the intersection among environmental sustainability, social justice, and well-being."[40] The term is used seven times in the third section, as an objection to growth linked to well-being: "Literature on degrowth, post-growth, and post-development questions the sustainability and imperative of more growth especially in already industrialized countries and argues that prosperity and the 'Good Life' are not immutably tied to economic growth."[41] The report also discusses "embracing post-development, degrowth, or non-material values that challenge carbon-intensive lifestyles and development models."[42]

The term also appears in the latest report from the IPBES, the "IPCC of biodiversity," which sees degrowth as one of the paths toward a more sustainable future. "The 'degrowth' pathway emphasizes strategies that reduce the material throughput of society, protecting human well-being through equitable distribution of material wealth rather than growth, reducing energy and resource consumption in the most industrialized countries as a means to achieve inter- and intra-generational equity and good quality of life for all."[43]

New degrowth groups are emerging. "Polemos-décroissance" in Montreal, "DegrowNYC" in New York, "Degrowth Switzerland" in Switzerland, the "Réseau étudiant pour la décroissance" in Lyon, a research laboratory on "post-growth innovation" at the University of Vigo in Galicia, the "Observatoire de la post-croissance et de la décroissance" at the University of Clermont Auvergne, and another on "Postgrowth welfare systems" at Lund University in Sweden. Since 2017, the "Maison commune de la décroissance" has been the most active association on the subject in France, with regular gatherings, an educational site, and an excellent book summarizing the topic.[44]

Other organizations are cautiously beginning to take a stance on the issue. In early 2021, the European Environment Agency (EEA) mentioned the term for the first time in a report called "Growth without Economic Growth,"[45] which stated that "post-growth and degrowth are alternatives to mainstream conceptions of economic growth that offer valuable insights." On France Inter, the president of the Muséum national d'Histoire naturelle Bruno David advocated for "moderation and slowing down our consumption."[46] In June 2022, the World Economic Forum published a rather positive article on the subject, describing degrowth as an "economic theory that matters right now."[47]

Nevertheless, few politicians use the term, in France or abroad. Bruno Clémentin and Vincent Cheynet launched a degrowth party in 2005, but it has remained more of an association than a genuine political party. Since 2009, the political group Europe Décroissance has participated in every European election, and a handful of candidates regularly run in legislative elections under the banner of degrowth.

Some political figures deploy the term here and there. In 2004, Communist Member of Parliament Patrick Braouezec advocated for "sustainable and solidary degrowth" for the first time in the Assemblée Nationale. Jean-Luc Mélenchon occasionally mentions it, for instance at the Assise de l'Écosocialisme in 2012, where he declared that "degrowth is not an option, but a necessity." More recently, in 2020, Irish President Michael D. Higgins proclaimed in a speech that "degrowth remains the only sustainable strategy for planetary survival."[48]

Others are more cautious: in 2016, Socialist presidential candidate Benoît Hamon campaigned as "agnostic when it comes to growth"; so did François Ruffin who, in an interview with

France Info, described himself as "a-growth." When politicians do mention degrowth, it is often to distance themselves from it. Emmanuel Macron, for instance, is "adamantly opposed" to degrowth, which he calls an "Amish model." Former Prime Minister Edouard Philippe was not a "defender of degrowth," his successor Jean Castex did not believe in "green degrowth," and, more recently Élisabeth Borne, in her general policy speech, affirmed that she did not believe "that the climate revolution will happen through degrowth."[49]

Even France's Green party is reticent. In 2004, they called for "equitable and selective degrowth." But during the 2007 primaries, the degrowth advocate Yves Cochet (one of the few to defend degrowth within the party) lost the election to Dominique Voynet, a proponent of sustainable development. Since then, the Greens have stopped talking about degrowth, with the exception of a brief reference to "solidary degrowth" in 2008 and a motion in 2011 on "12 concrete measures for a degrowth society: selective, solidary, and job-friendly."[50]

It would take until the presidential primary in 2021 for degrowth to reemerge, championed by Delphine Batho, who declared herself "the degrowth candidate," embracing "the necessary break with the pursuit of GDP growth."[51] A Green primary candidate for the 2022 presidential election, she forced the other candidates to take a stance on the issue. Éric Piolle described himself as agnostic, "neither a believer in growth, nor in degrowth." Yannick Jadot didn't "give a damn" about the issue, like Sandrine Rousseau, for whom degrowth "does not make much economic sense," and Jean-Marc Governatori, for whom growth or degrowth "is not the issue."[52] While they did not defend growth, these candidates did not lend degrowth any legitimacy. Delphine Batho came in third in the first round with 22% of the vote, behind Sandrine Rousseau (25%) and Yannick Jadot (27%), who won the second round and did not mention degrowth during his presidential campaign.

Fortunately, civil society isn't waiting for its politicians to wake up, and more and more people are seduced and convinced by ideas of degrowth, often discovered through books or documentaries.[53] I have personally experienced this phenomenon since the publication of my thesis, which led to over 200 invitations to speak on degrowth—from media, conferences, and podcasts, but also major corporations from different industry sectors like EDF, SNCF, Orange, Airbus, Thales, or Salesforce; from associations, numerous engineering and business schools (I was invited to teach an introductory course to HEC students), and even government agencies (I gave an introduction to ecological economics to senior officials from the General Secretariat of the Government, and was invited by the General Council for the Economy of the Ministry of Economics and Finance to talk about degrowth).

The term has started appearing in new and unexpected fields, like fashion. *Vogue Business* got the ball rolling with several articles[54] alluding to a new trend: "*defashion*." Pope Francis published the encyclical *Laudato si'*, which includes a paragraph that mentions degrowth,[xi] and the World Council of Churches organized a conference on "Degrowth—Living Sufficiently and Sustainably." Degrowth has inspired artists and architects, too. In late 2021, the Kunsthalle Museum in Münster, Germany, held an exhibit called "Nimersatt? Imagining Society without Growth." The theme of the Oslo Architecture Triennale in 2019 was "Enough: The Architecture of Degrowth." The Verbier Art Summit in 2017 was themed "Size Matters," and led to the publication of the collective volume titled *Size Matters! (De)Growth for the 21st Century Art Museum*.[55] Suddenly, after two

---

[xi] "We know how unsustainable is the behaviour of those who constantly consume and destroy, while others are not yet able to live in a way worthy of their human dignity. That is why the time has come to accept decreased growth in some parts of the world, in order to provide resources for other places to experience healthy growth."

decades of intellectual bashing, degrowth has the wind in its sails and is making its way into various spheres of public life, art, and media.

When we talk about degrowth today, we should consider the three progressive meanings of the concept. First, degrowth as *objection to growth*, aligned with the Meadows' concerns. A few decades later, we found ourselves in the red, and realized that the early pioneers were right: growth was indeed causing not only the destruction of the living world, but also worsening inequality and a widespread malaise. So *degrowth* was born as a desire not just to reduce the size of the economy, but also to escape growth altogether, to decolonize our imaginations and our societies from the productivist imperative of endless enrichment. This idea of degrowth spread across Europe and then the world, becoming increasingly complex. Having developed a robust critique, degrowth then formulated a utopia with *postgrowth*, an alternative society built on new values. The aim of the next two chapters will be to understand the concrete implications of degrowth as a period of transition and of post-growth as the desired destination.

6
A Transition Pathway
Degrowing the Economy

What is degrowth? While the question may be simple, the answer is far less so. Because degrowth is many things at once: a transition strategy, but also a movement, a mosaic of practices, a school of thought, a critical theory, and a field of study. In Chapters 2, 3, and 4, we explored it as an environmental, social, and political critique of economic growth. In Chapter 5, we examined it as a paradigm—that is, as the historical development of concepts and values that today serve as the guiding principles for a school of thought and set of practices. Now, it's time to operationalize degrowth as a transition pathway, meaning study it as a concrete phenomenon. What would economic degrowth entail, and how would we implement it?

A Downscaling of Production and Consumption

Producing and consuming less—that's without a doubt the essence of degrowth. A growing economy produces and consumes *more* from one year to the next, while a degrowth economy would produce and consume *less*.

To be more specific, and using the first chapter's analytical framework, we could speak of the *contraction* and *slowing down* of the economy as measured by GDP, and especially of its market sphere. Let's start with the first phenomenon. The monetary segment of production would contract after we abandon some of the harmful or useless activities that comprise it. Most advertising activities, for example, would be phased out, as would a great number of financial services,[i] and a significant portion of the service economy, which would be decommodified. The economy would necessarily be smaller, as these production and consumption activities would simply cease to exist, along with the extraction and pollution they entail.

This first type of reduction would be paired with a second: the economy would *slow down*. We would continue to produce and consume some of our commodities, but at a much slower pace and through different methods. It is worth differentiating, here, between *frugality* on the one hand, a form of renunciation (choosing to stop doing things that we used to do, like flying, buying SUVs, advertising, designing financial products, eating meat, and selling pesticides), and *restraint* on the other, a form of moderation (choosing to limit the things that we used to do: keeping the same phone for longer, vacationing closer to home, producing more slowly with low tech and renewable energy, working less). We would produce much of the same stuff as we do today, but the frequency and volume of production would be lower.

The automatic consequence of this degrowth by contraction and deceleration would be a decline in GDP. Let us be clear: this does not mean that an economy *in degrowth* is the same as an economy *in recession*. The decline in GDP is not the goal, just one of the consequences of degrowth policy. Equating a painful recession with a controlled policy of degrowth just because it provokes a decline in GDP is as absurd as comparing an amputation to a diet just because it results in weight loss.

---

[i] Definancialization, for example. Financial market authorities could be tasked with banning certain financial products, such as credit default swaps on the sovereign debt of Global South countries, credit cards with high interest rates, hedge funds that speculate in food products, and investments in extractive industries. We could also ban (or tax) certain forms of trading, like high-frequency trading.

The sectors made to shrink won't be cleaved and butchered; rather, picture a gradual reorientation of the economy, planned democratically, in which a portion of our resources, working time, energy, and materials would no longer be used to produce certain commodities (especially those that pollute and contribute little or nothing to our well-being), and could therefore be partially remobilized to society's benefit. We must dispel another misconception: reducing production through degrowth in no way means getting poorer. It is entirely possible to reduce an economy's monetary value added (GDP) while increasing its social and ecological value added—by increasing free time and improving ecosystem services, for example.

The decline in some forms of production will be partly offset by the rise in other activities. For example, fewer gas-powered cars and less parking lot construction, but more building renovations and bike repairs; fewer real estate agents and stockbrokers, but more caregivers and farmers. Still, the redeployment of our productive forces must have a negative net effect on GDP, if we want it to reduce the ecological footprint quickly enough (and free up the time essential to social prosperity). Given the coupling rates between GDP and environmental pressures, simply rearranging activities will not suffice—we have no choice but to reduce the economy's overall size.

Alas, the economy has no "production and consumption" switch we can flick up or down. Degrowth would be the macroeconomic manifestation of a deliberate policy, the result of a myriad of choices toward frugality and restraint by consumers, businesses, organizations, and public authorities. To orchestrate such a transition would require implementing *degrowth policies* in the same way that we currently implement growth policies. But while growth policies have long acquired an undemocratic character, degrowth policies can only succeed by fundamentally strengthening democracy (we'll return to this point).

Let's focus on one concrete proposal: the reduction of

working time. This is a policy of degrowth *through production*: dedicating less time to paid employment with the goal of reducing the overall output volume. Imagine that our ecological context requires us to halve the total size of the economy. We would therefore have to produce half as much, and thus work half as much. The true challenge of degrowth—and this will be this chapter's central argument—is to orchestrate this great slowdown in a way that it is ecologically sustainable, socially just, and democratically acceptable.

Take unemployment, for example. In a growth society where living power is tied to purchasing power, access to paid employment is vital. As employment is also one of the main pillars of personal identity and social relations in our society, unemployment is a triple burden. Yet, in theory, we can reduce economic activity by half without creating unemployment—in fact, we could even lower it. In Chapter 4, we saw that there are three ways to generate employment: producing more, working more slowly (i.e. reducing productivity), and working fewer hours. To maintain a portion of its paid employment, a degrowth economy would need to work more slowly, for less time, or both.

Thus, the less we produce and the higher our productivity per hour, the more we will need to reduce working hours and therefore share the available jobs. We should note, however, that it is quite unlikely that productivity will remain stable or increase in a degrowth society, at least under the classic definition of productivity measured in euros.[ii] Agroecology and

---

[ii] When it comes to productivity, the trend is already downward, and it is likely that it will fall significantly with a transition away from fossil energy, which will require an increase in manual labor. For example, industrial farming (high productivity per hour) will give way to local agroecology (low productivity per hour). Highly profitable activities (thus with a high productivity per hour) in finance, advertising, and international trade will give way to services where productivity is necessarily lower, like education, culture, healthcare, and eldercare.

soft mobility, for example, do not yield the same returns as their industrial counterparts in classic value-added terms, even though their social value added (job satisfaction, health, social relationships) and ecological value added (energy efficiency, environmental impact, resilience) is greater. Remember that a reduction in paid working hours does not necessarily mean a reduction in work in the anthropological sense. This was the main lesson of Chapter 3: the less time people devote to their paid job, the more they can participate in a multitude of productive and reproductive activities (though unpaid) outside the market sector.

That was an example related to production; here is one related to consumption. If, starting today, every city in France followed Grenoble's example and banned advertising in public spaces, and if advertising for highly ecologically-intensive products, like tobacco ads, were forbidden by the European Union (I am thinking, namely, of SUVs, meat and dairy products, air travel, and luxury goods),[1] there is little doubt that demand for these products would crumble. The economy would experience a decline in consumption (specifically targeting polluting products), as well as a decline in the production of advertisements, and thus in the working hours required to create them. The degrowth of these harmful activities would free up working time, making it available for other, more beneficial activities.

These are only two examples among many. In a review of the literature, we identified more than 380 concrete degrowth measures.[2] These include abandoning "big, useless and tax-funded projects"[3] (airports, highways, shopping malls, parking lots, new nuclear power plants, football stadiums, data centers, certain high-speed rail lines, etc.), imposing moratoriums on offshore drilling and creating ecosystem sanctuaries, introducing national well-being budgets, a progressive tax on financial assets adjusted to their carbon footprint, debt cancelation, banning some forms of advertising, prolonging product warranties and criminalizing planned obsolescence, banning pesticides, closing flight routes and rationing airplane tickets, reducing working hours and guaranteeing employment, generalizing the use of open-source software, a tax on road transport, a tax on financial transactions and a ban on certain financial products and high-frequency trading, a progressive tax on profits, dismantling large corporations like "too big to fail" banks, requiring strategic sectors like education, research, and healthcare to be not-for-profit, extending the logic of social housing to the entire real estate market, a tax on the highest value added for luxury goods, reciprocity networks and alternative currencies, providing essential services for free, capping salaries at four times the guaranteed minimum income, and rationing fossil fuels—just to name a few.

Each of these proposals would result, to varying degrees, in a degrowth of production and consumption, the beneficial contraction and slowdown of the economy as measured by GDP. The political effort would be the same as that currently exerted for growth policies, but with a radically different objective: (1) to reduce the ecological footprint, (2) in a democratic manner, (3) in the spirit of equality, (4) while securing our well-being. These are the four key elements of a degrowth strategy.

To Reduce Ecological Footprints

The prosperity of the economy is intrinsically linked to that of the environment. Just as a healthy organ cannot live long in a dying body, there can be no prosperous economy in an ecological desert—an economy cannot sustain itself in a collapsing biosphere (or at least not for long).

Just like the human body, the economy is a metabolism that consumes resources and ejects waste. From a strictly physical point of view, the economy does not produce or consume, it only transforms. To keep functioning, this economic superorganism can only draw on natural resources that already exist, and can never fully eliminate its waste, which, as undesirable as it may be, continues to exist in some transformed form. An economy's sustainability is therefore a matter of size, or more specifically, of proportion. To endure over time, the size of the economy must not exceed the regenerative capacities of the natural resources it consumes or the assimilative and recycling capacities of the ecosystems into which it ejects its waste.

A pond produces fish, the Earth's geology produces fossil fuels, the climate provides services like maintaining the chemical composition of the atmosphere. But this *biocapacity* (the capacity of a natural environment to replenish its resources and absorb waste) follows its own rhythm. A carrot takes 75 days to grow, a tree may take several decades, and a resource like oil forms over hundreds of millions of years. To be sustainable, an economy's ecological footprint (that is, its extraction from and impact on nature) must never exceed the biocapacity of the territory in question. This applies to the economy of a village with respect to its natural surroundings just as it does to the globalized economy with respect to the entire planet. This is the fundamental rule of any ecological economy: the economic speed of consumption-ejection must never outpace the ecological speed of regeneration-assimilation.

Such an overshoot, if prolonged, destroys biocapacity, leading to the irreversible degradation of the ecosystem and the depletion of natural resources. In other words, the overexploitation of a renewable resource renders it less and less renewable. Any community whose ecological footprint is greater than its biocapacity is in a state of *deficit* or *ecological overshoot*. If you were to exceed the load capacity of an elevator by two or three times its limit, you would risk an accident by putting the elevator out of order. The same goes for ecosystems, which also have a certain load capacity. Overfishing a fish population will lead to its extinction, and emitting too many greenhouse gases into the atmosphere exposes us to global warming, which is already disrupting many ecosystem services.

In a country like France, this load capacity is greatly overshot. In 2015, France had already breached at least 6 of the 7 planetary boundaries: greenhouse gas emissions, the use of phosphorus and nitrogen, material footprint, ecological footprint, and land use.[4] According to this study, the material footprint was 21.9 metric tons per capita in 2015—or more than three times the sustainable limit of 6.8 metric tons per person. France's ecological footprint was 4.8 global hectares (gha) per person, or double our biocapacity (2.4 gha), and greenhouse gas emissions were 3.4 times the threshold needed to stay on a serious mitigation trajectory. The numbers are conclusive: France is living far beyond its ecological means.

Since it is impossible to fully green an oversized economy (the lesson of Chapter 2), we must necessarily produce and consume less to slow the extraction of natural resources and the pollution of ecosystems. Hence the first defining characteristic of degrowth: a diet prescribed to the economy to reduce its ecological footprint and keep it in good environmental health.

Just like a diet, the reduction doesn't need to reach zero, but only a level below the ecologically sustainable thresholds. For each planetary boundary (climate, biodiversity, water, land, etc.), there is a sustainability threshold and a corresponding reduction pathway. And for each country, according to the extent of its overshoot, there is a degrowth trajectory. The degrowth required for the American economy will be more substantial than that for the Swedish economy, and Americans will not need to produce the same things as Swedes. What is certain is that the sooner a country starts to degrow, the lighter (and thus possibly more manageable) this degrowth will be. Conversely, the longer countries continue to grow beyond their ecological budget, the more abruptly they will be forced, sooner or later, to degrow, making it more difficult to plan for a transition that is just, democratic, and peaceful.

To be effective, this "diet" must be selective and target first and foremost goods and services with a high ecological impact. To reduce our carbon footprint (the use of coal, oil, and gas) and material footprint (the extraction of fossil fuels, minerals, metals, and biomass), we will need to prioritize reducing car use (which accounts for 26% of the average French carbon footprint and nearly half of the average French material footprint),[5] as well as cutting back on gas and oil heating, livestock farming for meat and dairy products, aviation, construction, and, lest we forget, military activities.

Once again, there is no "carbon emissions" or "land use" or "sand mining" switch to flick. Therefore, more specific degrowth policies will be required. Let's revisit the example of reducing working hours. A study of 29 developed countries from 1990 to 2008 shows that a 1% increase in working time comes with a 0.4% rise in energy consumption.[6] Since energy consumption is currently closely linked to greenhouse gas emissions (46% of France's energy mix in 2020 consisted of fossil fuels),[7] reducing working time—and with it production—is a quick way to kick-start degrowth and mitigate at least one of our six ecological overshoots.

Let's explore some of the other levers at our disposal. We can group them into three major categories: *prohibition levers*, *rationing levers*, and *taxation levers*. First, we could shut down a number of domestic airline routes and limit the number of flights,[iii] ban advertising for air travel, prohibit the sale of combustion-engine cars, and lower speed limits. The second option would involve *rationing* the use of fossil fuels through a system of carbon credits[8] or more targeted quotas, such as limiting

---

[iii] In early July 2022, the Dutch government announced a cap on the number of flights to Amsterdam-Schiphol airport, limiting them to 440,000 per year starting in 2023, an 11% reduction compared to 2019.

the right to fly.[iv] The third option, taxation, would increase the cost of activities we want to discourage, for instance through a "progressive tax on plane tickets"[9] (no tax on the first flight; a €150 surcharge on the second, with the amount increasing with each additional flight),[v] a tax on jet fuel, a Norwegian-style bonus-malus system that raises the cost of more heavy-duty and polluting cars and incentivizes the purchase of light electric vehicles, and all that while facilitating access to other activities, for example by making public transportation free.[vi]

These tools can be layered. For example, a progressive tax on airplane tickets could first be implemented alongside the closure of some domestic routes. Over time, this could give way to a rationing system for air travel, and later extend to the broader rationing of fossil fuel use on national soil, eventually leading to a complete international ban. The same logic applies to cars: a bonus-malus system based on pollution and weight, coupled with a ban on advertising for the most heavy-duty and polluting cars, could precede a ban on their sale, which in turn would be followed by a ban on all internal combustion vehicles.

The task is easier than it seems because the ecological burden is highly concentrated geographically. For example, 71% of global emissions can be traced back to just 100 companies, primarily in the energy extraction sector, with the 20 most polluting companies causing a third of these emissions.[10] The same

---

[iv] For example, the proposed law "aimed at imposing an individual carbon quota to limit air travel" (June 30, 2020) would set a maximum quota of air kilometers every five years, calculated in equivalent tons of carbon dioxide.

[v] We could also mention Switzerland, which in January 2022, introduced a progressive tax on airline tickets (the *Flugticketabgabe*) ranging from €28 to €112 depending on the flight's distance and ticket class.

[vi] We could cite the example of Luxembourg, which in March 2020 became the first country in the world to offer free public transportation across its territory. This same approach of providing free public transportation can be found in over sixty cities in France, including Niort (since 2017) and Dunkirk (since 2018).

is true for other pressures. In 2019, just 20 companies were responsible for a little over half of all plastic waste on the planet.[11] According to estimates by cartographer Cedric Rossi,[12] the vast majority of emissions are attributable to a few large industrial hubs, and the ten most polluting factories accounted for 34% of industrial emissions in 2021, or 7% of all French emissions. These companies are not solely responsible for these greenhouse gas emissions, of course, but their strong concentration would hypothetically allow for targeted interventions (we'll come back to this).

We see here the importance of addressing both *production and consumption*. There is no point in having consumers drive less if the decrease in emissions is offset by an increase in military activities (a B-52 bomber burns as much fuel in one hour as the average driver does in seven years). There is no use in halting the production of SUVs in France if we continue to import them from elsewhere, and no use in driving electric if we continue to export SUVs made in France abroad. The challenge is to coordinate degrowth, so that consuming less leads us to produce less, and vice versa.

Planned Democratically

Degrowth is not just any downscaling of production and consumption. Unlike the kind of chaotic recession symptomatic of a growth economy, degrowth is *planned*—meaning it is democratically discussed with society and organized in advance by public authorities and the economy's stakeholders according to a plan. It is not some unexpected, unbridled crisis to endure, but an anticipated, organized, and chosen transition.

We must not only distinguish between degrowth and recession but also between degrowth and collapse. "Degrowth by design" is neither recession nor "degrowth by disaster," which we could fittingly call *collapse*.[13] Recession (the slowdown of economic activity resulting in negative GDP growth) is a recurring accident in an economy dependent on growth to function (akin to losing weight due to illness). Collapse is the inevitable long-term outcome for a growth economy—the equivalent of dying after losing all body weight due to illness. In contrast, degrowth is the intended result of a deliberate, voluntary transition specifically aimed at downsizing (losing the weight necessary to be in good health *thanks to* a beneficial diet).

If degrowth must be planned, it is because the current economic system (capitalism) is not designed to degrow and is dominated by economic agents who deem its downsizing unacceptable. Like a shark that must always be in motion to breathe, our current economic system is only stable when it grows.[14] It therefore becomes extremely unstable in the current context, characterized by a general deceleration of growth rates (the infamous "secular stagnation"). It's hard to picture an oil company giving up the exploitation of profitable reserves to mitigate global warming, or an investment fund slowing down its activities to prevent a financial crash. Today, the for-profit business model is inherently opposed to any degrowth objective. But here's a point we too often forget: the propensity to grow is itself by design.

Nothing is ever produced or consumed in isolation. In this sense, every economy is planned in one way or another. Contrary to popular belief, neoliberalism, which characterizes the current global economy, is not the opposite of planning. In fact, it is a highly planned form of capitalism where large corporations decide what to produce, supported by the state, which actively facilitates the expansion of the economic sphere within society. Today, production is planned at four main levels. Business managers decide what to produce, often with profitability in mind. Not-for-profit organizations also plan their production, but according to broader criteria. As individuals, we plan our labor, generally with the aim of maximizing our purchasing power, as well as our consumption (itself already partially planned by advertising). And of course, the government plans a portion of production—the part conducted by government agencies—and participates in planning the rest of the economy by regulating it (currently, according to growth objectives).

What would planning for degrowth look like? Of the four levels mentioned above, the business level poses a problem. It is the disproportionate power held by large corporations, reinforced by a neoliberal ideology that makes profitability society's guiding star, which incites undesirable behaviors at the three other levels. The government is forced to defend the interests of major corporations; nonprofit organizations must scrape by on corporate handouts and public funding; and consumer behavior is predetermined by businesses through advertising and planned obsolescence practices. To be able to implement a degrowth strategy, we will need to regain control over the organizations that are actively blocking any effort toward moderation.

Let's take a concrete example. We know that fossil fuel companies must reduce oil and gas production by 74% by 2030.[15] To limit global warming to 1.5°C, we must forgo the exploitation of at least 60% of oil and gas reserves and 90% of coal reserves.[16] It's hard to believe that private, for-profit companies will voluntarily give up these potential profits. If that were plausible, they would surely have already done so. On the contrary, these companies do everything in their power to safeguard their margins and continue extracting.[vii] The alternative is to nationalize them (in whole or in part) and make the decision on their

---

[vii] Between 2010 and 2019, the five largest fossil companies (BP, Shell, ExxonMobil, Chevron, and Total) spent 251 million euros on lobbying against European environmental regulations (according to the European Union's Transparency Register, an online database that shows the financial resources dedicated to lobbying activities).

behalf. We might imagine a French public energy sector that would bring together EDF, Engie, Total, and other smaller suppliers to coordinate a national strategy for energy restraint and a quick transition to low-carbon energy.

By the same logic, we could establish a strategic transportation sector, which would involve nationalizing the SNCF (France's national railway company), highways, airports, and major airline and shipping companies. If banks keep refusing to finance the ecological transition,[viii] we will also need to make the decision for them. Democratic control of the big banks would allow us to generalize the policy of the Banque Postale and suspend financing for all companies developing new fossil fuel extraction projects.[17] The same applies to the pharmaceutical industry, telecommunication companies, and all other companies we aim to radically transform in the coming years. While the appropriate mode of governance for these organizations in the long term remains an open question (we will address this in the next chapter), their hierarchical control by a minority of shareholders focused on investment returns is fundamentally incompatible with the goal of an ecological transition through degrowth.

By transformation, we mean *closure*, *dismantling*, and *reconversion*, as described by the proponents of "ecological redirection."[18] The automobile industry must cease (either voluntarily or by mandate) designing, producing, and selling large gas-powered cars, and must focus instead on the limited production of light electric vehicles. Airline companies must close some national air routes and some airports and eliminate most international flights. Highway companies must abandon their expansion projects and dismantle part of their existing

---

[viii] In 2021, French banks continued to massively fund fossil fuels at a higher level than in 2016, including Société Générale, Crédit Agricole, and BNP Paribas, the fifth largest fossil fuel financier in the world ("Banking on climate chaos" report, 2022).

infrastructure. Banks must renounce all investment in fossil fuels and start winding down parts of the financial markets. Degrowth at the level of a national economy is the aggregate result of multiple closure, dismantling, and reconversion protocols at the corporate level.

Some may argue that these nationalization strategies imperil the productivity of these companies and the country's competitiveness (meaning, within the framework of a growth economy, profits and GDP). As we have already seen, we must redefine what we mean by productivity and abandon the ideology of competitiveness, given the emergency we face, which is ecological and social before economic. A country like France can afford to lose profits (especially those captured by an already wealthy minority), but it cannot afford to lose its biodiversity and ecosystems.

Others may argue that nationalizing a company does not guarantee sustainability (by observing, for example, that the three largest global emitters are three "public" companies in Saudi Arabia, China, and Russia).[19] First, we should note that these companies are run by authoritarian regimes. Second, planning *for degrowth* (taking control in order to close, dismantle, and reconvert) will have the opposite effect of planning *for growth* (taking control to optimize and accumulate). Between the government and private multinationals, which is more likely to act to protect the planet's interests and the common good?

Nationalizing is not the only answer, of course. Strategic sectors and communal goods and services lend themselves well to public management. For others, the goal must be to *cooperativize* companies, meaning to democratize their operations in the hope that a more participatory process will enable them to make decisions in the public interest. Once again, it seems more likely that a cooperative will decide to scale back some of its activities to preserve the habitability of our planet than a private, hierarchical, and profit-driven company would. From an ecological transition perspective, diluting decision-making power could help avoid situations where any attempt to transform a company that goes against profitability is immediately blocked by shareholders.

To cooperativize, a large company could start by creating an "inclusive ownership fund,"[20] a collectively owned fund managed by democratically elected representatives, into which companies would issue new shares. We could also cap the voting rights of non-managing shareholders, separate voting rights from financial rights, and completely rethink decision-making processes based on the experience of existing cooperatives.

IN A WAY THAT IS EQUITABLE

Degrowth must not only be ecologically effective: it must also be fair. To speak of degrowth achieved *in a way that is equitable* means applying the principle of "common but differentiated responsibilities,"[ix] that is, of equity: each person must contribute according to their circumstances. Consumers with the largest footprints will need to reduce their consumption and give up a portion of their income first; the most polluting companies will need to slow down their production and sacrifice part of their profits first; and the most ecologically destructive countries will have to make the greatest effort to reduce their GDP. Conversely, it is the most vulnerable groups (low-income individuals, small and struggling businesses and nonprofits, and countries of the Global South) that must benefit from the shift in economic structure.

[ix] This is Principle 7 of the United Nations Rio Declaration (1992): "In view of the different contributions to global environmental degradation, States have common but differentiated responsibilities. The developed countries acknowledge the responsibility that they bear in the international pursuit of sustainable development in view of the pressures their societies place on the global environment and of the technologies and financial resources they command."

The logic is one of "contraction and convergence": degrowth for the privileged few (the *contraction*) and growth for those who need it most (the *convergence*). In a world with tightening environmental constraints, we must share our ecological budgets more equitably. If the countries of the Global South need more resources to build infrastructure that is essential to well-being, we must degrow the economies of the Global North. In other words, the degrowth of rich countries is a sine qua non condition for the prosperity of poor countries.

If the ecological end goal of a degrowth strategy is an economy with a sustainable biophysical metabolism, its social end goal is an equitable society where everyone has enough to satisfy their needs without anyone consuming in excess. These two goals combined create a "safe and just space for humanity,"[21] in the words of economist Kate Raworth.

The first stage in this great transformation involves *contracting* the production and consumption of the most privileged populations. Geographically, the task begins in high-income countries. A few key figures for context: Europe and North America alone are responsible for half of the 2,450 billion metric tons of CO_2 emitted globally since 1850.[22] In 2010, the European Union's carbon footprint consumed 90% of the annual carbon budget available worldwide.[23] Together, the residents of the Global North have caused 92% of the CO_2 emissions in excess of the carbon budget allowed by the 350 ppm climate stability threshold.[24] If we do the same calculation for the use of materials (material footprint), high-income countries (which represent only 16% of the global population) are responsible for 74% of the excess consumption beyond the global limit of 50 Gt per year, a threshold set by scientists for the sustainable use of natural resources.[25]

But there's a catch: behind these average footprints hides a massive disparity, even within the wealthiest countries. In 1990, things were simple: rich countries polluted a lot, and poor countries polluted little. Thirty years later, the situation has radically changed. Carbon inequalities are no longer (or in any case, less) a matter of divergence between countries but of divergence between social classes. Today, the richest 10% of the global population are responsible for 47.6% of total emissions—four times more than the poorest half of humanity.[26] Wealth confers an "energy privilege"[27]: the richest 5% on the planet use more energy than the poorest half of humanity.[28] But in a world where we already consume too much energy, this privilege is as unsustainable as it is immoral: the most affluent decile have used 56% of the carbon budget for 1.5°C, while the poorest 50%, who logically should have priority access to available resources, have only used 4%.[29]

In France, the wealthiest 10% of households earn on average seven times more than the poorest 50%, and a household in this top decile emits an average of 24.7 tCO2e—five times more than the poorest half of the French population.[30] To reduce emissions by at least 55% by 2030, and by even more by 2050, the reduction in the footprint of the biggest consumers and producers will necessarily have to be more drastic than that of those who currently pollute the least. According to a report from France Stratégie,[31] the poorest 50% of households will need to reduce their carbon footprint by 4% by 2030, compared to 81% for the wealthiest 10%,[32] meaning those with a monthly income of more than 3,328 euros and assets exceeding 607,700 euros. According to calculations by engineer Clément Caudron,[33] it would be possible to halve France's GDP without even touching the incomes of the poorest half of the population. This is only an estimate, but it shows that a country like France has the leeway to reduce its GDP without increasing inequality.

This contraction can be achieved in different ways, some fairer than others. The current carbon tax system is regressive because it is proportional: less polluting households pay the same tax per ton as the most polluting households. But there are other, more equitable mechanisms. A carbon tax with a redistributive mechanism, under an "anti-energy poverty climate contribution"[34] model, would allow the most vulnerable half of French households to receive more than they pay. Alternatively, as Thomas Piketty suggests,[35] we could at a minimum adjust the income tax to neutralize the carbon tax's impact on the poorest households, or even implement a progressive tax on emissions (no tax on the first few tons, followed by a gradual tax increase up to a maximum footprint level, beyond which fines would replace taxation).

We should also consider the carbon footprint of financial capital, which today represents 70% of the emissions of the wealthiest 1%.[36] A report by Greenpeace/Oxfam[37] estimates that the financial assets of France's 63 billionaires have a carbon footprint equal to 152 million metric tons, equivalent to the footprint of the financial capital of half of all French households. The average French person can quit flying and stop eating meat, but it will be in vain if those who control companies keep investing in the production of all the things we urgently need to stop producing.

Another option involves introducing individual carbon accounts, following the "Tradable Energy Quotas"[38] model. Each year, the French carbon budget would be divided into units, with a portion allocated to each citizen as a personal carbon allowance, and the rest distributed to various companies, associations, and public authorities. Every time a consumer buys fossil fuel (gasoline, natural gas, or heating oil, for example), an equivalent quantity of carbon units would be deducted from their account, on top of the purchase price. Similarly, every time a business buys fossil fuel to produce, it would also need to use units. Consumers and organizations that do not use their entire carbon quota could resell the surplus units on a secondary market with regulated prices.

Let's revisit the example of aviation. In 2018, 1% of the global population caused 50% of the sector's emissions while more than 96% of people did not fly at all.[39] Just ten countries account for 60% of the sector's emissions.[40] Within the European Union, only the richest 10% of households fly.[41] In Great Britain, 60% of flights are taken by 10% of the population, while half of the population never flies.[42] The same is true in France: only a quarter of French people take a plane each year.[43]

The degrowth of aviation achieved *in a way that is equitable* would involve increasing the cost of flying for frequent flyers (with exceptions for humanitarian organizations, diplomats, scientists, etc.) to allow others who have never flown to benefit without jeopardizing climate stability. First and foremost, we would have to significantly reduce the use of private jets and eliminate business and first class seats, or at the very least, introduce a direct per-flight tax proportional to the distance traveled.[x] For commercial flights, we could set a total annual cap on flights (which would decrease along a decarbonization trajectory), and allocate them as fairly as possible according to how they are used.

Let's turn next to the *convergence* stage of a degrowth transition. To improve the situation in the Global South, countries in the Global North must completely rethink the international ramifications of their economic model. Today, globalization sustains a true "extractivist circuit"[44]: rich countries import natural resources at artificially low prices and do not compensate exporting countries for the damage caused by their extraction. To put an end to this "imperial mode of living,"[45] we must reverse the trend: reduce the volume of imports in proportion to

---

[x] This was one of the proposals from the Citizens Convention for Climate: a €360 tax on each private jet flight traveling under 2,000 km, and €1,200 for longer distances, with equivalent taxes for business class flights (€180 and €400) and for economy class (€30 and €60).

the decline in production and consumption, while simultaneously increasing financial flows from the North to the South.

This was the idea behind the Yasuni ITT initiative in Ecuador. From 2007 to 2013, the president at the time proposed selling "greenhouse gas non-emission rights" to countries that bought oil from Ecuador. In exchange, he pledged to protect Yasuni Park and the oil reserves underneath it. This is a concrete way to safeguard natural resources and finance the development of Global South countries while reducing consumption in rich countries. Global North countries would continue to pay for resources that would remain unextracted, turning them into something akin to World Heritage sites. It could be a way for industrialized countries to settle their climate debt.

While Securing Our Well-Being

An increase in GDP is correlated with an increase in well-being below a certain level of income per capita. Beyond this level, the effects reverse: GDP growth becomes harmful, especially when distributed inequitably. In other words, in a country like France, growth no longer brings happiness (Chapter 4). That said, a drastic and poorly organized decline in economic activity—essentially a recession—could degrade quality of life. Hence the fourth element: degrowth aims to reduce production and consumption *while securing our well-being*.

Picture a graph with two axes, mapping everything an economy produces.[46] The environmental axis would represent each product's contribution to the national footprint (the *ecological footprint*) while the social axis would represent its contribution to the public's well-being (the *well-being footprint*). The easiest way to lower the ecological footprint while maintaining our quality of life is to give up highly polluting products that contribute little to our well-being. If we aim to reduce air travel, for example, we should start with the frequent weekend trips taken by the richest households and not with humanitarian trips or family reunions. Similarly, if we wanted to reduce the number of large, polluting cars, we would start with private vehicles in big cities, not with ambulances or mountain rescues.

A quick international comparison reveals that there is enormous room for degrowth. For a similar quality of life, the average carbon footprint of a Costa Rican resident does not exceed 3 metric tons of CO2 equivalent, while that of a French resident is around 10 metric tons, and that of an American is almost 15.[47] To organize degrowth *while securing our well-being*, we need to learn from the countries that have managed to decouple well-being from ecological footprint (a far more important issue than decoupling from GDP). Another comparative study estimates that it is possible to reach high levels of well-being with low levels of energy demand (between 13 and 18 GJ per capita, or a tenth of the energy consumption of the average French resident).[48] In the 106 countries studied, the quality of public services, income redistribution, and democracy are statistically more effective strategies for improving well-being and are significantly less ecologically intensive than GDP growth.

A policy of "happy degrowth" would involve expanding access to quality public services, for example by making them free. Healthcare, education, public transportation, water management, internet access, phone service, and other essential goods and services would be collectively funded through contributions, following a universal basic services model, and managed as locally and democratically as possible with a not-for-profit approach. These goods and services would be priced progressively: essential items would be free, with prices on other items rising progressively to discourage waste and "misuse."[49]

Let's say it again: what really matters for well-being is not purchasing power but living power. What's the point of protecting consumers' wallets when the underlying logic of profit-driven production is to sell at the highest possible price? This is not a purchasing power problem, it is a *selling power* problem—which for large, quasi-monopolistic companies has become a selling *superpower*. Instead, we should regulate the prices of essential items to bring them closer to their actual production costs, which would deflate the sectors currently buoyed by the exorbitant margins of capitalist companies. Following the Viennese model, housing costs could be capped, and the same would apply to the price of drugs, insurance, and everything else without which we cannot live a decent life.

This gives us a clear roadmap for how to maintain and increase well-being during the economy's great slowdown. We can classify these actions into two major categories: deconsumption and non-production. Behind the issue of production lies the question of work and its utility. During lockdown, many people wondered whether their jobs justified the risk of spreading the virus by going to work. Today, the question is similar: does my job justify the risk of environmental collapse? And more broadly, at the level of each region and each company: what do we really need? It is a question of priority: we must slow the most polluting and least useful activities down in order to preserve those we consider essential, which we will then need to green as much as possible.

During these major industrial closures, guaranteed employment[50] could prevent involuntary unemployment. We might imagine expanding the "zero long-term unemployment zones"[51] program and creating *employment cooperatives* at the municipal level. These participatory democracy bodies would identify local needs or shortages and catalog the skills of residents eager to work, with the goal of creating jobs that meet both community needs and the aspirations of workers. These *employment commons* would become democratic forums for constantly adjusting economic activity.

The same logic applies to consumption. Let's recall one of the Citizens Convention on Climate's proposals: to include a disclaimer in all advertisements for the most polluting products, "Do you really need this? Overconsumption harms the planet."[52] Letting go of possessions (and desires) that we care little about would be a way to reorder our priorities and redistribute some of those objects—an economy where an organization like Goodwill would be more important than Amazon.

This process starts at the individual level with a practice of voluntary simplicity, a bit like the decluttering method popularized by Marie Kondo,[53] which involves assessing each possession with the question, "does this item spark joy?" The reflection then continues at the local level, by discussing which possessions we could pool to share their use (carpooling, neighborhood reuse centers, community tool libraries, little free libraries, online sharing networks, outdoor gyms, online encyclopedias, and even shared washing machines), and which items could become unnecessary if we organized to eliminate them (bottled water, hotels, and cars, made redundant by the existence of public fountains, home exchange networks, and public transportation).

Before lamenting the sacrifice, let's recognize that the activities most important for our well-being have a very low ecological footprint and are not typically considered either work or commodities: spending time with friends, walking in nature, reading and making music, or participating in political debates. Producing less would reduce working hours and free up time to create all the things that GDP does not measure, and enjoy the riches we already have. We could "work less to live better,"[54] give up designing bigger cars, building 5G towers, and developing space tourism to be able to devote ourselves to a civic and political life rich in meaning, even if lean in terms of GDP. Economic degrowth would thus mean "immense intellectual, hedonistic, humanistic, and ecological growth,"[55] a tremendous step forward for our societies.

Degrowing an economy means *downscaling production and consumption to reduce the ecological footprint in a democratically planned and equitable way, while securing our well-being.* A smart degrowth strategy would allow us to fall back below sustainable ecological thresholds while generating a triple social dividend: a more participatory economy where we decide together what we want to produce and consume, less poverty and inequality, and a quality of life more resilient to geopolitical, economic, and ecological shocks. It's a "happy coincidence," as Jason Hickel says: what we must do to survive is also what we should do to be happy.[56]

What defines degrowth as a concept is the combination of these four aspirations in a single transition strategy. Every transition has a destination; we will now explore what the economic system toward which degrowth leads might look like.

7
A Societal Project
Toward a Post-Growth Economy

The previous chapter defined degrowth as the *downscaling of production and consumption to reduce ecological footprints, planned democratically in a way that is equitable while securing well-being*. But an economy is not meant to keep degrowing until it completely disappears. The downscaling of production and consumption is merely a transitional phase—a means to an end. It is therefore necessary to clarify the destination of this transformative process of degrowth, meaning the economic system that would replace the growth economy we know today.

It makes sense to call this next phase *post-growth*,[1] a word we can associate with the same ideas as those of researchers who speak of a society *of* degrowth (that is, an economy operating according to the values associated with degrowth). It's a *steady-state economy, in harmony with nature, where decisions are made collectively, and where wealth is equitably shared to enable prosperity without growth*. Here again, we find the four cardinal principles defined in the previous chapter (sustainability, democracy, justice, well-being), but from a different perspective: no longer as criteria for a temporary transition, but as the operating principles of an enduring economy.

A Steady-State Economy

A *growing* economy produces and consumes more and more, while a *degrowing* economy produces and consumes less and less. As its name suggests, a steady-state economy is stable. Economic activity may fluctuate slightly up or down, based on needs and productivity, but it does not fundamentally change in size. We have seen that both recession and degrowth lead to a reduction in GDP, but with completely opposite effects. Similarly, a post-growth steady-state economy would have a stable GDP, much like what economists call "secular stagnation," the deceleration or halt in growth rates, as observed in Japan since the mid-1990s.

Unlike in Japan, where a growth economy can no longer grow, the size of a post-growth economy would not be chosen at random. Like a diet that targets a specific weight to optimize a person's health and well-being, degrowth is a strategy that strives to achieve a theoretical economic size that guarantees well-being and social justice (the social floor) without exceeding the load capacity of ecosystems (the ecological ceiling). This brings us back to the fundamental two-fold question that has guided us throughout this book: "What do we really need to be happy?" and "What can we really afford to produce to preserve the habitability of our planet?"

This should be the goal of any economy. Yet today, we associate production with *accumulation* (more and more), when we should be associating it with contentment (enough). A contentment economy would produce what we really need—nothing more, since human needs are fundamentally finite. Of course, new needs may appear, which would require a rise in production, just as others may disappear, leading to a decline in production. We produce more masks during a pandemic, and production slows down once the crisis is over. The economy as a whole would experience phases of (mild) growth and (mild) degrowth—in the original sense of degrowth as a decrease in production—depending on the social and environmental context. This would be a "steady-state economy," as defined by economist Herman Daly.[2]

Let's immediately dispel a common misconception: the stagnation of production in no way means the end of innovation and progress. In a post-growth steady-state economy, productivity gains are not used to increase production, as they are today, but rather to reduce working time and improve working conditions. If certain jobs can be automated, we can collectively utilize the productivity gains to reduce working hours, freeing up time for non-economic activities. This is a form of progress that improves quality without necessarily increasing quantity.

To remain steady, an economy must break free from the imperatives of growth, from all the pressures to continuously produce and consume more. As we saw in the first chapter, these pressures come from three main actors: governments (through growth policies), businesses (through the pursuit of profit), and consumers (through the pursuit of income). A post-growth economy must rid itself of all the institutions that encourage the "more and more," such as using GDP as the target for economic policy, the for-profit business model, and advertising that encourages consumption.

We can easily picture an economy that could function without growth. A functional economy mobilizes natural resources (but not too many) to produce (useful) goods and services and distribute them (equitably), while investing in new (necessary) activities. A post-growth economy undergoes a systemic transformation during the degrowth phase. To borrow Herman Daly's analogy,[3] it would be like turning a plane (which can only fly by moving forward) into a helicopter that can hover in place. This is a vast project that can be divided into four areas of transformation: (1) rethinking our relationship to the living world, (2) transforming the way we produce, (3) harmonizing the distribution of wealth, and (4) redefining prosperity.

In Harmony with Nature

We saw it in the last chapter: living in harmony with the rest of the living world is a matter of sustainability. It's the principle of good stewardship: we do not consume more than ecosystems can produce and we do not emit more than they can absorb. In short, we respect their health. The load capacity of ecosystems (*biocapacity*) sets extraction and pollution thresholds that must not be exceeded. This is the well-known definition of "sustainable development": development that meets present needs without compromising the ability of future generations to meet their own.[4] We could also invoke Hans Jonas's categorical imperative: "act so that the effects of your actions are compatible with the permanence of genuine human life on Earth."[5] The idea is the same: economy and ecology must co-exist peacefully.

A steady-state economy can only produce more if it manages to improve how it uses its "ecological budget," or if that budget increases. If we find a way to improve the efficiency of solar panels or discover a new energy source, we can afford, if need be, to consume more electricity. Conversely, if an ecosystem is deteriorating faster than expected, we will need more degrowth to preserve it. In other words, production can fluctuate up and down according to the state of natural resources and our technological and institutional capacity to use them. Thus, the most decarbonized and dematerialized goods and services benefit from a broader production frontier than those heavily dependent on materials and fossil energy.

The goal of eco-innovation is to decouple socially beneficial production as much as possible from environmental pressures, that is, to reduce the economy's *ecological codependency*. Our method of production must be as circular as possible in terms of its use of materials, and as renewable as possible in terms of energy. Every time the economy succeeds in circularizing a new production process (deposit-return schemes, for example), it makes materials available for other potential production. Every time an energy source is replaced by an alternative with a smaller ecological footprint, the economy generates an energy surplus that becomes available for use. We will come back to this soon, but it is important to remember that this additional production is merely a possibility. Producing more is a political decision, not fate. It is entirely possible to imagine an economy that uses its efficiency gains to work less and to protect ecosystems—that is, a form of technical progress that facilitates leisure and allows for the rewilding of nature.

This is indeed one of the core values of a post-growth economy: a new relationship with the living world. Thus far, we have looked at sustainability through an economic lens. Nature renders us a service and it is therefore in our interest to preserve it. The term "natural resources" suggests that nature's value derives from its utility in the production process, and the term "natural capital" treats nature as a whole like an investment we should make profitable. When we speak of "ecosystems," we interpret the living world through the language of engineering, viewing nature as a machine that we could break and then repair. Imagine just how different our behavior would be if we treated ecosystems like *natural societies inhabited by living beings*. Burning down a forest or destroying a coral reef would be more akin to genocide than breakdown.

A post-growth economy needs a new "natural contract."[6] It would start with a question economists never ask: "Which humans does nature need?"[7] We must develop an "ecological conscience," as American philosopher Aldo Leopold described in *The Land Ethic*.[8] It's the idea of an "expanded community," the same one we find in the philosophy of *buen vivir*.[9] The society we live in is not only human but also animal, vegetal, and mineral. In an ecological economy, we are all members of this community of living things. This is the idea of "multispecies conviviality,"[10] a mode of interaction where we view our natural surroundings as a subject endowed with rights.

We know this ecologically sympathetic attitude well, because we all grew up with it. The pig in *Babe* isn't pork, the rat in *Ratatouille* isn't vermin, the creatures in *Finding Nemo* aren't fish stocks, and the fox in *Fantastic Mr. Fox* isn't fur. Some people see their cats and dogs as members of the family, others fight to save sharks, a river, or a forest, and more and more people are becoming vegetarians out of sympathy for animals. We already feel this ecological sympathy, but it is often sacrificed in a production process that stifles the sentiment. There is no room for animal love in a slaughterhouse or an industrial farm; people work there to earn a living, and that's at least something.

We must put our ecological sympathy into action by granting rights to nature in the same way that we have gradually granted them to ourselves. In France, the law already prohibits causing unnecessary suffering to animals; it protects certain species and certain habitats. Let's go further. Let's simply ban industrial livestock farming, cruel hunting practices, and recreational activities that harm animal health. Let's give animals the right to life and well-being,[i] which would also forbid us from destroying their habitats. Instead of setting vague sustainable development objectives, let's protect nature with a Universal Declaration of the Rights of the Living World.

This is the logic behind conservation initiatives like UNESCO World Heritage Sites.[ii] Granting World Heritage status to a forest, a coral reef, a lagoon, a marsh, or a chain of volcanoes protects them from the greed for short-term profits and

---

[i] For example, Quebec's Animal Welfare and Safety Act, in effect since 2015, grants animals the right to "well-being" and safety from "distress," but unfortunately does not yet apply to farm animals.

[ii] As of 2019, there were 213 natural heritage sites out of a total of 1,121 sites. These benefit from an international legal status that protects them against any form of alienation.

the exploitation that comes with it—they become *sanctuaries of life*. The wealth of societies far exceeds their GDP: an economy *in harmony with nature* is an economy that bestows value (but not necessarily a price) on everything that is not human.

If a river is granted legal personhood, and a company pollutes that river, it is not a predetermined tax that must be paid but an unpredictable fine or an even greater penalty. It is a crime of "ecocide," defined by a committee of international experts as "committing illegal or arbitrary acts knowing that there is a real probability that these acts will cause serious, widespread, and lasting environmental harm."[11] In the event of litigation, the penalty should be determined by a court, taking into account the injury caused to the river itself and to all those whose subsistence depends on it, both now and in the future. Placing the governance of nature under the jurisdiction of the legal system (rather than the market) is a way to reintegrate the market economy into society.

The idea is simple but its implications are radical: what if the best way to be in harmony with nature is to redefine the divide between humans and non-humans, which our modern economies have taken to an extreme?

Where Decisions Are Made Collectively

In the previous chapter, we saw that degrowth requires planning production based on needs (the *well-being footprint*). But why stop planning once the degrowth phase ends? What good would it do us to return to the current model, which indiscriminately and undemocratically increases the production of both useful and useless things? If an economy's objective is to satisfy, we should be constantly making sure that it produces what people actually need.

Yet, to know what people need, they must have a voice. They

must be able to collectively discuss what to produce and how to produce it, and thus extend the democratic process to the economy as a whole. This is the ideal of *economic democracy*, found in theories like Murray Bookchin's "libertarian municipalism," Abdullah Öcalan's "democratic confederalism," and Joseph C. Kumarappa's "economy of permanence."[12] The essential idea is this: to combine direct, deliberative, and participatory local democracy with representative democracy at higher levels, such as the regional, national, or supranational level.

At the local level, "neighborhood round tables" like those that have existed in Montreal since the 1960s, where neighbors work together on collective projects. At the municipal level, "participatory budgets" in the tradition of those that emerged in Porto Alegre in the 1980s, to decide how to allocate the municipal budget. At the company level, multi-stakeholder co-management councils that invite local stakeholders (workers, users, local communities, neighbors, etc.) into the decision-making process related to product choices, production technologies, and prices. At the national level, regular public assemblies and citizen-initiated referendums. At the international level, multilateral organizations like the African Union, European Union, and United Nations.

The goal is not to plan the economy down to the very last detail, but to allow for more inclusive deliberation on production choices. It is relatively quick and simple to produce based on prices and for the sake of profits, especially in a hierarchical company where only a handful of individuals make decisions. It is much more complicated to produce based on needs and for the sake of well-being, while incorporating the interests of an expanded community of stakeholders. It requires identifying needs that, unlike demand, are not directly visible or measurable, and discussing the balance between several, sometimes conflicting, interests when setting product prices.

Imagine an economy where each company is legally required

to define a clear *production mission*,[iii] which justifies to the public what its activity consists of and why it is useful to the satisfaction of needs. Ideally, the mission would be clear, sincere, described in precise terms, and followed by action. The mission would be defined by a convention of stakeholders, modeled on citizens' assemblies. Each company would have a *mission committee* that would internally monitor the alignment between the company's activities and its mission, and companies would be regularly audited by "existence tribunals"[13] that would assess this alignment, as is already the case for France's *Sociétés Coopératives d'Intérêt Collectif*, or SCICs (multi-stakeholder cooperatives for public interest).

The mission-driven company model would replace the profit-driven company model. This seemingly superficial change may be more revolutionary than it appears. Instead of assuming that all businesses are beneficial in the name of some purported principle of "free enterprise," we could flip the logic: to exist, a company must have a mission (and a concrete plan for achieving it) that aligns with the needs of a region and its population. The democratic selectivity of production would be two-fold: with respect to the ends (what do we want to produce?) and to the means (how do we want to produce it?). This would allow us not only to avoid wasting precious resources on minority or non-essential needs, but also to discourage production techniques that are socially and/or environmentally harmful.

Where there's a mission, there are *impact indicators*. While traditional business accounting is primarily financial, there are alternatives. The core idea is to find a balance between at least three major goals: *sustainability* (the ecological burden),

---

[iii] The Pacte Law (n° 2019-486) gives companies the option of having a "raison d'être" linked to a socio-environmental mission included in their bylaws. The law adds to Article 1835 of the French Civil Code: "Bylaws may specify a raison d'être, comprised of the principles that the company adopts and for which it intends to allocate resources in carrying out its activity."

conviviality (the well-being of stakeholders), and *productivity* (the efficiency of production). There is a hierarchy between these goals. The first condition for a company's long-term viability is to be environmentally sustainable. Next, we must ensure that its social utility is positive—a company that enriches a minority of shareholders through bullshit jobs and useless gadgets would most likely have a negative well-being footprint if all its stakeholders were to evaluate it. And lastly, once sustainability and conviviality are ensured, we can worry about the company's productivity, which can only be improved as long as it does not compromise the other two goals.

In a capitalist economy, a company's shareholders and managers push for productivity, even if it comes at the expense of conviviality and sustainability. In a democratic economy, stakeholders are required to meet sustainability and conviviality goals before optimizing productivity. This is the mode of production that resonates most with common sense. If I cultivate my garden, I obviously pay attention to productivity because I don't want to spend my life growing tomatoes, but I take other important criteria into account first. For example, I refuse to use pesticides and herbicides out of respect for the soil and animals, and I garden in a calm and pleasant manner, even if it would be theoretically possible to do it faster and more efficiently.

It's an *artisanal mindset*, rooted in the common sense of homemade craftmanship. Craftsmanship does not mean producing by yourself with limited resources. It is a mode of production that is autonomous in the sense that it is self-organized, and that it demonstrates the "technological discernment" needed to select only the tools deemed useful and desirable. As for working time, reducing *per-hour productivity* is no regression if it increases *per-hour conviviality*. Here's a better alternative to GDP: instead of aiming to grow by $x\%$ per year, let's aim to reduce working time by $x\%$ per year. Let's maximize *Gross Domestic Naptime* and measure our economy's performance by the hours of unwanted labor it helps us avoid. The same logic applies to sustainability: we could reduce *per-hour productivity* by abandoning certain industrial fishing techniques, which would represent economic progress in the long term, as it would preserve biodiversity. "How to produce?" then becomes the combined pursuit of these three different goals, hence the importance of workplace democracy to be able to mediate between different interests.

A concept that captures this new philosophy of production is "low tech,"[14] which designates a group of technologies as *useful* (meeting essential needs), *accessible* (available to the widest possible audience), and *durable* (eco-designed, durable, repairable, and recyclable). These are "tools for conviviality,"[15] as philosopher Ivan Illich described them: decentralized, democratic, and adaptable methods of production that allow us to produce efficiently without undermining collective life. While production techniques in a productivist system are predetermined by the imperative of profit, a post-growth economy selects its tools based on much broader criteria. Who cares if the voice commands used in warehouses improve labor productivity if they make employees miserable?

While there is a constant baseline of fundamental human needs, some needs are not set in stone—they can change over time. This is why a well-being economy (centered on needs) must necessarily include institutions that facilitate deliberative democracy.

The model of hierarchical and authoritarian private companies must give way to multi-stakeholder workplace democracy. This is the logic behind cooperatives, which are legally required by their members to uphold the principle of "democratic governance."[iv] To fast track, we might say that a good

---

[iv] Article 1 of Law n° 2014-856 of July 31, 2014: "A cooperative is an enterprise formed by multiple individuals voluntarily assembled with an aim to satisfy their economic and social needs through their joint effort and contri-

way to democratize the economy would be to transform all private companies into cooperatives: production cooperatives; user cooperatives like consumer co-ops; and allocation cooperatives like credit unions. The word "cooperative" here means something much broader than "company," and closer to the concept of *commons*, those "institutions governed by stakeholders linked to a common or shared (material or immaterial) resource that serves a social purpose, collectively guaranteeing the fundamental abilities and rights (access, management, and decision-making) of the stakeholders, as well as their responsibilities (preservation, openness, and enhancement) toward the shared resource."[16]

Collectively deciding what to produce also means collectively deciding how to finance new projects. Today, a company can obtain funding either through bank credit or by raising equity capital. Banks demand interest and shareholders demand dividends, both creating a profit imperative. In an economy without growth, companies would have to be able to get financing from actors who do not require continually positive financial returns. Bank credit could be organized through not-for-profit cooperative banks, which would evaluate each new production project according to its contribution to the public interest (its alignment with the company's raison d'être). Instead of giving credit to the most profitable projects (as is the case today), these new *banking commons* would prioritize projects that generate well-being and social justice and that respect nature.

We might imagine the creation of Benoît Borrits's "socialized investment funds," or of Bernard Friot's "investment accounts," a *financial reciprocity* network that would operate by the same logic as social security.[17] Each company contributes

---

bution of the necessary resources. It operates in every sector of human activity and adopts the following principles: voluntary and open membership, democratic governance, the economic participation of its members, the training of those members, and cooperation with other cooperatives."

a portion of its value added, and these contributions are reallocated to companies according to their investment needs as non-repayable grants. In this system, we would pool part of the economic surplus through a decentralized network of investment committees.

No matter the economic rung, the logic is the same: *commoning*. For a steady-state economy in harmony with nature to prosper, decisions about extraction, production, distribution, consumption, and elimination must necessarily be made together. One of these decisions—and by no means a minor one—is about the distribution of wealth.

Where Wealth Is Equitably Shared

In a steady-state economy with limited ecological budgets, not everyone can always have *more*. This is not a problem if everyone can have *enough*. We can all live decently with the wealth we already have—and even with much less, as has long been the case—provided that the wealth is shared equitably. This is the key theme of this section: sharing (which I use here in an economic rather than philosophical sense, meaning the set of policies regulating the allocation of resources among people). Sharing takes place at three levels: before production (the *predistribution* of inherited wealth), during the production process (the *distribution* of value added), and afterward (the *redistribution* of accumulated wealth).

"Each player starts the game with . . . " We all know the rule from Monopoly. This is a *predistribution* policy—a property right given to each participant irrespective of their success in the economic game. Everyone should be able to meet their most basic needs. Today in France, we protect the poorest households from energy insecurity with an "energy voucher," and we guarantee basic cultural purchasing power for young people with a "culture voucher."[v] More broadly, there is a whole insurance infrastructure that partially protects individuals from unemployment and poverty. What if we took things further by extending the logic of social security to include "economic security"?[18]

To start, a *guaranteed minimum inheritance*. This is the "universal capital endowment" in Thomas Piketty's participatory socialism model.[19] At the age of twenty-five, each individual would receive an inheritance equal to 60% of the average level of wealth (about 120,000 euros), financed through a tax on private property. This property tax would have seven progressive brackets, ranging from 0.1% for those with half of the average wealth, up to 90% for wealth exceeding several thousand times the average.

This guaranteed inheritance would allow us, for example, to distribute access to housing more fairly. In France, 24% of households own 68% of privately held housing.[20] Those who inherit fortunes can invest their savings into real estate and get richer by renting to others who, meanwhile, find it impossible to buy a home and become dependent on their purchasing power, especially in cities where rents are high.

Next step: sharing value added. The goal is to bring an end to the "profit-driven ownership of the means of production."[21] As highlighted in the previous section, profit-oriented companies will be phased out in favor of mission-driven cooperatives. These cooperatives will be structured according to the principles of "limited-profit" and shared ownership, already practiced by multi-stakeholder cooperatives like France's SCICs.

In practice, this means that a company's value added is

---

[v] Since 2018, an energy voucher for an amount between €48 and €277 is automatically delivered to French households below a certain income level; they can use it to pay for electricity, natural gas, firewood, or heating oil, as well as energy renovations. Since 2021, every young person receives a €300 culture voucher when they turn eighteen years old, to be spent within 24 months on books, concerts, theater, museums, music, etc.

equitably distributed among the various internal and external stakeholders who participate, directly or indirectly, in production (through deliberation in a general assembly, in accordance with the rule: "one person, one vote"). Following the logic of *self-set salaries* (extended here to all incomes derived from production, not just those of employees), the stakeholders are the ones who decide their remuneration (within the legal bounds of minimum and maximum incomes). This means the end of profit-driven, private ownership of the means of production, because no individual can appropriate a company's profits (except, of course, in the case of sole proprietorships, whose revenues would nonetheless be capped).

Several models of deliberative distribution already exist. For example: the Dutch digital services company Incentro. After participating in a workshop to better understand the company's financial situation, employees choose their salary for the following year, providing a one-paragraph justification in a shared document. The employees discuss, first in small groups, then together, what is best for them, for their coworkers, and for the company, before finally making an individual decision on their salary amount. What if we expanded this self-remuneration process to all stakeholders that deserve compensation? Within a not-for-profit company, setting salaries is no longer a battle between employees and managers. It becomes a routine task at the heart of a workplace democracy. This same logic of self-determination (taking decisions together) can be applied to a whole range of other decisions like working hours, time off, price setting, and ultimately, everything.

The last mechanism for sharing wealth in a post-growth economy involves *redistribution*. Let's revisit Thomas Piketty's second proposal (after his wealth tax): a progressive income tax structured into seven brackets, set as a function of average income. A household earning half the average income would only be taxed at 10% (including social security contributions and any carbon tax); one that earns five times the average income would be taxed at 50%; and so on progressively, up to the highest incomes, which would pay up to 90% on income in excess of several thousand times the average (we could even add a statutory cap on income and wealth).

This redistributive system would allow us to fund a *guaranteed minimum income* set at the poverty line, automatically received by all individuals living below that threshold. A portion of this basic income could be paid in alternative currencies, following the model of "food social security" (a monthly allowance of 150 euros earmarked for basic food products, delivered as food vouchers) and another part would be paid in the national currency. This would be a modular basic income, as proposed by advocates of an "unconditional autonomy allowance."[22] With disbursements in alternative currencies, every citizen would have a minimum level of purchasing power earmarked for the consumption of specific items to which public policy does not already guarantee free access.

To Enable Prosperity Without Growth

An economy that panics at the slightest, even minimal, drop in GDP is a rather feeble one. This brings us to the central objective of post-growth: an economy's capacity to achieve and maintain a high quality of life *without* growth. This was the brilliant idea of Tim Jackson, who introduced the concept of "prosperity without growth" in 2009, and Jean Gadrey, who developed the idea of a "post-growth society" the following year (others also spoke of "independence from growth" or "growth without economic growth").[23] Unlike capitalism, which can only be stable with growth (and even then, with poor results when it comes to well-being, justice, and sustainability), a post-growth economy must be able to function and prosper without being forced to grow.

But what exactly does "function" mean? The underlying question is one of prosperity, and thus of the indicators we use to measure it. An economy cannot prosper without growth if prosperity itself is defined by growth. Therefore, we must redefine our understanding of prosperity and adopt new measures to assess it. The "*loi Sas*" of April 2015 requires the French government to submit an annual report to Parliament on "new indicators of wealth"—at least in theory. In practice, the 10 indicators the government adopted are far too narrow, and there have only been three reports (2015, 2016, and 2017), always very short, superficial, self-congratulatory, and largely ignored during budget votes. A "complete failure," according to sociologist Dominique Méda.[24] The foreword to the 2017 report, signed by Prime Minister Édouard Philippe, reveals its true colors: the purpose of the report is to evaluate the government's reforms "to assess their alignment with our intent of steering France toward greener and more inclusive growth."[25]

We've got to come up with something better. In 2019, New Zealand started using "well-being budgets," a dashboard of 65 economic, social, and environmental indicators. There are numerous similar initiatives,[26] all united around the same goal: to replace GDP with a holistic vision of prosperity. For example, economist Éloi Laurent envisions a dashboard divided into three sections: well-being here and now (equality among people and regions), well-being in the future (long-term sustainability), and well-being elsewhere (global responsibility).[27] The objective of a post-growth economy is to advance this triple agenda.

To prosper without growth means, first of all, to pose the question of well-being. What do we need to live a happy life? This approach, profoundly philosophical, is completely ignored in discussions about growth, which focus on *having* (possessions and purchasing power) and completely overlook *being* ("capabilities," in the Amartya Sen sense, and living power).[28] The growth ideology is an obsession with having, focused on ownership and fixated on money. We must replace it with a different way of living, based on human relationships, intellectual and spiritual fulfillment, and a harmonious relationship with the world around us.

There are many concepts to describe this paradigm shift: "power of restraint," "frugal abundance," "eco-sufficiency," "alternative hedonism" and "frugal hedonism," "simple living," or more common terms like *voluntary simplicity*, *anti-consumerism*, *post-materialism*, *deconsumption*, and *minimalism*.[29] In Quebec, where the idea of voluntary simplicity gained traction in the late 1990s, the Office Québécois de la Langue Française defines it as "a lifestyle that involves reducing one's consumption of goods in order to lead a life more centered on core values." "*Lagom*," as the Swedish say. Not too much, not too little—the happy medium.

To make this restraint possible, we must organize it collectively. If I am given direct access to a healthy diet, doctors and dentists, and housing, I do not need a high salary to buy food, pay for healthcare, and rent a house. How we structure access to goods and services predetermines our options for moderation. For an economy to prosper without growth, the ownership of essential infrastructure cannot be too concentrated (especially if that ownership is profit-driven, since it then creates a growth imperative). Healthcare, education, transportation, energy, food, housing: these sectors should all be managed as democratically as possible, in the cooperative spirit of a not-for-profit model.

What would an economy more centered on the Swedish concept of *lagom* look like? It's an economy without bullshit jobs (imagine if everyone who took no pleasure in their job and felt disrespected there stopped doing it), without unwanted advertising or planned obsolescence, where we only produce what we really need. An economy rid of profit-driven production and its rentiers, with honest prices regulated by floors and ceilings that fluctuate around production costs; an economy of shared free services, where we do not have to own something to be able to use it. It's a common sense economy, after all: why create jobs (that fulfill no one) to produce (in an ecologically unsustainable way) in order to increase purchasing power (without increasing living power), all just to consume (things we could do without)?

In an economy where we produce and consume together, and no longer against one another (the race for competitive advantage and the consumption of positional goods), we will realize that we need far fewer things to be happy. We don't want products or dollar bills: what we want is to enter into "resonance"[30] with the world around us. We want to make love, spend time with our families, have fun with our friends, play music and read books, enjoy meeting our neighbors, create new knowledge, experience the joys of nature, cook delicious food, debate politics. The things we use to achieve these ends are only means. The ends themselves are social. That is why we need a "relational economy."[31] *Fewer things, more relationships*, as degrowth advocates say.

We must degrow the economy to establish *a steady-state economy in harmony with nature, where decisions are made collectively, and where wealth is equitably shared, to enable prosperity without growth*. To put it simply, we could call it an economy of better, where "more" or "less" becomes irrelevant. A democratic economy, where decisions are informed by ecological sympathy, where production is centered on needs and well-being, where everyone is rich and no one is poor. An economy whose purpose would be a new form of prosperity—the pursuit of meaning and happiness through frugality and respect for the living world.

8
Controversies
12 Critiques of Degrowth

Explaining what degrowth is can be a tough job. Not because it is a complicated idea (we have just seen that it is relatively simple), but because the concept is constantly misrepresented by a handful of poorly informed commentators.

According to Emmanuel Macron, degrowth would mean "stopping everything."[1] It has already been implemented in Venezuela, Greece, and the USSR, and even in Sub-Saharan Africa, claims Melchior, a website providing educational resources for economics and social science teachers. It is synonymous with "giving up" for former Transportation Minister Jean-Baptiste Djebbari, and with "social chaos" for entrepreneur Bertrand Piccard. Brune Poirson, former Secretary of State for the Ecological Transition, describes it as a "fatal alternative," and former Prime Minister Michel Rocard warns that it would "lead us straight to civil war."[2]

The slander is abundant: "*The Hunger Games* applied to real life," "doomsday fanatics," and of course, the good old "Luddites" and proponents of a return to "caveman life." The blatant exaggeration in these criticisms makes them sound ridiculous. But what are degrowth's critics really afraid of?

OFF-PUTTING?

After a detailed presentation of my research to the European Commission, the examiners tasked with evaluating my project asked me just one question: "Don't you think the word degrowth is a little off-putting?" Clément Viktorovitch, a communications specialist, agrees: advocating for degrowth is like "swimming against the tide."[3] Bruno Latour similarly prefers to talk about "prosperity," because he finds it hard to imagine a crowd chanting "degrow, degrow, degrow!"[4] Jean Gadrey also avoids the term, which he considers "an obstacle to the proliferation of the powerful ideas it contains."[5]

And yet, the word is on the cover of this book. A "*mot obus*," as Paul Ariès calls it,[6] designed to provoke discussion on subjects that would surely not have been broached if we had talked about a *green economy* (inequality and capitalism, for example). Degrowth is "a word of dissensus,"[7] explains Vincent Cheynet, one of the creators of the term *sustainable degrowth*. Transition necessarily involves disagreement. If everyone agreed, we would end up with the system we already have. To dismantle a system, one must use explosive language that is difficult to co-opt. So, as long as the term disturbs, it is doing its job of conceptual demolition.

Another of the term's strengths is its clarity. Show a 1.5°C trajectory curve to a twelve-year-old and ask them if it looks more like degrowth or "green," "circular," and "eco-economic" growth. We can add adjectives like *sustainable*, *equitable*, *prosperous*, *joyful*, *convivial*, *peaceful*, etc. But the idea remains: produce and consume less. The term addresses the problem head on instead of sweeping it under the rug, as *positive economy*, *common good economy*, or *well-being economy* would. It would be patronizing to think we should protect people by only showing them watered-down concepts, rid of all nuance, which obscure rather than reveal the scientific truth. After all, how can we solve a problem if we cannot talk about its cause with adequate language? The term "degrowth" has the advantage of summarizing the problem's cause and identifying a concrete solution.

Let's not put the cart before the horse. We are not going to move from ecologically overshooting capitalism to steady-state ecosocialism with the snap of a finger. Talking about *post-growth* and a *steady-state economy* today, while we are immersed in a growth economy, is jumping the gun. It's like calling Alcoholics Anonymous the "sobriety and abstinence club." Yes, we want an economy that can prosper without growth. But for it to do so without destroying the environment, it will have to be a lot smaller than it is today. We will have to accept degrowth.

Some believe the term frightens people. But again, is anyone on a diet afraid of losing weight? Obviously not—sometimes downsizing is a good thing. That is the case with GDP today. Should we have abandoned the option of "lockdown" because the word sounded scary? A better question to ask is why "degrowth" scares people. Could it be because we have been bombarding people for decades with the idea that growth is good for jobs, purchasing power, and social security? Given the scientific facts about the link between environmental degradation and our economic activities, it's the word "growth" that should frighten us.

Once we understand that degrowth is not a recession but rather a transition toward a democratic, sustainable, just, and joyful economy, why fear the word? No matter the term we prefer to use (moderation, sufficiency, frugality, degrowth, deceleration), the actions to undertake remain the same: we must produce and consume less, all while organizing this great slowdown in a way that avoids social harm.

Painful?

Entrepreneur Bertrand Piccard is against degrowth because it would force the population to make "sacrifices in terms of comfort, mobility, and standard of living."[8] Columnist Ferghane

Azihari protests that it would "bring suffering."[9] "Imagine having to live without airplanes, without phones, without the internet—basically, without pleasure or well-being," laments Clément Viktorovitch.[10]

First, an increase in GDP no longer translates into gains in well-being. In France, a study by INSEE shows that levels of happiness begin to stagnate once monthly income exceeds 2,100 euros.[11] We should also add that growth does not increase the average quality of life, because it primarily benefits those who are already wealthy.

We must dispel Philippe Charlez's unfounded fear that "the temptation of degrowth would mechanically reduce the global average life expectancy from 75 to 66 years."[12] In Portugal, GDP per capita is 65% lower than in the United States, yet life expectancy is higher, at 81.1 years, compared to 78.7 in the United States.[13] Not only is it entirely possible to reduce the size of the economy while improving public health (since life expectancy does not depend on GDP beyond a certain threshold), but doing so is more urgent and necessary than ever to prevent it from further deteriorating (let's not forget that the Covid-19 pandemic was first and foremost an ecological crisis).

Moreover, it is growth that comes with its daily dose of sacrifice and suffering: the free time we waste working against our will or stuck in traffic, the habitats that disappear and the species that perish in our race for extraction, the terrible psychological malaise of workers subjugated to the imperatives of productivity, the marginalized unemployed we sacrifice on the altar of profitability, or the social injustices we ignore in order to maintain our competitive advantage.

Production is not a magical phenomenon, and the material abundance it creates is not free. If there is indeed a painful and sacrificial phenomenon today, it is GDP growth. The argument I have made throughout this book is that, in a country like France, the costs of growth have far outstripped its benefits, that the economy has become a "diseconomy," that productivity has turned into "counter-productivity," and that we have a clear interest in slowing down.

Slowing down production and consumption (remember: first in rich countries and for the most privileged among us) means preserving a part of our precious social and ecological capital. It is the only way to guarantee conviviality (free time and meaningful work), justice (the reduction of inequalities), and sustainability (a thriving natural environment). After all, what good are airplanes, a new phone every year, and 6G in a world on fire where everyone hates each other?

We must be realistic: this will not be easy. The restraint that degrowth requires is like withdrawal for a person addicted to a hard drug. It demands profound changes in culture, mobility, nutrition, housing, and many other areas. There will be both new freedoms (working less and more enjoyably, a private life protected from advertising propaganda, a rich community and political life) and what, for now, look like sacrifices (traveling less far, more slowly, and without taking the plane, giving up meat, buying new things less often). There is a whole way of life to reinvent.

But we have no choice (Chapter 2). Even if this materialist detox cure proves unpleasant to crazed consumers, delaying climate action out of fear of upsetting an ultra-rich minority is obscene in a world where poverty persists. Should we have opposed the abolition of slavery because it represented a sacrifice for slave owners? The central question, too often forgotten in current debates about restraint, is about equitably sharing both the effort and the benefits moderation entails.[14]

INEFFECTIVE?

"French tree huggers are not equipped to fight global warming," asserts the editor in chief of *L'Opinion*.[15] Michael

Liebreich, an energy consultant, thinks that degrowth would only reduce global emissions by a few percentage points.[16] For Robert Pollin, an American advocate of the Green New Deal, degrowth is not a viable strategy because we do not have time to swap economic systems.[17] For the blogger Noah Smith, degrowth is "a fantasy that distracts us from real efforts to save the planet."[18]

It's the world turned upside down. Those who argue that producing *less* will allow us to pollute *less* are expected to prove their case to those who, despite overwhelming scientific evidence (and the most basic common sense), believe that to pollute *less* we should produce *more*. Climate denial on that level is no longer belief but superstition.

Lockdown, though painful, demonstrated that reducing economic activity does indeed reduce the ecological footprint. Global greenhouse gas emissions fell by 5.4% in 2020, the fastest decline ever observed.[19] Noise, light, air, water, and soil pollution dropped spectacularly, to the point that some big city residents could see mountains on the horizon or stars in the sky for the first time in their lives. We could finally hear the songs of all sorts of species in places where they had been inaudible. It was possible to get around by bike in cities where we would normally have to risk our lives to brave the cars.

Yet, in absolute bad faith, some pointed to the "minor drop in emissions" during lockdown to conclude that "degrowth doesn't work." Even if we mustn't confuse a recessionary episode like lockdown with a planned, equitable, and peaceful period of degrowth, it nonetheless provides objective evidence of the link between economic slowdown and a reduction in the ecological burden.

What we must recreate is the effect (degrowth), but we don't need to repeat the same strategy (lockdown). Returning to the diet versus amputation analogy: we want to lose weight, but preferably without having to saw off a leg. If we were to talk about a climate *lockdown*, it would not be a matter of confining people but rather of renouncing certain polluting activities along with the lifestyles that depend on them. The goal is not to put the economy on pause, like some sort of red light, green light game for capitalism, but to transition toward a different economic system.

Let's take this moment to reiterate that being agnostic about growth is not enough. The current secular stagnation, which Olivier Pastré[20] wrongly interprets as a degrowth utopia, has only drawbacks: it consists of unstable economies struggling to function, even at ecologically unsustainable levels of production and consumption. Even if all additional GDP growth were perfectly green (which empirical evidence contradicts), the fact remains that the economy's current size far exceeds planetary boundaries, making a significant reduction in production both essential and urgent.

The empirical data and theoretical works at our disposal show that there will be no actual decoupling between GDP and the ecological footprint. Nevertheless, Dominique Seux claims that "the question is not growth or degrowth, but the decarbonization of the economy."[21] He forgets that decarbonization is only one of nine planetary boundaries we must respect. And even if decarbonization alone were enough (an easier aim than dematerialization, for example), we couldn't do it without degrowing. Either we produce more or we pollute less—we will have to choose.

Let's at least agree on this: reducing production does not mean we stop greening it.[22] We can combine less with better; mix moderation with eco-efficiency. Let's apply the IPCC's "avoid-shift-improve" approach: avoid everything we can do without, shift from heavily polluting products to less polluting ones, and concentrate our eco-innovation efforts on improving everything that we can neither avoid nor shift away from. But we must set our priorities in the right order. If the most sustainable resources are the ones we do not use, we should start by *avoiding* the production and consumption of as many things as possible,[i] leaving us with a smaller economy that can then be greened.

Impoverishing?

For Bruno Le Maire, the logic is implacable: "If you have degrowth, you will have less wealth, and you will have more poverty."[23] It is a "road that leads to famine, destitution, and poverty," an "environmental agenda to impoverish the French people,"[24] that would drive us to "absolute ruin." "Imagine this degrowth world for the poor countries that even today lack access to hospitals, roads, and basic incomes."[25]

Let's begin with what should be obvious: degrowth should only apply to those who already have enough, starting with the richest. We do not ask someone struggling to feed themselves to go on a diet. Reduce production and consumption in France for those who can afford it, yes, but not in places like Madagascar or Syria. To be equitable, degrowth must be selective and target those who contribute most to ecological overshoot. The biophysical downsizing of rich countries is specifically aimed at allowing others to develop under the best possible conditions. What would we rather: use the rest of our carbon budget so some people in France can drive SUVs and fly every weekend (without it enhancing their quality of life)? Or build water pipelines and schools in countries that lack them?[ii]

---

[i] According to a study cited in the latest IPCC report, moderation strategies would allow us to reduce the footprint of construction by 78%, of transportation by 62%, of food by 41%, and of industrial production by 41%. For example, stopping meat consumption could reduce food-related emissions by 40% (Felix Creutzig *et al.*, "Demand-side solutions to climate change mitigation consistent with high levels of well-being," *Nature Climate Change*, 2021).

[ii] Let's remember here that the wealthiest 10% of the global population (about 550 million people, roughly equivalent to the population of the European Union) consume as much energy as the poorest 80% (Yannick Oswald

Let's also stop holding on to the myth that GDP growth is some miracle cure for poverty. Poverty rose in France between 2006 and 2016 and continues to rise, despite economic growth.[iii] Growth policies, which are ineffective, often unjust, and unsustainable in the long term, are a deeply inadequate answer to the destitution of those who are worn down and dejected by the market economy.

The wealth has been there for a while, it's just poorly distributed. In 2021, 56% of the national disposable income was enough, if equitably redistributed, to satisfy the needs of the entire French population and enable everyone to participate in social life.[26] This means that right now, and without any infrastructural change, we could degrow by 44% without generating poverty—*if, and only if,* we shared the wealth we already have.

Finally, confusing moderation with poverty is intellectually dishonest. Producing gadgets and putting extra hours into bullshit jobs should not be considered enriching, even if it makes GDP go up. A degrowth transition would destroy financial "wealth" (which isn't real wealth) to transform it into social wealth (reclaimed free time, a vibrant democracy, flourishing social relationships, meaningful work) and ecological wealth (clean air, a stable climate, fertile soil, an abundant biodiversity). After six years of studying the absurdity of the growth ideology, I have found no better expression than this famous Native American proverb: "When the last tree is cut down, the last fish eaten, and the last stream poisoned, you will realize that you cannot eat money."

---

et al., "Large inequality in international and intranational energy footprints between income groups and across consumption categories," *Nature Energy*, March 16, 2020).

[iii] According to the *Rapport sur les inégalités* (2019) by the Inequality Observatory, in 2016, there were 5 million people living on less than 855 euros per month (half of the median income), or 9% more than in 2006.

Selfish?

Max Roser, creator of the platform *Our World in Data*, says it over and over: "without economic growth, there is *no chance at all* to leave poverty behind."[27] The argument is again simplistic: "if there is degrowth in rich countries, there will be degrowth in poor countries,"[28] states Denis Olivennes. Christine Kerdellant, managing editor of *Usine Nouvelle*, has the same concern: "if Western countries decide to degrow, poor countries will collapse."[29]

First observation: the poor only get crumbs. In the study "Growth isn't working," the New Economics Foundation calculated that between 1990 and 2001, for every $100 of growth in global per capita income, only $0.60 went to those who live on less than $1 a day.[30] Ten years later, a new study reached the same result: between 1999 and 2008, 95% of growth went to the wealthiest 40%—while the poorest 30% received only 1.2%.[31] At this rate, eradicating poverty would take between one and two centuries and would require multiplying global GDP by 173 (an ecological impossibility). For a sense of scale, redistributing less than a third of the annual income of the world's wealthiest 1% (6 trillion dollars) would be enough to eradicate poverty below the $7.40-a-day line.[32]

Another crucial element: what one hand gives, the other takes away. Between 1985 and 1999, the net monetary flow between the Global North and South favored the former, with a wealth transfer of over 600 billion dollars due to the burden of debt.[33]

And that's not all: international trade takes place at the expense of poor countries. Marxists call this phenomenon "unequal exchange": rich countries pressure poor countries to obtain inexpensive resources and then sell back their finished products at high prices. In 2015, for every hour of work that a poor country imported from a rich one, it had to export 13 to pay for it (the ratio is 5:1 for materials and 3:1 for energy).

In one year, this translates to the net appropriation of 12 billion tons of raw materials, 822 million hectares of land, 21 exajoules of energy (equivalent to 3.4 billion barrels of oil), and 392 billion hours of work.[34] This appropriation amounts to 10.8 trillion dollars—enough money to end extreme poverty 70 times over.

Moral of the story: we were wrong to think that our growth was feeding a virtuous cycle of beneficent globalization; it is quite the opposite. The GDP growth of rich countries deprives the Global South of resources it could have used to develop, and tacks on the burden of environmental degradation.[iv] What we too quickly call "growth" is more like "accumulation by dispossession,"[35] or let's be frank, by plunder.

Degrowth is a strategy to reverse the trend, to implement *disaccumulation through reparations*. Rich countries will degrow, and part of the financial wealth they relinquish will be given to countries in the Global South as compensation for decades of unequal exchange and environmental harm.

Austeritarian?

Some intellectuals on the left find the idea of degrowth suspect, accusing it of being "a form of ecological austerity for working-class people"[36]—just "austerity by another name."[37] This is the argument of ecosocialists like Leigh Philipps,[38] who sees degrowth as a form of "ecological austerity," and Matt Huber,[39] for whom "an ecological politics of less overlaps perfectly with a wider neoliberal focus on austerity that calls on all of us to tighten our belts."

[iv] According to the *Climate Vulnerability Monitor*, Global South countries bear 82% of the total cost of global warming, amounting to 571 billion dollars up to 2010. A more concrete figure: 98% of the 400,000 annual deaths associated with climate crises are residents of poor countries.

We should recall that austerity is a neoliberal strategy that involves restricting public spending and lowering certain taxes *to stimulate economic growth*. Given that this growth primarily benefits those who are already wealthy and impacts the most vulnerable disproportionately, we could say austerity imposes collective restraint to allow for the individual enrichment of a small minority. Degrowth is precisely the opposite: selective individual restraint (in proportion to each person's capabilities and responsibilities) that allows for a shared, collective abundance of social and ecological wealth.

Beyond this misunderstanding lies a real question. Even if it is not geared toward austerity, would degrowth contract the public budget? Mechanically yes—if and only if the revenue base remains anchored to GDP. But we can easily change this method of financing.

As we saw in Chapter 4, public services form their own economic domain that does not depend on the private sector's charity. It's actually quite the opposite: private companies benefit, more or less freely, from highly valuable social and ecological capital: roads, power grids, worker education and training, ecosystem services, healthcare and social security systems, protections for trade, to name a few. What if instead we recognized that it is the public, social, and ecological sectors that fund the private sector? The austerity question is not a technical issue, but a political one, tied to our collective interpretations of value and the social conventions that govern how we share it.

It is absurd to think we should grow the whole economy, filled with things we do not need, just to scrape together a few crumbs to reinvest in the things we want.[40] Must we sell more and more polluting SUVs to collect a few euros of VAT[v] to fund treatments for respiratory diseases? Do we really need a burgeoning advertising sector to pay our teachers'

---

[v] Value-Added Tax [Translator's Note].

salaries? Who, outside tobacco lobbies, would dare argue that we should increase cigarette sales to fund cancer treatments? This strategy of expanding the problem to finance its solution is a dead end.

The only truly limiting factors of production are available time, energy, and raw materials; the rest of our economic categories are merely social convention. In other words, we know how to create money, but we do not know how to stretch time or fabricate ecosystems. We cannot produce food out of nothing. We can, however, produce healthy and quality food without money.

Since the degrowth of harmful production will free up working time, energy, and materials, it can be paired with an expansion of public services and the commons in general. From an ecological and social wealth perspective, slowing down the market economy (we could call it austerity applied to capitalism and to those who profit from it the most) is good news: less environmental degradation and more resources available for the sectors that contribute meaningfully to well-being but have so far struggled to thrive in a system obsessed with profitability.

Yes, we should revisit the state's funding model (and many other things, for that matter), but to claim that we cannot degrow (a biophysical imperative) because it would lower VAT revenues (a social convention) is as absurd as saying we shouldn't stop a car heading at full speed toward a wall because it would cut off the music on the radio. There are countless ways to redistribute wealth. We could imagine a system without a VAT, as Thomas Piketty does in his "participatory socialism"[41] model, and far more progressive, selective, and participatory funding methods that would strengthen the resilience of public action.

Capitalist?

Economist Jean-Marie Harribey criticizes degrowth theorists for abandoning the Marxist critique of capitalism in favor of an abstract target, growth.[42] Frédéric Lordon shares the same criticism, arguing that "degrowth advocates who are not capable of articulating an 'exit from capitalism' are clowns."[43] For the ecosocialist Daniel Tanuro, degrowth creates "the illusion of a gentle alternative, less risky and less exacting" than an exit from capitalism.[44]

Let's be clear: since its inception, the degrowth movement has been fundamentally anti-capitalist. Capitalism is a system where production is specifically structured to maximize monetary surplus, that famous *capital accumulation*, based on the private ownership of the means of production and on wage labor. It is therefore a system that cannot degrow without falling into crisis[45]—"capitalism can no more renounce growth than a crocodile can go vegetarian."[46]

If we want to exit growth, we will necessarily have to exit capitalism and thus reduce the social importance of the institutions that comprise it: wage labor, commodities and markets, private ownership of the means of production, and profit-driven businesses. Degrowth is not today's economy in slow motion or in miniature, it is a transition pathway toward a post-capitalist economy where these practices would retreat to the margins of the economic structure.

The divide between ecosocialism and degrowth is unwarranted. It stems from an artificial and somewhat ridiculous stance, typical of a trigger-happy left that would rather spot differences than pursue common objectives. A joint statement by representatives from both communities titled "For Ecosocialist Degrowth"[47] conveys this message. Ecosocialism is socialism without extractivism, productivism, and consumerism—"socialism without growth."[48] Degrowth is the strategy required to reduce the size of the economy so that it can function in a sustainable way. Degrowth is the necessary transition for countries in ecological overshoot, while post-growth (or ecosocialism) is the economic model and societal project that will enable a steady-state economy to prosper once its biophysical metabolism has been slowed down.

Why, then, insist on *degrowth*? For one, because no economic growth is sustainable in the long run, whether the economy is capitalist, socialist, anarchist, or tribal. "Socialist oil is no more ecological than capitalist oil,"[49] writes Paul Ariès. Whatever the proponents of "luxury communism"[50] may say, nothing material can grow forever, no matter the structural model.

Yes, we must exit capitalism. But that alone will not be enough if a new, non-capitalist economic structure falls back into the trap of limitless expansion. Eco-Marxist critics of degrowth must admit that growth is not just the product of capitalism but also the result of a metaphysics of limitlessness that pervades imperialism, colonialism, extractivism, productivism, consumerism, materialism, transhumanism, and more. A true anthropological transformation, far more radical than anti-capitalism, is indispensable.

Let's also admit that growth is a trendier starting point, as evidenced by the popularity of growth/degrowth debates in the media, which far exceeds that of capitalism/anti-capitalism debates. Capitalism is an abstract concept that is rarely discussed in public debate. Growth, on the contrary, is on everyone's lips. If we admit that modern societies (and the economies that go with them) are obsessed with growth, isn't it necessary to start from square one, a "critique of growth," before we can talk about social and ecological justice? Return to sender: critics of capitalism who cannot articulate "degrowth" have not read the IPCC reports carefully.

Anti-Innovation?

François Fillon thinks that degrowth means "curbing the highest capabilities of the human mind."[51] Édouard Philippe opposes it because he believes in science.[52] Guillaume Duval, while editor in chief of *Alternatives Économiques*, accused degrowth of being reactionary and promoting a "back in the good old days" nostalgia for traditional agrarian societies.[53] In a scathing letter to Greta Thunberg, Quebecer historian Marc Simard[54] asked who would want to go back to the pre-industrial era.

As if today's economy harnessed the full potential of the human mind. We allocate our collective resources to a startup founder chasing the next food delivery unicorn (not exactly the challenge of the century) while giving almost nothing to a brilliant researcher developing a revolutionary system to save the planet.[vi] Technical progress does not magically solve all the world's problems; it is a practice embedded in an economic system that predetermines which innovations will be developed.

In an economic system where we invent to get rich, the problems innovation addresses are primarily those of the most privileged and rarely the most urgent (how to increase the productivity of super trawlers and beef cattle, how to design the fastest high-frequency trading algorithms, how to better harvest personal data for advertising).

Local currencies, mutual aid networks, Wikipedia, co-ops, recovered factories, free stores, street libraries, participatory democracy initiatives, walking school buses—these are innovations that should capture our attention but remain underfunded. Inventing a way to collectively organize digital restraint,

---

[vi] If you really want to experience a blow to the human spirit, try applying for funding to research degrowth (I know what I'm talking about).

a bike-sharing service, or a nudge that encourages people to fly less, for example, is innovation too (even if it does not maximize shareholder profit). Why study geo-engineering to invent robots that collect microplastics from the oceans when we could fix the problem at its source by simply ceasing to produce plastic?

Degrowth will not prohibit innovation, but will completely change its content. What if, instead of designing useless ads, all communications experts took on more important issues? Fewer money problems (how to increase my income, boost profits, or grow GDP), and more socio-environmental problems (how to reduce food waste, protect endangered species, or make democracy more participatory). We must also improve our ability to "de-innovate,"[55] that is, to close and dismantle an entire infrastructure that pollutes and makes us unhappy.

It is actually quite paradoxical to label an innovative transition strategy as "anti-innovation." The human genius[56] is capable of conquering new planets and creating artificial intelligence, but not of regulating the housing market or designing a carbon rationing system? As if it were impossible to create a better economic system than the one we have today, even if we can easily improve everything else. Apple has developed 34 new versions of its iPhone since 2007. Is it really beyond our creative capabilities to invent even just one new economic system?

Anti-Business?

"Asking a business executive if he is in favor of growth is like asking a farmer or a gardener [if he wants] his plants to grow," explains Florent Menegaux, CEO of Michelin.[57] When a journalist asked Bertrand Piccard if companies listen to him, he answered that they do, because he doesn't talk about some "utopia of environmental preservation through degrowth" that "scares everyone."[58] Even Philippe Wahl, president and CEO of the French postal service, opposes it: "for us postal workers, growth is the solution."[59]

Degrowth is not anti-business but anti-profit-chasing. It criticizes companies organized around the imperative to grow revenue, profits, and capital, and that sacrifice conviviality and sustainability to endlessly increase their margins. Making money off the backs of exploited workers and a ravaged environment is not true enrichment, especially if the value these activities add is captured by the privileged few.

Remember that degrowth is a macroeconomic phenomenon. It would be the result of specific policies whose effects would differ by sector and by company. There is no point in expanding companies that contribute little to our collective well-being and that pollute a lot. Similarly, there is no use in downsizing companies that contribute a lot to our collective well-being and pollute little. Yes to the expansion of organic farms, Feeding America, and Doctors Without Borders; no to the expansion of Amazon and ExxonMobil. The goal of degrowth as a production readjustment strategy is precisely to downsize companies with negative social utility to free up resources for those with positive social utility.

We must ditch the capitalist cliché that all companies should strive to grow like plants. That is certainly not the case for cooperatives in a social and inclusive economy, whose success is measured in more than just profit. Small family businesses do not operate like *gazelles* (high-growth companies), stopping at nothing to snatch up any extra dollar. They are often stationary, fluctuating slightly with demand but not seeking exponential growth.

The neighborhood baker who already has a sufficient customer base may not want to put in extra hours, hire more staff, or build a second bakery. If the first bakery allows them to make a living, enjoy their work, and feed the community, why work more?

There are over 22,000 cooperatives in France and only 668 publicly traded companies. Of the 4.5 million companies on French soil, only 292 are large corporations (with over 5,000 employees and more than 1.5 billion euros in revenue). The average company in France is not a gazelle hoping to become a unicorn, but a small business that aspires only to satisfy the needs of its stakeholders, without necessarily wanting to become a multinational. Given that large corporations are responsible for the majority of harmful activities, degrowth is, above all, about reducing the importance these behemoths have claimed in economic life.

Against Our Nature?

During the presentation of a Climate Plan by France's Public Investment Bank in April 2022, its president, Nicolas Dufourcq, rejected degrowth because "growth is in our DNA."[vii] According to entrepreneur Bertrand Piccard, "human beings always want to have more,"[60] and for economist Xavier Timbeau, growth is the natural consequence of human behavior, "something people do on their own."[61]

To think that we have always worshiped money and pursued its accumulation is to know little of human history. Economic

---

[vii] "It is also a civilization of growth. And that growth, it's in our DNA. And we are not going to change that. So we must find a way to stay true to our growth DNA. I'm telling you that BPI France does not believe in degrowth; Covid showed us that quite clearly. We now know that we would need to lockdown every two years to have a shot, through degrowth, at reaching the minimum targets of the Paris Agreement. So it's just not feasible. Our growth DNA, it's here to stay; the carbon-based society needs to become a thing of the past, and that needs to happen as quickly as possible." (Nicolas Dufourcq, presentation of the Public Investemant Bank's Climate Plan in April 2022).

growth in human societies only really began in 1820 in industrializing countries.[62] GDP was only invented in 1930, and its use only spread internationally after World War II. Anthropologists show that many societies, past and present, aspire for equilibrium rather than growth. This is not surprising. Nothing in nature grows forever. Our bodies stop growing at a certain age, and even trees ultimately reach a maximum height. It is one of the most fundamental characteristics of living things: all growth has a beginning and an end.

Human beings may be animated by an unquenchable existential thirst, a desire for transcendence that pushes us to certain achievements. Wanting to improve one's lot is a sound aspiration, but producing more is not always the best means to that end. The pursuit of progress and a better life cannot be reduced to curves mapping exponential growth, especially not of income.

The very idea of increasing happiness indefinitely would rile many philosophers. Happiness is not a matter of quantity but rather of quality. In a context of ecological collapse and major social crisis, if we were truly driven by the desire to improve our situation (or at least to avoid making the world uninhabitable), the great majority of us should prioritize degrowing toward a steady-state economy that could prosper without growth.

What would an alien observer say, watching us ravage the planet to collect points on an indicator we made up ourselves? It's as stupid as friends killing each other over a game of Monopoly. This obsession with economic growth, distinctive of contemporary productivist systems, is a historical and anthropological anomaly. To attribute it to some inherent human nature is to shut down political debate by attempting to legitimize an ideology as universal law.

We are neither selfish nor altruistic. I will not counter the tale of the calculating individual with one of the inherent kindness and generosity of human nature. The behaviors causing our troubles today are determined by social convention, nothing more. Business leaders are no more greedy monsters than senior officials are passionless bureaucrats or advertising executives are crooks. We all play a specific role in the grand theater of economics. To transform it, the first step is to admit that these roles can change, that the banality of economic evil is not our fate. We are at the first step.

Unacceptable?

For John Molyneux, degrowth will be unacceptable to the majority of workers who face unemployment and austerity.[63] This is the central argument of Luc Ferry, who incessantly repeats that degrowth is unworkable in a democracy, and that implementing it would be to "oppose the majority opinion of citizens who generally have little interest in seeing their incomes fall."[64]

And yet, degrowth has the wind in its sails. In 2021, the Barometer for Responsible Consumption showed that 52% of people surveyed believed "that we must completely rethink our economic system, and dispel the myth of infinite growth."[65] In 2020, 67% of participants in another survey declared they were in favor of degrowth, defined as "the reduction of the production of goods and services to protect the environment and the well-being of humanity."[66]

Another survey in 2019 asked, "What is the most effective way to solve current and future ecological and climate problems?" To this, 54% of respondents answered that "we must fundamentally change our lifestyle, our modes of transportation, and drastically reduce our consumption."[67]

In a May 2020 survey, 55% of respondents chose "an economic and social structure geared toward equilibrium" based on the principle of "less but better" (72% among those aged 18-24), ranking higher than all other options. In another survey from June 2021, 47% of participants said that we should prioritize "the environment, even if that could slow economic growth and cause people to lose their jobs."[68]

In 2021, 75% of French people agreed with the statement that "the economy should prioritize the health and well-being of people and nature rather than only focusing on profit and increasing wealth."[69] And even a survey by the Medef (the French Business Confederation) in 2020 concluded that 67% of French people were in favor of "degrowth."[70]

During the Grand Débat National,[viii] I analyzed some of the proposals online. Of the 153,798 contributions on the theme of ecological transition, 540 included the word "degrowth" in their title, a term used more frequently than "green economy" (only 61 posts), "green growth" (40), "circular economy" (126), or even "sustainable development" (529).[71] Also noteworthy was the Citizens' Convention on Climate, which, according to *Le Point*, "chose degrowth."[72] During its first working session in October 2019, "the obsession with growth" was identified as the chief obstacle to ecological transition.[73]

I don't see how degrowth can be democratically unworkable if the majority of the population sees it as progress. Those who worry about their purchasing power today are the ones who will see their living power improve with degrowth. The only group likely to resist degrowth is the small minority who still manage to enrich themselves under capitalism, to the detriment of everyone else and of nature as a whole.

[viii] The Grand Débat National (Great National Debate) was a large-scale public consultation initiated by French President Emmanuel Macron in January 2019 in response to the widespread Yellow Vest (*Gilets Jaunes*) protests [Translator's Note].

Totalitarian?

Like "Godwin's law" (the longer a debate goes on, the more likely that someone will be compared to a Nazi), there is the "Goulag law"[74]: when talking about ecology, you will likely be accused of supporting the Soviet Union (or some other dictatorial regime). For Philippe Charlez, energy specialist at the Institut Sapiens, "degrowth legitimizes totalitarian practices."[75] A "degrowth dictatorship," according to Rémi Godeau, editor-in-chief of *L'Opinion*; the "unhealthy desire to determine people's happiness for them," according to Bruno Le Maire.[76]

To call capitalism democratic is to misunderstand it. In France, the wealthiest 10% of households possess more than half of all wealth.[77] The few who control the means of production decide what to produce without consulting anyone. This is not a democratic system, but a plutocratic one: economic planning by the wealthy.

The richer you get, the more you can weigh in on political decisions and shape the rules of the game to your advantage.[78] Producing and consuming more allows the powerful to get richer, an imperative imposed upon us which they try desperately to legitimize by associating it with our collective well-being. And even if we could vote with our wallets without being influenced by ads, the biggest wallets would still set the trend.

Determine people's happiness for them is actually an excellent characterization of advertising, a kind of "invisible dictatorship"[79] that pushes people to buy. Sweden bans advertisements aimed at children under the age of twelve, and France limits advertising for alcohol and tobacco. Every time a law of this kind is proposed, industry lobbies spend millions to portray these common sense measures as a slippery slope to dictatorship. Would it really be so terrible to impose a default ad blocker on internet browsers, or to ban aerial advertising, the distribution of flyers in mailboxes, and billboards in public spaces?

It's the same story today—and has been for the past twenty years—with climate change. The specter of a "green dictatorship" that haunted sustainable development in the 1980s has returned today to protect the status quo.

Yes, degrowth requires the courageous mobilization of all of society's strength. We must fall back below ecological ceilings, in one way or another, and that will not happen without effort, complaints, or even legitimate social conflicts. Nature imposes boundaries that it would be irresponsible not to respect, and our freedom to produce and consume must from now on be subordinated to this ecological imperative.[ix] But we remain free to use resources however we want to below these thresholds, and to organize the degrowth transition in a way that is as fair, convivial, and democratic as possible.

Degrowth is a "fighting word"[80] used both by those who indict the existing system and those who defend it. Amid the swarm of controversies surrounding the concept, we find both clichés that pollute the debate and critiques that stimulate it.

No, degrowth is not a perpetual recession, a pandemic lockdown, an apologia for poverty, a reactionary impulse, a hatred of business, a rejection of innovation, or a form of eco-dictatorship. But yes, some of the issues it raises are worth discussing, like the relationship between ecology and capitalism, our choice of terminology and its democratic acceptability, the role of the state in this transition and the consequences

---

[ix] During a televised debate on the subject, a journalist asked: "In a world that aims to degrow, do I still have the right to go on Amazon and buy whatever I want, whenever I want?" The answer is no, but that has nothing to do with degrowth. Every society imposes limits on production and consumption. Amazon does not have the right to sell movies with pedophilic content, and if someone had bought thousands of masks just for themselves at the height of the pandemic they would have faced public outrage.

of degrowth on public finances, or the ties of dependency between countries of the Global North and countries of the Global South.

These discussions are already underway, and the more of us participate, the better. To brush degrowth aside without truly making the effort to understand it (as many of the people cited in this chapter do) is to refuse to participate in one of the most important debates of our time.

Conclusion
Deserting Capitalism

Etymologically, the term "radical" comes from the Latin *radix* (root): to be radical is to get to the root of the problem. Degrowth, in this sense, is radical indeed, because it doesn't just put a bandage on the wounds of capitalism; rather, it identifies the mechanisms that inflict them. Instead of "greening GDP," "creating jobs," and "maintaining purchasing power," it sheds light on the underlying forces driving our societal choices and compels us to rethink our relationship with the world—with nature, justice, the meaning of life, and well-being.

At the core of all these questions is growth, that totem of modern societies that has become as much an individual obsession as a collective one. Tuning into a political debate, one can only be aghast at the cult that politicians from all sides, journalists, and economists continue to create around GDP. High-income countries like France stubbornly insist on chasing "fairy tales of eternal economic growth," even if it endangers the health of ecosystems and the quality of life of everyone who depends on them.

GDP is an incomplete map that only captures a small part of a vast social and ecological landscape. What a neoclassical economist hastily calls "production" is in fact only the appropriation of wealth that already existed in another form before being mobilized for the market economy. Beyond a certain threshold, GDP growth stops being value *added* and becomes value *stripped away*, a kind of plunder of the social and ecological sphere. We destroy the living world and our collective life to produce ads, SUVs, and meals delivered by precarious workers on bicycles, and we dare call it "wealth creation." To insist on growing without limit is not development, it is bulimia.

The absurdity of the situation will baffle future generations, who will wonder how we came to organize our society around a single monetary indicator, just as we now mock the tribes that performed human sacrifices to influence the weather.

Most economists firmly believe in the future greening of GDP and of growth, despite decades of epic fails (hot messes, literally). Scientists have crunched the numbers every which way without finding any justification for this optimism. It is astounding, by contrast, to observe how this tremendous mass of data, these thousands of warnings all point to a very simple truth: the economy can never fully decouple from nature. For better or for worse, we are confined in a biosphere with finite limits. Trying to keep an economy in a state of perpetual growth within a limited environment is like a child wearing kids' shoes into adulthood. Today, and until evidence to the contrary, every additional percentage point of GDP brings us closer to an ecological future that scientists describe as *ghastly*.[1]

Even if it were biophysically possible, this exponential growth of monetary activities would still be undesirable. There are only 24 hours in a day and our attention is limited. We strive to grow the marvels we can sell, to the detriment of other kinds of wealth, maybe the real kinds, that national accounting does not record.

Yet all these efforts for a growth that destroys nature and drains us don't even deliver on their promises. The economy grows but poverty persists. GDP points accumulate but the purchasing power of most of the population stagnates or declines. Growth creates activities that almost nobody needs and jobs that almost nobody wants. Financial markets are booming and yet public services are stalled. The economy expands, but quality of life diminishes. A 1996 United Nations report aptly sums it up: the growth we are experiencing is "jobless, ruthless, voiceless, rootless, and futureless."[2]

The message of this book is clear: we must say "goodbye to growth."[3] We must "exit growth,"[4] dismantle the "growth regime,"[5] demystify "the mystique of growth"[6]; disbelieve to be able to degrow. To put it simply, we must imagine an economic life beyond the blind productivism that only counts dollar bills. What can we still afford to produce and consume? Degrowth is an ecological necessity, but it is also a social and existential opportunity. Yes, slow down to survive, but more importantly, slow down to *live well*, to truly exist.

When I talk about common laundry rooms, insect hotels, local currencies, and limited-profit cooperatives, my economist colleagues look at me like I have suggested we move to Mars (and in their eyes, Elon Musk's proposed space project might actually seem more realizable). It is paradoxical that, on the one hand, the ideology of growth celebrates innovation with the fervent conviction that everything can always be improved by technology and, on the other hand, when it comes to the system itself, the capitalist economy introduced in the 19th century is considered rigid, immutable, and unsurpassable. We must demolish this static dogma, this Thatcherian *there is no alternative* that sees present-day capitalism as the end of history. That is not the case. The economy, like every social construct, is malleable; and in human affairs, where there's a will, there's a way.

The task remains to imagine what economy we hope to create. We urgently need a *pedagogy of miracles*—a sort of inverted pedagogy of disaster. Imagine if there were as many movies about the end of capitalism as there are movies about the end of the world. A *Black Mirror* episode that ends well. *The Day After Tomorrow* in a world where animals and humans live in Disney-esque harmony. *Ecotopia*, *The Dispossessed*, *News from Nowhere*, and other utopian classics adapted into TV shows.

The imagination is a muscle, and ours has atrophied,

weakened by the lack of vision of a generation of economists who couldn't think outside the lines of their Excel spreadsheets. It's about time we retake control of our future, step out of line, exercise creativity, and broaden the horizon of what's possible. We must educate our desire for a different economy, free the future from the endless cycle of productivist economic systems, be they capitalist or socialist; we must *révolutionize* the economy (to borrow *rêve*, the French word for dream), that is, dream up a future for it that is radically different from the present.

"They did not know it was impossible, so they did it": a famous quote by Mark Twain that should be printed in capital letters in every economics department. No more neoclassical killjoys who use their calculators to dismiss any project that does not respect the Maastricht Treaty's debt-to-GDP ratio. We need "disruptive thinking"[7] now and massive "civil resistance"[i] to break our economic model out of the small habits that destroy the living world and collective life. We do not need docile economists who act like capitalism's friendly plumbers, but architects of alternative economies. No more repairs; time for design.

The real challenge of the early 21st century is to invent an economic system that guarantees "well-being for all within planetary boundaries,"[8] as the latest IPCC report puts it. We could also say, echoing Serge Latouche, "frugal abundance in an inclusive society."[9] A joyful, nonviolent, participatory, resilient, just, and sustainable economy. An economy centered on quality and no longer on quantity, where conviviality prevails

---

[i] Let's cite the collective Dernière Rénovation's call to action: "At this moment in History—our moment—resistance is a last resort against the forced march of our societies toward the greatest episode of human suffering in History, all around the world. It is no longer just a matter of disobedience or stepping aside; it is now a moral imperative for all citizens who are able to join the resistance, take control of our destiny, and save whatever can still be saved."

over productivity. Out with hubris and excess, in with temperance and parsimony; out with competition and speed, in with cooperation and resonance; out with domination and exploitation, in with autonomy and care. An economy that performs, in the simplest way possible, its economic function (the parsimonious coordination of our contentment) without colonizing the rest of social life or destroying the living world.

A different economy—we are not the first to want it. More and more researchers and engaged citizens are designing and experimenting with alternatives. The Via Campesina movement reinvented peasant agriculture under principles of sustainability and sovereignty. Transition Towns has revived interest in ecological municipalism, while the ecovillage movement is reimagining new ways of living together. New Zealand is moving beyond GDP with its well-being budgets, and countries like Ecuador and Bolivia are amending their constitutions to recognize nature as a legal subject. The French, for their part, are not as reticent as one might think about truly innovative initiatives: limited-profit cooperatives have multiplied in recent years, as have local currencies (more than 80), Zero Long-Term Unemployment Zones, and a whole array of other extremely valuable tools. We aren't starting from scratch.

As for concepts, the models abound: *participatory economics*, the *well-being economy*, the *donut economy*, the *economy for the common good*, the *permacircular economy*, *economic democracy*, *participatory socialism*, and *ecosocialism*.[10] It is a vast undertaking, but there's no lack of ideas: a *convivial* economy composed of *frugal associations*, *contributive permacompanies*, and *relational societies*, driven by an *alternative hedonism* and the pursuit of *resonance*; a *low-tech* economy with a *work less to live better* culture, structured into *decentralized bioregions* and *sociocratic circles*, following the model of *libertarian municipalism*.[11] There are many others. Each of these concepts is a piece of the puzzle that will help us invent the economy of tomorrow. All that's left is to fit them together into a coherent system.

Because no, hope alone is not enough to change the world. If "revolution is the active passage from dream to reality" (famous graffiti from May 1968), let us dream, but let's dream without having to wake up after. Let's draw up plans for the boldest utopias without fearing the changes they will impose. Some of us intuit that the reality imposed upon us is just a representation like any other: no less artificial, no less suspect than a façade painted over unsightly machinery. While most people prefer the bliss of ignorance and the media's soothing lullaby, some do not shy away from the challenges of introspection and are willing to shake the convictions of the old world. This book is for those who will choose the red pill and realize that the matrix of capitalism and growth exploits and destroys us.

Of course, transforming an economy is no small feat. An economy cannot be assembled like kit furniture, and let's be honest, any answer to the "how" question will always be somewhat disappointing. What's important is that we already have all the tools at hand. The literature on degrowth offers countless concrete policy measures—in a recent study, we identified 380 specific instruments: the reduction of working hours, universal basic income, guaranteed employment, taxes on financial transactions, bans on certain forms of advertising, energy rationing, carbon accounts, and hundreds more. The transition toolkit is increasingly well-stocked and only waiting to be put to use.

And by the way, this transition isn't waiting on politicians. If degrowth is a systemic transformation, a societal project, it will require the mobilization of all actors. There is no magic button to transform the economy overnight, like a quick-change artist swapping costumes. We must produce and consume differently, and to do so, we must reinvent our mode of social organization. The group Masse Critique often says that their cycling events *do not block traffic, they are the traffic*. It's the same for the economy: we aren't blocking the economy, we are the economy. Our mission: to "take back the economy,"[12] take back control to shape an economy that is democratic, convivial, fair, and sustainable.

To those who will say we're not ready, that we need more data and better models, I say: no. We could spend centuries theorizing the economy in a million different ways. It has already been fifty years since the Meadows developed their model, and many economists still refuse to admit that economic growth has biophysical limits (they will probably never admit it, or only when it's far too late). Let's not be like the one in John Locke's aphorism, "who would not use his legs, but sit still and perish, because he had no wings to fly."

What is certain is that we do not need to stimulate the economy. We must take "preventive measures against the old world," as Bruno Latour says.[13] Stimulating the economy means reactivating the monstrous machine that is slowly eating away at the world. To continue with business as usual is to head for certain death. The time has come to send capitalism back into the void from which it came. Let's be clear: let it die,[14] as an obsolete system destined to join its productivist peer, the state socialism of the Soviet Union, in the history books. "Outraged"[15] at the social and ecological injustice of all productivist-extractivist systems, we are now on strike against this economy that destroys life.

Like the brave graduates of Agro Paris Tech,[16] we are deserting. "These jobs are destructive, and choosing them means causing harm while serving the interests of a privileged few. Yet these were the career paths presented to us throughout our studies at Agro Paris Tech. Meanwhile, they never told us about the graduates who believe that these careers are more a part of the problem than the solution and who chose to desert. We are speaking to those who have doubts. [. . .] We want to tell you that you are not the only ones who feel like something's off—because something really is off. [. . .] We refuse to serve this system and have decided to seek other paths, to chart our own course."

The American economy is experiencing a "Great Resignation," young people in China are "lying flat," the "anti-productivity" movement is growing, and French graduates are flipping the tables. In addition to material shortages and ecosystemic cataclysms, the workforce is now becoming scarce. People no longer want to work for a system that ravages the world to enrich the privileged few. They're right. We will not give our time, energy, and skills to this system. We will not collaborate.

"I have doubts and I'm stepping away," as a Centrale Nantes student said in another call for desertion.[17] If some companies want to wage war on the living world and on humanity, we refuse to participate. We will protect nature and those who depend on it with all our might. Let's dare to "rethink our growth model" and explore "sober and prosperous models for degrowth,"[18] as one HEC student suggests. Let's listen to the students at Polytechnique and build a "more pleasant, more peaceful society, slowed down by choice."[19] Deserting does not mean leaving the whole of society behind, only capitalism—void of meaning and running out of steam.

I'll stop there. It's time for a nap.

Notes

Introduction

[1] David Wallace-Wells, *The Uninhabitable Earth: Life After Warming*, Tim Duggan Books, 2019.

[2] Lucas Chancel, "Climate change and the global inequality of carbon emissions 1990-2020," World Inequality Database, October 2021.

[3] D. Kenner, *Carbon Inequality: The Role of the Richest in Climate Change*, Routledge, 2019.

[4] Hervé Kempt, *Que crève le capitalisme*, Seuil, 2020, chapter III.

[5] Timothée Parrique, "Look Up: Climate change is not a crisis, it's a beating," *Parole*, March 24, 2022.

[6] Rox Nixon, *Slow Violence and the Environmentalism of the Poor*, Harvard University Press, 2011.

[7] Jason W. Moore (ed.), *Anthropocene or Capitalocene? Nature, History, and the Crisis of Capitalism*, PM Press, 2016; Richard V. Norguard, "Economism and the Econocene: A Coevolutionary Interpretation," *Real-world Economics Review*, 2019; Éloi Laurent, *Sortir de la croissance: mode d'emploi*, Les liens qui libèrent, 2021.

[8] Serge Latouche, *Justice sans limites. Le défi de l'éthique dans une économie mondialisée*, Fayard, 2003.

[9] Joseph Bullington, "GDP: A countdown to doom," *In These Times*, September 4, 2021.

[10] Dominique Méda, *La Mystique de la croissance: comment s'en libérer*, Flammarion, 2013.

[11] In *Pourquoi sommes-nous capitalistes malgré nous?* (2022, p. 26), sociologist Denis Combi offers a nice definition: "To denaturalize means to restore an exotic quality to our most quotidian economic behaviors, to make them appear foreign to us, external to us, and thus open to rational analysis. [. . .] It's also being willing to see their element of strangeness in a wholly different sense: as shocking, bizarre, and, frankly, quite often absurd."

[12] I reprise the nice triad *"rejet-projet-trajet,"* proposed by Michel Lepesant in *Politique(s) de la décroissance: propositions pour penser et faire la transition*, Éditions Utopia, 2013, p. 23.

1. The Secret Life of GDP

[1] The webpage "La croissance" on the FACILEECO portal of the Ministère de l'Économie, des Finances et de la Relance's website.

[2] Tim Jackson, *Prosperity Without Growth: Foundations for the Economy of Tomorrow*, 2017.

[3] Manfred Max-Neef, *Human Scale Development: Conception, Application, and Further Reflections*, The Apex Press, New York, 1991.

[4] Amartya Sen, *Development as Freedom*, Oxford University Press, 1999.

[5] https://www.pactedupourvoidevivre.fr

[6] Éloi Laurent, *Sortir de la croissance: Mode d'emploi*, 2021, Les Liens qui libèrent, p. 190.

[7] A few vital works on the history of GDP: Lorenzo Fioramonti, *Gross Domestic Problem: The Politics Behind the World's Most Powerful Number*, 2013; Dirk Philpsen, *The Little Big Number: How GDP Came to Rule the World and what to do about it*, 2015; Joseph E. Stiglitz, Amartya Sen, and Jean-Paul Fitoussi, *Mismeasuring our Lives: Why GDP doesn't add up*, 2010; Matthias Schmelzer, *The Hegemony of Growth: The OECD and the Making of the Economic Growth Paradigm*, 2016; Rutger Hoekstra, *Replacing GDP by 2030: Towards a Common Language for the Well-being and Sustainability Community*, 2019; Diane Coyle, *GDP: A brief but Affectionate History*, 2014; Philipp H. Lepenies, *The Power of a Single Number: A Political History of GDP*, 2016; Ehsan Masood, *The Great Invention: The Story of GDP and the Making (and Unmaking) of the Modern World*, 2014.

[8] "System of National Accounts," United Nations, 2008. The definition of GDP is at p. 8, that of value added at p. 103, and that of production at p. 97.

[9] To better understand the calculation of GDP: Heu?reka, *Tout sur l'économie, ou presque*, Payot, 2020.

[10] France Bénévolat, "L'évolution de l'engagement bénévole associatif en France, de 2010 à 2019," March 2019.

[11] "System of National Accounts," United Nations, 2008.

[12] *Ibid.*, Chapter VI: The production account, p. 98.

[13] Annex 1: Glossary, of the AR6 WGIII report, p. 23.

[14] Éloi Laurent, *Sortir de la croissance . . .*, *op. cit.*, p. 16 and p. 61.

[15] R. M. Solow, "The economics of resources or the resources of economics," *The American Economic Review*, vol. 64, n° 2, 1974, p. 11.

[16] Paul Fauconnet and Marcel Mauss, *Sociologie*, 1901, in Marcel Mauss, *Œuvres*, t. III, *Cohésion sociale et division de la sociologie*, Paris, Éditions de Minuit, 1969, pp. 139-177.

[17] Milton Friedman, "The Social Responsibility of Business Is to Increase Its Profits", *The New York Times Magazine*, September 13, 1970.

[18] During a visit to Rouen's university hospital in April 2018, President

Emmanuel Macron responded to a nurse who was voicing concern about the hospital's lack of funding: "Investing money without taking the steps to modernize, support, transform, sometimes applying common sense, that's not helping people. Because in the end, the funds, it's you who pays for them too, you know. There is no magic money."

[19] Bruno Le Maire, *L'Ange et la Bête: mémoires provisoires*, Gallimard, 2021, p. 327.

[20] Article 1 of Decree n° 2022-826 from June 1, 2022, relating to the responsibilities of the Minister of the Economy, Finance, and Industrial and Digital Sovereignty.

[21] https://www.gov.uk/government/publications/growth-duty

[22] Daniel A. Hirschmann, *Inventing the Economy. Or: How We Learned to Stop Worrying and Love the GDP*, Sociology Thesis, University of Michigan, 2016.

[23] Matthias Schmelzer, *The Hegemony of growth . . .* , *op. cit.*

[24] Olivier Godechot, *Les Traders. Essai de sociologie des marchés financiers*, La Découverte, 2005.

[25] Quelques ennemis du meilleur des mondes (coll.), *Sortir de l'économie*, 2013, p.5.

[26] Frédéric Lordon, *Figures du communisme*, La Fabrique, 2021, p. 87.

[27] Stéphane Foucart, *Des marchés et des dieux: quand l'économie devient religion*, Grasset, 2018.

[28] Éloi Laurent, *La Raison économique et ses monstres*, Les Liens qui libèrent, 2022, p. 15.

[29] Rowan Williams, "Face it: Marx was partly right about capitalism," *The Spectator*, September 27, 2008.

[30] Dominique Méda, *La Mystique de la croissance . . .* , *op. cit.*

[31] Here's how Luc Boltanski and Ève Chiapello define the *spirit of capitalism* in the 1999 book *Le Nouvel Esprit du capitalisme* (Gallimard, "Tel", 2011, p.45): "That set of beliefs associated with the capitalist order, which help to justify that order and to support, by legitimizing them, the actions and attitudes that are consistent with it."

[32] J.K. Gibson-Graham, *The End of Capitalism (As We Knew It). A Feminist Critique of Political Economy*, University of Minnesota Press, 1996, p. 40.

[33] Denis Colombi, *Pourquoi sommes-nous capitalistes malgré nous?*, Payot, 2022, p.12.

[34] *Ibid.*, pp. 283-284.

[35] H. Welzer, "Mental Infrastructures: How growth entered the world and our souls," Heinrich B ll Stiftung, 2011.

[36] Michel Foucault, *Naissance de la biopolitique. Cours au collège de France (1978-1979)*, Gallimard-Seuil, 2004.

[37] Céline Marty, *Travailler moins pour vivre mieux*, Dunod, 2021, p. 27.

[38] Walt Whitman Rostow, *The Stages of Economic Growth*, Cambridge University Press, 1990 [1960].

[39] Eva Sadoun, *Une économie à nous*, Actes Sud, 2022, p. 37.

[40] Yves-Marie Abraham, *Guérir du mal de l'infini*, Écosociété, 2019.

2. The Impossible Decoupling

[1] See the "planetary boundaries" page on the Stockholm Resilience Center's website.

[2] G. Grossman and A. Kruger. "Environmental Impacts of a NAFTA Agreement." National Bureau of Economic Research, Working Paper 3914, 1991; G. Grossman and A. Krueger. "Economic growth and the environment." *Quarterly Journal of Economics*, 1995; T. Panayotou *et al.* "Is the Environmental Kuznets Curve Driven by Structural Change? What Extended Time Series May Imply for Developing Countries." 2000; N. Shafik and S. Bandyopadhyay. "Economic growth and environmental quality: time series and cross-country evidence." The World Bank, 1992.

[3] Timothée Parrique *et al.*, "Decoupling debunked: Evidence and arguments against green growth as a sole strategy of sustainability," European Environmental Bureau, 2019.

[4] H. Haberl *et al.*, "A systematic review of the evidence on decoupling of GDP, resource use and GHG emissions," *Environmental Research Letters*, vol. 15, n° 6, 2020.

[5] WWF, "Living Planet Report 2020."

[6] IPBES, "Global assessment report on biodiversity and ecosystem services," 2019.

[7] Nature France, "Comment évoluent les écosystèmes et habitats en France?"

[8] F. Krausmann *et al.*, "From resource extraction to outflows of wastes and emissions: The socioeconomic metabolism of the global economy, 1900–2015," *Global Environmental Change*, 2018.

[9] T. O. Wiedmann *et al.*, "The material footprint of nation," *PNAS*, 2013.

[10] K. Bithas and P. Kalimeris, "Unmasking decoupling: Redefining the Resource Intensity of the Economy," *Science of The Total Environment*, 2019.

[11] Data from the University of Vienna: http://www.materialflows.net/visualisation-centre/country-profiles/

[12] "L'environnement en France—édition 2019" report.

[13] IEA, "The role of critical minerals in clean energy transition," May 2021.

[14] Nate Aden, "Reducing Carbon Emissions While Growing GDP," *World Resource Institute*, April 2016.

[15] A. J. Turner *et al.*, "A large increase in U.S. methane emissions over

the past decade inferred from satellite data and surface observations," *Geophysical Research Letters*, 2016.

[16] R. W. Howarth *et al.*, "Methane and the greenhouse-gas footprint of natural gas from shale formations," *Climatic Change*, 2011.

[17] Wiedmann and Lenzen, "Environmental and social footprints of international trade," *Nature*, 2018.

[18] Wiedmann *et al.*, "The material footprint of nations," *PNAS*, 2013.

[19] *The Carbon Bankroll: The Climate Impact and Untapped Power of Corporate Cash*, Climate Safe Lending Network, May 2022.

[20] IPCC AR6 WGIII, "Mitigation of climate change," Chapter 2, p. 39.

[21] "Chiffres clés du climat—édition 2021," Ministère de la Transition écologique, p. 28.

[22] *Ibid.*, p.44.

[23] These numbers come from the database Materialflows.net held by the University of Vienna.

[24] Ministerio de Consumo, *Sostenibilidad del consumo en España*, May 2022.

[25] Principaux partenaires de la France à l'exportation et à l'importation, Annual data 2020, Insee, July 2021.

[26] World Bank data.

[27] Online data from the International Energy Agency, "Data and statistics."

[28] Haut Conseil pour le Climat, "Dépasser les constats. Mettre en œuvre les solutions," June 2022, p. 33.

[29] Anderson *et al.*, "A factor of two: How the mitigation plans of 'climate progressive' nations fall far short of Paris-compliant pathways," *Climate Policy*, 2020 (The global climate budget calculated by the authors of the study is 656 GtCO2).

[30] Friedlingstein *et al.*, "Global Carbon Budget 2021," *Earth System Science Data*, 2022.

[31] Data from the University of Vienna: http://www.materialflows.net/visualisation-centre/country-profiles/

[32] The 17.1 t comes from the University of Vienna's online database and the 3-6 t limit from Hickel *et al.*, "National responsibility for ecological breakdown: A faire-shares assessment of resource use, 1970-2017," *The Lancet*, April 2022.

[33] Le Quéré *et al.*, "Drivers of declining CO2 emissions in 18 developed economies," *Nature climate change*, 2019.

[34] S. Keen *et al.*, "A note on the role of energy in production," *Ecological Economics*, 2019.

[35] J.M. Pearce, "Optimizing greenhouse gas mitigation strategies to suppress energy cannibalism," 2nd Climate Change Technology Conference, Ontario, Canada, May 2009.

[36] C. A. S. Hall et al., "EROI of different fuels and the implications for society," *Energy Policy*, 2014.

[37] Capellán-Pérez et al., "Dynamic Energy Return on Energy Investment (EROI) and material requirements in scenarios of global transition to renewable energies," *Energy Strategy Review*, 2019.

[38] A. Fabre, "Evolution of EROIs of electricity until 2050. Estimation and implications on prices," *Ecological Economics*, 2019.

[39] O. Vidal, *Matières premières et énergie*, ISTE Éditions, 2018, p. 82.

[40] M. Fischer-Kowalski et al., "Methodology and indicators of economy-wide material flow accounting," *Journal of Industrial Ecology*, 2011.

[41] C. Benjamin et al., "How do fuel taxes impact rebound effect? Empirical evidence from French households," *Économie et Prévision*, 2019.

[42] S. B. Bruns et al., "Estimating the economy wide rebound effect using empirically identified structural vector autoregressions," *Energy Economics*, 2021.

[43] A. Berner et al., "Do energy efficiency improvements reduce energy use? Empirical evidence on the economy-wide rebound effect in Europe and the United States," *Energy Economics*, 2022.

[44] "L'environnement en France: rapport sur l'état de l'environnement," February 2021.

[45] Numbers cited in Guillaume Pitron, *L'Enfer numérique: voyage au bout d'un like*, Les liens qui libèrent, 2021, p. 212.

[46] C. C. M. Kyba et al., "Artificially lit surface of Earth at night increasing in radiance and extent," *Science Advances*, 2017.

[47] C. L. Magee and T. C. Devezas, "A simple extension of dematerialization theory: Incorporation of technical progress and the rebound effect," *Technological Forecasting and Social Change*, 2017.

[48] Mireille Campana et al., "Réduire la consommation énergétique du numérique," Ministère de l'Économie et des Finances, December 2019.

[49] "Faut-il vraiment passer à la 5G?", *Alternatives économiques*, n° 404, September 2020.

[50] ADEME, "La face cachée du numérique—réduire les impacts du numérique sur l'environnement," January 2021.

[51] France Nature Environnement, "L'empreinte cachée des smartphones," September 2017.

[52] A December 2020 report from the Haut Conseil pour le Climat estimates the carbon impact of 5G deployment between 2.7 MTCO2e and 6.7 MTCO2e in 2030, which represents between 18% and 45% of digital's carbon footprint in 2020.

[53] Mathieu Ecoiffier, "Une analyse de la baisse des émissions de CO2 dues à la combustion d'énergie en France depuis 1990," Insee, December 2017, p. 50.

[54] Haut Conseil pour le Climat, "Renforcer l'atténuation, engager l'adaptation," June 2021.

[55] Guillaume Pitron, *L'enfer numérique . . .* , *op. cit.*

[56] A. S. G. Andrae and T. Edler, "On global electricity usage of communication technology: Trends to 2030," *Challenges*, 2015.

[57] C. Preist *et al.*, "Evaluating sustainable interaction design of digital services: The case of YouTube," *Proceedings of the 2019 CHI Conference on Human Factors in Computing Systems*, 2019.

[58] D. Kamiya, "The carbon footprint of streaming video: Fact-checking the headlines," IEA, 2020.

[59] Guillaume Pitron, *L'enfer numérique . . .* , *op. cit.*, p. 168.

[60] K. Devine and M. Brennan, "Music streaming has a far worse carbon footprint than the heyday of records and CDs—new findings," *The Conversation*, 2019.

[61] C. Mora *et al.*, "Bitcoin emissions alone could push global warming above 2°C," *Nature climate change*, 2018.

[62] "Training a single AI model can emit as much carbon as five cars in their lifetimes," *MIT Technology Review*, June 6, 2019.

[63] The carbon footprint of Google's financial capital is 38 times higher than the footprint linked to its activity—it is 55 times for PayPal, 10 times for Netflix, and 3.3 times for Microsoft (*The carbon bankroll: The climate impact and untapped power of corporate cash*, Climate Safe Lending Network, May 2022).

[64] B. Fix, "Dematerialization through services: Evaluating the evidence," *BioPhysical Economics and Resource Quality*, 2019.

[65] "Circularity gap report," 2022, p. 22.

[66] M. Reuter *et al.*, "Limits of the circular economy: Fairphone modular design pushing the limits," *World of Metallurgy*, 2018.

[67] Eurostat Data Browser, "Recycling rate of e-waste," February 2021.

[68] To take this further: Guillaume Pitron, *L'enfer numérique . . .* , *op. cit.*, p. 59.

[69] Geyer *et al.*, "Production, use and fate of all plastics ever made," *Science Advances*, 2017.

[70] M. S. Chowdhury *et al.*, "An overview of solar photovoltaic panels' end-of-life material recycling," *Energy Strategy Rev.*, 2020.

[71] Minderoo Foundation, "The plastic waste makers index: Revealing the source of the single-use plastics crisis," 2021.

[72] Flore Berlingen, *Recyclage, le grand enfumage. Comment l'économie circulaire est devenue l'alibi du jetable*, Rue de l'Échiquier, 2020, p. 38.

[73] IDDRI, "Livre blanc Numérique et Environnement," 2018.

[74] C. Jenik, "Quelle est la durée de vie d'un smartphone?," *Statista*, March 2017.

[75] Federec, "Rapport annuel," 2019.

[76] Baromètre unifié du marché publicitaire, "Les marché publicitaires en 2019," 2020.

[77] "Circularity gap report," 2022, p. 22.

[78] Ademe/Federec, "Évaluation environnementale du recyclage en France," April 2017, p. 99.

[79] Aghion *et al.*, "Carbon taxes, path dependency, and directed technical change: Evidence from the auto industry," *Journal of Political Economy*, 2016.

[80] J. Halloy and N. Nova, "Au-delà du low tech: technologies zombies, soutenabilité et inventions," in *Low Tech: face au tout-numérique, se réapproprier les technologies*, Ritimo, 2020, pp. 120-128.

[81] Jean-Baptiste Fressoz, "Pour une histoire désorientée de l'énergie," 25e journées scientifiques de l'environnement, February 2014.

[82] R. York, "Do alternative energy sources displace fossil fuels?," *Nature climate change*, 2012.

[83] The Shift Project, "Le plan de transformation de l'économie française," 2022, p. 50.

[84] IRENA, "Global energy transformation: A roadmap to 2050," 2018.

[85] M. Mills, "The 'new energy economy': An exercise in marginal thinking," The Manhattan Institute, 2019.

[86] "The Fiber Year 2016. World Survey on Textiles and Nonwovens," *The Fiber Year*, 2016.

[87] D. Bugden, "Technology, decoupling, and ecological crisis: Examining ecological modernization theory through patent data," *Environmental Sociology*, 2022.

[88] *Aviation et climat*, ISAE-SUPAERO, September 2021.

[89] Tim Jackson, *Prosperity without Growth*, Routledge, 2017, pp. 96-100.

[90] J. Hickel and G. Kallis, "Is green growth possible?", *New Political Economy*, 2019, pp. 8-9.

[91] D. Strumsky *et al.*, "Complexity and the productivity of innovation," *Systems Research and Behavioral Science*, 2010.

[92] Maura Bonaiuti, "Are we entering the age of involuntary degrowth? Promethean technologies and declining returns on innovation," *Journal of Cleaner Production*, 2018.

[93] N. Bloom et al., "Are Ideas Getting Harder to Find?," *American Economic Review*, 2020.

[94] Timothée Parrique, "Decoupling in the IPCC AR6 WGIII," Timothée Parrique blog, April 8, 2022.

[95] IPCC AR6, "Mitigation of Climate Change," Chapter 2, "Decoupling of emissions from economic growth" section.

3. Market Versus Society

[1] Katrine Marçal, *Le Dîner d'Adam Smith. Comment le libéralisme a zappé les femmes et pourquoi c'est un gros problème*, Les Arènes, 2019.

[2] For an introduction to feminist economics, Hélène Périvier, *L'Économie féministe*, Les Presses de Sciences Po, 2020. See also *Le Capitalisme patriarchal* by Silvia Federici, La Fabrique, 2019; and Stefania Barca, *Forces of Reproduction: Notes for a Counter-Hegemonic Anthropocene*, Cambridge University Press, 2020.

[3] Suzanne de Brunhoff, *État et capital*, FM/Fondations, 1976.

[4] Cécile Brousse, "Travail professionnel, tâches domestiques, temps 'libre': quelques déterminants sociaux de la vie quotidienne," *Insee*, 2015.

[5] "Le travail domestique: 60 milliards d'heures en 2010," *Insee*, n° 1423, November 22, 2012.

[6] Fritjof Capra, *The Web of Life: A New Synthesis of Mind and Matter*, HarperCollins, 1996.

[7] Jonathan Crary, *24/7: Late Capitalism and the Ends of Sleep*, Verso, 2014.

[8] Christian Arnsperger, *Éthique de l'existence post-capitaliste. Pour un militantisme existentiel*, Cerf, 2009, p. 131.

[9] Robert Solow, "A Contribution to the theory of economic growth," *The Quarterly Journal of Economics*, February 1956.

[10] Alf Hornborg, *Global Magic: Technologies of Appropriation from Ancient Rome to Wall Street*, Palgrave Macmillan, 2016, p. 15.

[11] To better understand the concept: Yves Crozet, "Économie de la vitesse: Ivan Illich revisité," *L'Économie politique*, "Les révolutions de la mobilité," 2017.

[12] J. P. Dupuy, "À la recherche du temps gagné," 1975, annex to Ivan Illich's book, *Énergie et équité*, reissued in *Œuvre complètes*, vol. 1, Fayard, 2003, pp. 433-440.

[13] For a quick overview of Ivan Illich's ideas: Thierry Paquot, *Ivan Illich et la société conviviale*, Le Passager Clandestin, 2020.

[14] "The higher our social position, the faster we get around, going from 40 kilometers per hour to 64 kilometers per hour." (Tom Dubois *et al.*, *Pour en finir avec la vitesse*, L'Aube, 2021, p. 62.). This is all the more true for aviation: 75% of the sector's energy is associated with the flights of the wealthiest 10% (Tim Gore, "Combattre les inégalités des émissions de CO_2: la justice climatique au cœur de la reprise post-COVID-19," Oxfam, September 21, 2020).

[15] Karl William Kapp, *Les Coûts sociaux de l'entreprise privée*, Les Petits Matins, 2015 [1950].

[16] J. P. Manno. *Privileged Goods: Commoditization and Its Impact on Environment and Society*, CRC Press, 2000.

[17] Data for real estate jobs (https://fr.statista.com/statistiques/485918/emplois-salaries-activites-immobilieres-france/); data for the number of researchers (https://www.enseignementsup-recherche.gouv.fr/fr/grands-chiffres-de-rd-45890).

[18] Dirk Jacobs and Andrea Rea, "Gaspillage de talents. Les écarts de performance dans l'enseignement secondaire entre élèves issus de l'immigration et les autres d'après l'étude PISA 2009," GERME, 2011.

[19] David Harvey, *The New Imperialism*, Oxford University Press, 2003.

[20] N. Fraser, "Contradictions of Capital and Care," *New Left Review*, n° 100, July-August 2016.

[21] David G. Meyers, *The American Paradox: Spiritual Hunger in an Age of Plenty*, Yale University Press, 2000.

[22] Ezra J. Mishan. *The Costs of Economic Growth*, London, Staples Press, 1967.

[23] Herman Daly, *Beyond Growth: The Economics of Sustainable Development*, Boston, Beacon Press, 1996; J. Drewnowski, "The Affluence Line," *Social Indicators Research*, vol. 5, n° 3, 1978, p. 263-278; M. Max-Neef, "Economic growth and quality of life: A threshold hypothesis," *Ecological economics*, vol. 15, n° 2, 1995, pp. 115-118.

[24] Guillaume Pitron, *L'enfer numérique . . .* , *op. cit.*, p. 124.

[25] J. P. Manno, *Privileged Goods . . .* , *op. cit.*, 2000.

[26] Michael Sandel, *Ce que l'argent ne saurait acheter. Les limites morales du marché*, Seuil, 2016.

[27] *Ibid.*

[28] Richard M. Titmuss, *The Gift Relationship*, London, Allen and Unwin, 1970.

[29] U. Gneezy and A. Rustichini, "A fine is a price," *Journal of Legal Studies*, vol. 29, 2000.

[30] Jacques Généreux, *La Dissociété: à la recherche du progrès humain*, Seuil, 2011.

[31] Karl Polanyi, *The Great Transformation*, Farrar and Reinhart, 1944, p. 73.

[32] G. Dale, *Karl Polanyi: The Limits of the Market*, Cambridge, Polity Press, 2010, p. 45.

[33] David Graeber, *Debt: The First 5,000 years*, Brooklyn, Melville House, 2011.

[34] Karl Marx, *Capital. Book I*, first chapter, 1867.

[35] The "Wait in Line" section on the TaskRabbit website: "Waiting in line: not for you? Hire a Tasker to wait in line at a restaurant, for a special event, at the post office, or anywhere else.")

[36] Stefano Bartolini, *Pour une société fraternelle: En finir avec l'égoïsme, la compétition et la surconsommation*, Pocket, 2015.

4. False Promises

[1] "La transition environnementale est-elle compatible avec la croissance économique?", debate with Bruno Le Maire, Delphine Batho, and Antoine Frérot, *Le Monde*, January 27, 2021.

[2] Jean-Philippe Delsol, "La décroissance ou le chemin de la pauvreté," *Contrepoints*, May 28, 2020.

[3] Observatoire des Inégalités, *Rapport sur les inégalité en France 2021*, 2021; Observatoire National de la Précarité Énergétique, "Suivi annuel de la précarité énergétique," November 2018; Franck Le Morvan and Thomas Wanecq, "La lutte contre la précarité alimentaire: évolution du soutien public à une politique social, agricole et de santé publique," Inspection générale des affaires sociales, December 2019.

[4] "Revenus et patrimoine des ménages—Éditions 2021," *Insee*, May 27, 2021.

[5] Observatoire National de la Pauvreté et de l'Exclusion Sociale, "Les budgets de référence: une méthode d'évaluation des besoins pour une participation effective à la vie sociale," 2014-2015 report.

[6] Pierre Concialdi, "What does it mean to be rich? Some conceptual and empirical issues," *European Journal of Social Security*, 2018.

[7] Thomas Piketty, "De l'inégalité en France," Le blog de Thomas Piketty, *Le Monde*, April 18, 2017.

[8] Observatoire des Inégalités, *Rapport sur la pauvreté en France*, 2e édition, 2020-2021, p. 12.

[9] Drees, "Minima sociaux et prestations sociales: ménages aux revenus modestes et redistribution, édition 2020," September 22, 2020.

[10] https://www.livingwage.org.uk

[11] Fondation Copernic, *Vers une société plus juste: manifeste pour un plafonnement des revenus et des patrimoines*, 2019, p. 55.

[12] *Ibid.*, p. 42.

[13] Pour une mise en œuvre du droit à des moyens convenables d'existence, CNLE, June 2012, p. 29.

[14] Les économistes atterrés, *De quoi avons-nous vraiment besoin?* Les liens qui libèrent, 2021, p. 95.

[15] François-Xavier Devetter, "Conditions de travail," Dares, 2013.

[16] Observatoire des Inégalités, *Rapport sur les riches en France, op. cit.*

[17] You can take the test online with your own salary: https://www.inegalites.fr/Salaire-etes-vous-riche-ou-pauvre

[18] Figures shared by the Observatoire des Inégalités.

[19] Observatoire des Inégalités, Rapport sur les riches en France, *op. cit.*, p. 49.

[20] Thomas Piketty, "De l'inégalité en France," Le blog de Thomas Piketty, *Le Monde*, April 18, 2017.

[21] Observatoire des Inégalités, *Rapport sur les riches en France, op. cit.*, p. 10.

[22] Kate Pickett and Richard Wilkinson, *The Spirit Level: Why More Equal Societies Almost Always Do Better*, Allen Lane, 2009.

[23] "Le niveau de vie des ménages agricoles est plus faible dans les territoires d'élevage," *Insee*, October 2021.

[24] Observatoire des Inégalités, "Un million de travailleurs pauvres en France," January 5, 2021.

[25] "France, portrait social—édition 2019," *Insee*, 2019.

[26] Les économistes atterrés, *De quoi avons-nous vraiment besoin?, op. cit.*

[27] Proposition de loi pour une limite décente des écarts de revenus, n° 3094, June 16, 2020.

[28] Les économistes atterrés, *op. cit.*, p. 231.

[29] "À quel point la suppression de l'ISF est-elle un échec?," *Alternatives économiques*, October 2021.

[30] "24% des ménages détiennent 68% des logements possédés par des particuliers," *Insee*, November 2021.

[31] Attac, *Ce qui dépend de nous: Manifeste pour une relocalisation écologique et solidaire*, 2020, p. 69.

[32] Thomas Piketty, *Capital et idéologie, op. cit.*

[33] Denis Payre, "Coup de griffe contre l'écologie de la décroissance," Europe 1, October 2, 2020.

[34] A few key works for approaching the question: André Gorz, *Métamorphoses du travail, quête de sens*, 1988; Juliet Schor, *The Overworked American*, 1992; Dominique Méda, *Le Travail, une valeur en voie de disparition*, 1995; Kathi Weeks, *The Problem With Work*, 2011; David Frayne, *Le Refus du travail*, 2018; David Graeber, *Bullshit Jobs*, 2019; et Céline Marty, *Travailler moins pour vivre mieux*, 2021.

[35] David Graeber, *Bullshit jobs: la théorie*, Les liens qui libèrent, 2019.

[36] Nicolas Kayser-Bril, *Imposture à temps complet: pourquoi les bullshit jobs envahissent le monde*, Éditions du Faubourg, 2022.

[37] These numbers are available on the Journal du Net's Encyclopédie des Salaires: https://www.journaldunet.com/business/salaire

[38] https://globalwomenstrike.net/open-letter-to-governments-a-care-income-now/

[39] Sophie Swaton, *Revenu de transition écologique: mode d'emploi*, PUF, 2020.

[40] The initial proposal comes from Bernard Friot (*L'Enjeu du salaire*, 2012, for example), revived with a twist by Frédéric Lordon in *Figures du communisme* (2021), and from a degrowth perspective by Denis Baryon in *L'Écologie contre le revenu de base. Un salaire universel pour la décroissance* (2021).

[41] V. Liegey, S. Madeleine, C. Ondet, A.-I. Veillot, *Un projet de décroissance. Manifeste pour une dotation inconditionnelle d'autonomie*, Utopias, 2013.

[42] Claire Hédon *et al.*, *Zéro chômeur: l'expérience de 10 territoires*, Éditions Quart Monde/Éditions de l'Atelier, 2019.

[43] Pavlina Tcherneva, *La Garantie d'emploi. L'arme sociale du Green New Deal*, La Découverte, 2021.

[44] Jean-Marie Harribey, "Dans les services monétaires non marchands, le travail est productif de valeur," *La Nouvelle Revue du travail*, 2019.

[45] This point is developed in detail in Antoine Monserand's thesis: *The Macroeconomics of Degrowth* (2022).

[46] Pour un système universel de retraite, préconisations de Jean-Paul Delevoye, Haut-Commissaire à la réforme des retraites, July 2019, p. 111.

[47] Commission d'enquête sur le coût économique et financier de la pollution de l'air, Sénat, 2015.

[48] https://vaincreleburnout.fr/chiffres-cles/

[49] Martin Hagve, "The money behind academic publishing," *Tidsskriftet*, August 17, 2020.

[50] Étienne Nouguez, *Des médicaments à tout prix: sociologie des génériques en France*, Presses de Sciences Po, 2017.

[51] Vasilis Kostakis *et al.*, "The convergence of digital commons with local manufacturing from a degrowth perspective: Two illustrative cases," *Journal of Cleaner Production*, October 2018.

[52] Éric Berr *et al.*, *La Dette publique: précis d'économie citoyenne*, 2021, p. 83.

[53] Thomas Piketty, *Capital et Idéologie, op. cit.*, p. 647.

[54] "Que faire de la dette? Un audit de la dette publique de la France," CAC, 2014.

[55] Anne-Laure Delatte, "La croissance économique est-elle nécessaire au développement?", France Culture, July 22, 2019, 1:35.

[56] R. Easterlin, "Does economic growth improve the human lot? Some empirical evidence," *Nations and Households in Economic Growth*, 1974.

[57] A. L. Fanning *et al.*, "The social shortfall and ecological overshoot of nations," *Nature Sustainability*, 2021.

[58] "World happiness report," 2021, p. 20. See also OECD, "How's life? 2020: Measuring well-being," and in particular "Box 1.5. The relationship between GDP growth and well-being," p. 54.

[59] The results are detailed in Éloi Laurent, *Sortir de la croissance . . .*, *op. cit.*, p. 143: 26% for per capita GDP, and 34% (social ties), 21% (healthy life expectancy), 11% (freedom to make life choices), generosity (5%), and trust in institutions (3%).

[60] Robert Waldinger, "What makes a good life? Lessons from the longest study on happiness," Ted.com, November 2015.

[61] Bronnie Ware, *The Top Five Regrets of the Dying: A Life Transformed by Dearly Departing*, Hay House Inc., 2012.

[62] S. Preston, "The changing relation between mortality and level of economic development," *Population Studies*, 1975.

[63] Jason Hickel, *Less is More: How Degrowth Will Save the World*, Penguin, 2020, pp. 174-175.

[64] Éloi Laurent, *Sortir de la croissance...*, op. cit., p. 90.

[65] "L'espérance de vie par niveau de vie," *Insee*, February 2018. Note that these discrepancies are exacerbated when we look at healthy life expectancy (and not just life expectancy in general): Observatoire des Inégalités, "Les inégalités d'espérance de vie entre les catégories sociales se maintiennent," April 14, 2020.

[66] K. Pickett and R. G. Wilkinson, *Pour vivre heureux, vivons égaux: comment l'égalité réduit le stress préserve la santé mentale et améliore le bien-être de tous*, Les liens qui libèrent, 2020; R. G. Wilkinson, *L'Égalité c'est la santé*, Demopolis, 2020; R. G. Wilkinson, *L'inégalité nuit gravement à la santé*, Cassini, 2002.

[67] Cited in: P. Servigne, "L'inégalité économique, un agent socialement toxique," *Barricade*, 2010, p. 4.

[68] Éloi Laurent, *Sortir de la croissance...*, op. cit., p. 114.

[69] https://www.pactedupouvoirdevivre.fr

[70] Amartya Sen, *Development as Freedom*, Oxford University Press, 1999.

[71] Cécile Brousse, "Travail professionnel, tâches domestiques, temps 'libre': quelques déterminants sociaux de la vie quotidienne," *Insee*, 2015.

[72] James Duesenberry, *Income, Saving, and the Theory of Consumer Behavior*, Harvard University Press, 1949.

[73] Robert H. Frank, *Luxury Fever: Why Money Fails to Satisfy in an Era of Excess*, 1999.

[74] Robert H. Frank. *Choosing the Right Pond: Human Bahaviour and the Quest for Status*, New York, Oxford University Press, 1985.

[75] Hervé Kempf, *Que crève le capitalisme*, op. cit., p. 7.

[76] Jean Gadrey, "Le théorème du gâteau qui doit grossir et le retour des propibes," Debout!, Le blog de Jean Gadrey, *Alternatives économiques*, September 28, 2009.

5. A Brief History of Degrowth

[1] For more on André Gorz: Françoise Gollain, *André Gorz et l'écosocialisme*, Le Passager clandestin, 2021; André Gorz, *Leur écologie et la nôtre: anthologie d'écologie politique*, Seuil, 2020; Arno Münster, *André Gorz ou le socialisme difficile*, Nouvelles Ligne, 2008; Willy Gianinazzi, *André Gorz, une vie*, La Découverte, 2016; Christophe Fourel *et al.*, *Le Moment Gorz: André*

Gorz en personne, Bord de l'eau, 2017; and Christophe Fourel *et al.*, *André Gorz: Un penseur pour le XXIe siècle*, La Découverte, 2009.

² A. Sutter, "The birth of 'décroissance' and of the degrowth tradition," 2017.

³ To learn more about Nicholas Georgescu-Roegen: J. Grinevald, "La révolution bioéconomique de Nicholas Georgescu-Roegen," *Revue Stratégies énergétiques*, "Biosphère et société," 1993; J. Gowdy and S. Mesner, "The evolution of Georgescu-Roegen's bioeconomics", *Review of Social Economy*, 1998. On the link with degrowth: S. Ferrari, "De la bioéconomie à la décroissance: proximités et distances entre Nicholas Georgescu-Roegen et Serge Latouche," *Revue francophone du développement durable*, 2015, and S. Ferrari, *Nicholas Georgescu-Roegen et la bioéconomie*, in the collection "Les précurseurs de la décroissance" (out in February 2023). As well as more technical works: Antoine Missemer, *Nicholas Georgescu-Roegen, pour une révolution bioéconomique*, ENS Éditions, 2015, and Kozo Mayumi, *The Origin of Ecological Economics. The Bioeconomics of Georgescu-Roegen*, Routledge, 2001.

⁴ For a retrospective on his work, see the BBC documentary "The Limits to Growth" (June 2022), the "podcast sismique" episode with Dennis Meadows ("The end of growth?", November 2021), a conversation between Dennis Meadows and Richard Heinberg ("Interview de Dennis Meadows, pour le 50e anniversaire des 'Limites à la croissance'" on *Anticiper.org*), the article by Jørgen Stig Nørgrd *et al.*, "The History of *The Limits to Growth*," *Solutions*, 2016, and a text by Donella Meadows, edited by Dennis Meadows after her death, "The history and conclusions of *The Limits to Growth*," 2007.

⁵ Two books by Daniel Cérézuelle to explore Bernard Charbonneau: *Bernard Charbonneau ou la critique du développement exponentiel*, Le Passager clandestin, 2018; and *Nature et liberté, introduction à la pensée de Bernard Charbonneau*, Éditions de l'Échappée, 2022. See also the website "La Grande Mue" (https://lagrandemue.wordpress.com).

⁶ You can find a version of the text in *L'Inactuelle: revue d'un monde qui vient*, "Grand texte: Bernard Charbonneau 'La décroissance fait croître le bonheur'", October 12, 2019.

⁷ The article is available on Reporterre's website: "Le président de la Commission européenne: 'Il faut réduire notre croissance,'" October 21, 2011.

⁸ To look further: Peter A. Victor, *Herman Daly's Economic for a Full World: His Life and Ideas*, Routledge, 2022. See also an episode of the "Metabolism of Cities" podcast with Herman Daly ("From Steady State to Ecological Economics," October 2021).

⁹ To explore the history of ecological economics: Inge Røpke, "The early history of modern ecological economics," *Ecological Economics*, 2004. For a panorama of its current state: *Routledge Handbook of Ecological Economics*, edited by Clive L. Spash in 2017.

¹⁰ Two books to explore the intellectual tradition of degrowth: Cédric Biagini, *Aux origines de la décroissance: 50 penseurs*, L'Échappée, 2020; Serge Latouche, *Les Précurseurs de la décroissance, une anthologie*, Le Passager clandestin, 2016.

[11] Timothée Duverger, *La Décroissance, une idée pour demain*, Sang de la Terre, 2011.

[12] Yves Cochet, *Pétrole apocalypse*, Fayard, 2005; Matthieu Auzanneau, *Pétrole. Le déclin est proche*, Seuil, 2021.

[13] To explore Serge Latouche's ideas on degrowth: *Le Pari de la décroissance* (Fayard, 2006); *Vers une société d'abondance frugale, contresens et controverses sur la décroissance* (Fayard/Mille et une nuits, 2011); *Petit traité de la décroissance sereine* (Mille et une nuits, 2007); *Les Précurseurs de la décroissance, une anthologie* (Le Passager clandestin, 2016); *La Planète des naufragés, la décroissance avant la décroissance* (Libre et Solidaire, 2016); *L'Occidentalisme du monde* (La Découverte, 2005); *L'Invention de l'économie* (Albin Michel, 2005); and *Entre mondialisation et décroissance, l'autre Afrique* (Dedalo Bari, 2009).

[14] To explore Pierre Rabhi's ideas: his autobiography *Du Sahara aux Cévennes ou la reconquête du songe* (Albin Michel, 1983), and his main works: *Manifeste pour la Terre et l'humanisme* (Actes Sud, 2008), *Vers la sobriété heureuse* (Actes Sud, 2010), *La Convergence des consciences* (Éditions Le Passeur, 2016), *La Tristesse de Gaïa* (Actes Sud, 2021).

[15] He would then publish *La Décroissance: un nouveau projet politique* (2008), *Désobéir et grandir: vers une société de décroissance* (2009), *La Simplicité volontaire contre le mythe de l'abondance* (2010), and *Gratuité vs capitalisme* (2018).

[16] The full list is available here: https://timotheeparrique.com/academic-articles/

[17] For a summary of this literature, see Giorgos Kallis *et al.*, "Research on degrowth," *Annual review of Environment and Resources*, 2018. For a complete overview, see Matthias Schmelzer *et al.*, *The Future is Degrowth*, Verso, 2022.

[18] Isabelle Stengers, *Another Science is Possible: A Manifesto for Slow Science*, Wiley, 2018.

[19] There are more and more of them: a course at a public university in Scotland ("Degrowing the economy, regrowing our lives"), at the University of Melbourne ("Consumerism and the growth economy"), at the University of Copenhagen ("Degrowth in Europe: Foundations in theory and pathways to practice"), at the University of Oslo ("Debates in post-development & degrowth"), at the Norwegian University of Life Sciences ("Political ecology of scarcity, limits, and degrowth"), and at the center for socio-environmental studies in Madrid ("Decrecimiento. Introducción desde una perspectiva latinoamericana" in 2021 and "Decrecer para vivir bien" in 2022).

[20] Luc Semal, *Militer à l'ombre des catastrophes. Contribution à une théorie politique environnementale au prise des mobilisations de la décroissance et de la transition* (2012); *Measuring Progress Towards a Socially Sustainble Steady State Economy* (2012) by Dan O'Neill; *Small Business Transition Towards Degrowth* (2020) by Iana Nesterova; *The Hegemony of Growth* (2013) by Matthias Schmelzer; *From Degrowth Theory to Concrete Actions* (2019) by Inês Cosme; *Macroeconomics Without Growth* (2016) by Steffen Lange; *La Décroissance au prisme de la modélisation prospective* (2016) by François Briens;

The Macroeconomics of Degrowth (2022) by Antoine Monserand; *Democracy Without Growth* (2015) by Viviana Asara; *Relationship-to-Profit* (2012) by Jennifer Hinton; *A Piece of Land is a Piece of Gold* (2021) by Aaron Vansintjan; *Alternatives to Money-As-Usual in Ecological Economics* (2014) by Kristofer Dittmer; *Beyond GDP* (2021) by Jonas Van der Slycken; *Property Beyond Growth* (2011) by Samuel Alexander.

[21] Sustainable Development Commission, "Prosperity without growth? The transition to a sustainable economy," 2009.

[22] Dominique Méda. *La Mystique de la croissance . . .* , *op. cit.*, chapter V: «Une croissance sans modération.»

[23] Dominique Méda, *La Mystique de la croissance. Comment s'en libérer* (Flammarion, 2013), *Faut-il attendre la croissance?* (La Documentation française, with Florence Jany-Catrice), *Vers une société post-croissance* (L'Aube, 2017, with Isabelle Cassiers and Kevin Maréchal).

[24] Posted on Antonio Guterres's account on June 17, 2022 at 5:48 p.m.

[25] Alberto Garzón, "The limits to growth: Eco-socialism or barbarism," *LaU Review*, April 2022.

[26] Fabrice Bonnifet, "L'équilibre des trois piliers du développement durable n'existe pas," *TFI Info*, May 23, 2022.

[27] Cathérine Lehmann *et al.*, "Green growth, a-growth or degrowth? Investigating the attitudes of environmental protection specialists at the German Environmental Agency," *Journal of Cleaner Production*, February 2022.

[28] Timothée Parrique, "Le GIEC enterre la stratégie de la croissance verte," *Timotheeparrique.com*, May 5, 2022. For a more detailed analysis: Timothée Parrique, "Decoupling in the IPCC AR6 WGIII," *Timotheeparrique.com*, April 8, 2022.

[29] L.T. Keyber and M. Lenzen, "1.5°C degrowth scenarios suggest the need for mitigation pathways," *Nature Communications*, May 2021.

[30] Gilles Raveaud, "Crise gigantesque en approche?," *Thinkerview*, April 1, 2021.

[31] Luca Cigna, "Why comparative political economy should take the post-growth debate seriously," *LSE*, February 19, 2022.

[32] Prophil, "Entreprise & post-croissance—réinitialiser nos modèles économiques, comptables et de gouvernance," 2021.

[33] EELV, "Motion pour la création d'une commission EELV sur la société post-croissance," March 14, 2017.

[34] Romain Jeanticou, "La décroissance, une idée en pleine croissance," *Télérama*, November 1, 2021.

[35] Timothée Parrique, "Décroissance, un projet de société?," *Sismique*, July 8, 2021.

[36] Mathilde Goupil, "L'article à lire pour tout comprendre à la décroissance, prônée par certains candidats à la primaire écologiste," *Franceinfo*, September 3, 2021; Rémi Noyon and Sébastien Billard, "Faut-il avoir peur de

la décroissance?," *L'Obs*, May 17, 2021; Maxime Ferrer, "La décroissance: d'où vient ce concept politique qui fait débat à la primaire écologiste?," *Le Monde*, September 3, 2021.

[37] A few of these articles: *The Guardian* ("In the midst of an economic crisis, can 'degrowth' provide an answer?," April 2020); *Bloomberg* ("These folks think eternal economic growth will lead to unstoppable climate change," August 2020); *New Yorker* ("Can we have prosperity without growth?," February 2020); *Vice* ("Covid-19 broke the economy. What if we don't fix it?," June 2020); *Rolling Stone* ("Can we learn to live with less? Covid-19 and the debate on 'degrowing the economy,'" August 2020); *Vox* ("How affluent people can end their mindless overconsumption," November 2020); *The Washington Post* ("As covid-19 has exposed, our obsession with economic growth is harming people," November 2020); *BBC* ("How shorter workweeks could save Earth," August 2019); *New Republic* ("Giving Up on economic growth could make us cooler and happier," May 2021); *CNBC* ("A guide to degrowth: The movement prioritizing wellbeing in a bid to avoid climate cataclysm," February 2021); *The Economist* ("The economics of the climate," October 2021); *New York Times* ("Do we need to shrink the economy to stop climate change?," September 2021); *Foreign Policy* ("GDP didn't save countries from Covid-19," April 2021); *Scientific American* ("The delusion of infinite economic growth," June 2021); *Popular Science* ("What is 'degrowth' and how can it fight climate change?," July 2021), and many others.

[38] Rémi Noyon and Sébastien Billard, "En France, la décroissance est la cible d'un véritable tabassage intellectuel," *L'Obs*, April 21, 2021.

[39] Timothée Parrique, "Degrowth in the IPCC AR6 WGIII," *Timotheeparrique.com*, March 5, 2022; and "Degrowth in the IPCC AR6 WGIII," *Timotheeparrique.com*, April 6, 2022.

[40] GIEC AR6 WGII, 2022, chapter XVIII, pp. 81-82.

[41] *Ibid.*, chapter I, p. 41.

[42] *Ibid.*, chapter XVII, p. 14.

[43] IPBES, "Summary for policymakers of the methodological assessment regarding the diverse conceptualization of multiple values of nature and its benefits," July 2022, p. 26.

[44] Maison commune de la décroissance, *La Décroissance et ses déclinaisons, pour sortir des clichés et des généralités*, Éditions Utopia, 2022.

[45] European Environment Agency, "Growth without economic growth," January 11, 2021.

[46] Bruno David, "On est sur la trajectoire d'une 6e extinction des espèces," *France Inter*, May 22, 2022.

[47] Victoria Masterson, "Degrowth—what's behind the economic theory and why does it matter right now?," *WEF*, June 15, 2022.

[48] Michael D. Higgins, "President delivers keynote address at Engineers Ireland conference on climate action," October 21, 2020.

[49] Emmanuel Macron, « Emmanuel Macron défend la 5G contre le 'modèle amish,'" *France 24*, September 19, 2020; Édouard Philippe, "Séance

du mercredi 12 juin 2019," Assemblée nationale; Jean Castex, "Les propositions de Castex pour 'a croissance écologique, pas décroissance verte,'" *YouTube—The Huffington Post*, July 15, 2020; Élisabeth Borne, policy address to the Assemblée Nationale, July 6, 2022.

[50] EELV, "12 mesures concrètes pour une société de décroissance: sélective, solidaire et favorable à l'emploi!," April 21, 2011.

[51] Génération écologique, "La profession de foi de Delphine Batho," September 13, 2021.

[52] Timothée Parrique, "Réponse aux verts qui parlent de décroissance," *Thimotheeparrique.com*, September 13, 2021.

[53] *Volem rien foutre al païs* (2006), *Simplicité volontaire et décroissance*, vol. 1 and 2 (2007), *C'est par où la décroissance?* (2008), *Life After Growth. Economics for Everyone* (2009), *10 entretiens filmés pour mieux comprendre la décroissance* (2011), *Sacrée croissance!* (2014), *L'Urgence de ralentir* (2014), *Minimalism: A Documentary About the Important Things* (2015), *A Simpler Way: Crisis as Opportunity* (2016), *Decrecimiento: del mito de la abundancia a la simplicidad voluntaria* (2017), *System Error* (2018), *Prêts pour la décroissance?* (2020), *Fairy Tales of Growth* (2020).

[54] Vogue Business Team, "Facing fashion's overproduction issue: Solutions, new models and alternatives," *Vogue Business*, April 30, 2021; Rachel Cernansky, "Want to be sustainable? Try going small," *Vogue Business*, April 8, 2021.

[55] Nina Siegal, "At museums, maybe it's time for 'de-growth,'" *The New York Times*, March 11, 2017.

6. A Transition Pathway

[1] WWF. "Le trop-plein de SUV dans la publicité," March 2021. As a reminder, the average SUV uses 20% more energy than a classic car, and SUVs represented 45% of global car sales in 2021—if SUVs were a country, it would be the sixth largest polluter in the world ("Global SUV sales set another record in 2021, setting back efforts to reduce emissions," IEA, 2021).

[2] Nick Fitzpatrick, Timothée Parrique and Inês Cosme, "Exploring degrowth policy proposals: A systematic mapping with thematic synthesis," *Journal of Cleaner Production*, 2022.

[3] Camille, *Le petit livre noir des grands projets inutiles*, Le passager clandestin, 2015; Des plumes dans le goudron, *Résister aux grands projets inutile et imposés*, Textuel, 2018.

[4] Andrew L. Fanning *et al.*, "The social shortfall and ecological overshoot of nations," *Nature Sustainability*, November 2021. The most recent data for France (2015) is available at https://goodlife.leeds.ca.uk

[5] Carbone 4, "Empreinte carbone française moyenne, comment est-elle calculée?," 2022. As there is no estimate of the carbon footprint per sector in

France, I drew from a study about Finland (Michael Lettenmeier, "Eight tons of material footprint—suggestion for a resource cap for household consumption in Finland," *Resources*, 2014).

[6] Jared B. Fitzgerald *et al.*, "Energy consumption and working hours: A longitudinal study of developed and developing nations, 1990-2008," *Environmental Sociology*, June 2015.

[7] Ministère de la Transition Écologique, "Chiffres clé de l'énergie—édition 2021."

[8] For a detailed description of specific proposals, see the 2011 parliamentary report by David Fleming and Shaun Chamberlin, "Tradable energy quotas: A policy framework for peak oil and climate change." In France, see Mathilde Szuba's work—her thesis *Gouverner dans un monde fini* (2014), "Le rationnement, outil convivial," in *Politiques de l'anthropocène* (2021), "Régimes de justice énergétique" in *Penser la décroissance* (2013), as well as an interview where she sumarrizes the idea ("Carte carbone: plutôt qu'une taxe, un quota pour chaque citoyen?," *Socialter*, 2019).

[9] Alex Chapman *et al.*, "A frequent flyer levy: Sharing aviation's carbon budget in a net-zero world," *New Economics Foundation*, July 10, 2021.

[10] CDP, "The Carbon Majors Database—CDP Carbon Majors Report 2017," July 2017.

[11] "The Plastic Waste Makes Index: Revealing the source of the single-use plastic crisis," Minderoo Foundation, 2021.

[12] Cédric Rossi, "Carte des émissions françaises de gas à effet de serre EU-ETS 2019," data.gouv.fr, May 18, 2021.

[13] Peter Victor, *Managing Without Growth: Slower by Design, Not Disaster*, Edward Edgar Publishing, 2008.

[14] The shark analogy comes from the documentary *The Great Simplification* (2022). It's what German sociologist Hartmut Rosa calls "dynamic stabilization," in "Dynamic stabilization, the triple A. Approach to the good life, and the resonance conception," *Questions de communication*, 2017, for example.

[15] IISD, "Rich countries must end oil and gas production by 2034 for a fair 1.5°C transition," March 22, 2022.

[16] Dan Welsby *et al.*, "Unextractable fossil fuels in a 1.5°C world," *Nature*, September 8, 2021.

[17] La Poste, "La Banque Postale accélère sa stratégie de décarbonation," October 14, 2021.

[18] Emmanuel Bonnet, Diego Landivar, and Alexandre Monnin, *Héritage et fermeture: une écologie du démentèlement*, Divergences, 2021.

[19] Mickaël Correia, *Criminels climatiques: enquête sur les multinationales qui brûlent notre planète*, La Découverte, 2022.

[20] Peter Gowan and Mathew Lawrence, "Democratic ownership funds," *Common Wealth*, June 12, 2019.

[21] Kate Raworth, *Doughnut Economics: Seven Ways to Think Like a 21st-Century Economist*, Random House Business, 2017.

[22] Lucas Chancel, "Climate change and the global inequality of carbon emissions 1990-2020," October 2021.

[23] S. Sala *et al.*, "Environmental sustainability of European production and consumption assessed against planetary boundaries," *Journal of Environmental Management*, 2020.

[24] J. Hickel, "Quantifying national responsibility for climate breakdown: An equality-based attribution approach for carbon dioxide emissions in excess of the planetary boundary," *The Lancet*, 2019.

[25] J. Hickel *et al.*, "National responsibility for ecological breakdown: A fair-shares assessment of resource use, 1970-2017," *The Lancet*, 2022.

[26] Lucas Chancel, "Climate change and the global inequality of carbon emissions 1990-2020," *World Inequality Database*, October 2021.

[27] J. Hickel and A. Slamersak, "Existing climate mitigation scenarios perpetuate colonial inequalities," *The Lancet*, July 2022.

[28] Y. Oswald, A. Owen, JK. Steinberger, "Large inequality in international and intranational energy footprints between income groups and across consumption categories," *Nature Energy*, 2020.

[29] "Confronting carbon equality," Oxfam Media Briefing, September 21, 2020.

[30] "World Inequality Report 2022," World Inequality Lab, "France," p. 193.

[31] Johanna Barasz and Hélène Garner (coord.), "Soutenabilités! Orchestrer et planifier l'action publique," France Stratégie, May 2022, p. 53.

[32] Observatoire des Inégalités, "Rapport sur les riches en France," 2022, p. 13.

[33] Clément Caudron, *Il est urgent de ralentir*, Borrego, 2022, Chapter 17.

[34] Audrey Berry and Éloi Laurent, "Taxe carbone, le retour, à quelles conditions?," OFCE/SciencesPo, June 2019.

[35] Thomas Piketty, *Capital et idéologie*, Seuil, 2019, chapter XVII, "La question de la taxation progressive des émissions carbone."

[36] Lucas Chancel, "Climate change and the global inequality of carbon emissions 1990-2020," subpart "Taxing fossil assets."

[37] Greenpeace/Oxfam, *Les milliardaires français font flamber la planète et l'État regard ailleurs*, 2022.

[38] David Fleming and Shaun Chamberlin, "Tradable energy quotas: A policy framework for peak oil and climate change," All-Party Parliamentary Group on Peak Oil, and The Lean Economy Connection, 2011.

[39] Stefan Gössling and Andres Humpe, 2020, "The global scale, distribution and growth of aviation: Implications for climate change," *Global Environmental Change*.

[40] United States, China, United Kingdom, Japan, Germany, United Arab

Emirates, India, France, Australia, and Spain (Possible, "Elite Status; Global inequalities in flying," 2021).

[41] Diana Ivanova and Richard Wood, "The unequal distribution of household carbon footprints in Europe and its link to sustainability," *Global Sustainability*, 2020.

[42] David Banister, *Inequality in Transport*, Alexandrine Press, 2018.

[43] Tom Dubois *et al.*, *Pour en finir avec la vitesse*, Éditions de l'Aube, 2021, p. 74.

[44] Ajay Singh Chaudhary, "The extractive circuit," *The Baffler*, November 2021.

[45] Ulrich Brand and Markus Wissen, *The Imperial Mode of Living: Everyday Life and the Ecological Crisis of Capitalism*, Verso, 2021.

[46] Yannick Oswald *et al.*, "Large inequality in international and intra-national energy footprints between income groups and across consumption categories," *Nature Energy*, March 16, 2020.

[47] Our World in Data, "CO2 country profiles for 2019."

[48] Jefim Vogel *et al.*, "Socio-economic conditions for satisfying human needs at low energy use: An internatinoal analysis of social provisioning," *Global Environmental Change*, 2021.

[49] Paul Ariès, *Le Mésusage: essai sur l'hypercapitalisme*, Parangon/Vs, 2007.

[50] Pavlina R. Tcherneva, *La Garantie de l'emploi: l'arme sociale du Green New Deal*, Paris, La Découverte, 2021.

[51] Claire Hédon *et al.*, *Zéro chômeur: dix territoires relèvent le défi*, Éditions Quart Monde, 2019.

[52] Final report from the Convention Citoyeene pour le Climat, Proposition C2.2 "Réguler la publicité pour limiter fortement les incitations quotidiennes and non-choisies à la consommation," p. 28.

[53] https://konmari.com

[54] Céline Marty, *Travailler moins pour vivre mieux: guide pour une philosophie antiproductiviste*, Dunod, 2021.

[55] Aurélien Barrau, *Le Plus Grand Défi de l'humanité*, Michel Lafon, 2019.

[56] Jason Hickel, *Less is More: How Degrowth will Save the World*, Penguin, 2020.

7. A Societal Project

[1] The term is already used by many, starting with Jean Gadrey, who in *Adieu à la croissance* (2010) already called for building a "*société post-croissance*" ("post-growth society"), a term that would also be developed by Dominique Méda (e.g., *Vers une société post-croissance*, 2018). We should also mention Aurore

Lalucq's *"société prospère de la post-croissance"* ("prosperous society of post-growth," see *Reconquête. Au nom de l'intérêt général*, 2020). Same enthusiasm in Anglophone literature: Tim Jackson titled his lastest book *Post Growth: Life After Capitalism* (2021) and Kate Soper called hers *Post-Growth Living* (2020). Note also the "Observatoire de la post-croissance et de la décroissance" associated with the University of Clermont Auvergne, the "Post Growth Institute" in the United States, the international "Postgrowth Economics Network," and the conference circuit in European Parliament on post-growth.

[2] H. Daly, *Steady-State Economics; The Economics of Biophysical Equilibrium and Moral Growth*, W. H. Freeman, 1977.

[3] Herman Daly, "This pioneering economist says our obsession with growth must end," *The New York Times*, July 2022.

[4] *Our Common Future* [or *Rapport Brundstland*], 1987.

[5] Hans Jonas, *Le Principe responsabilité. Une éthique pour la civilisation technologique*, Éditions du Cerf, 1990 [1979], p. 40.

[6] Michel Serres, *Le Contrat naturel*, François Bourin, 1990.

[7] Isabelle Delannoy, "De quels humains la nature a-t-elle besoin?," *Time for the Planet*, April 19, 2021.

[8] Aldo Leopold, *A Sand County Almanac*, Oxford University Press, 1949.

[9] Alberto Acosta, *Le Buen Vivir: pour imaginer d'autres mondes*, Utopia, 2018.

[10] Lars Gertenback *et al.*, "Eating ourselves out of industrial excess? Degrowth, multi-species conviviality and the micro-politics of cultured meat," *Anthropological Theory*, 2021.

[11] "Une proposition de définition universelle du crime d'écocide," *Actu Environnement*, June 23, 2021.

[12] Murray Bookchin, *Pour un municipalisme libertaire*, Atelier de création libertaire, 2018; Abdullah Öcalan, *The Political Thought of Abdullah Öcalan. Kurdistan, Women's Revolution, and Democratic Confederalism*, Pluto Press, 2017; Joseph C. Kumarappa, *Economy of Permanence: A quest for a social order based on non-violence*, Sarva Seva Sangh Prekashan, 1945.

[13] Joseph Sournac, Lucas Deutsch, and Yoan Brazy, "Pour sauver la planète, faut-il abolir la liberté d'entreprendre," *Maddyness*, December 27, 2021.

[14] https://lowtechlab.org/fr

[15] Ivan Illich, *Tools for Conviviality*, Harper & Row, 1973.

[16] Édouard Jourdain, *Les Communs*, "Que sais-je?," 2021, p. 13.

[17] Benoît Borrits, *Virer les actionnaires: pourquoi et comment s'en passer?*, 2020, p. 113; *Coopératives contre capitalisme*, p. 133; *Au-delà de la propriété*, p. 148; Bernard Friot, *L'enjeu du salaire*, La Dispute, 2012. The difference between the two systems is that Borrits's *"sécurité économique"* ("economic security") mutualizes only a part of value added, while Friot's *"salaire à vie"* ("wage for life") mutualizes all of it.

[18] The term "*sécurité économique*" ("economic security") comes from the initiative https://securiteeconomique.org

[19] Thomas Piketty, *Capital et idéologie, op. cit.*, chapter XVII.

[20] Mathias André *et al.*, "24% des ménages détiennent 68% des logements possédés par des particuliers," *Insee*, November 25, 2021.

[21] Frédéric Lordon, *Figures du communisme*, La Fabrique, 2021.

[22] Vincent Liegey, Stéphane Madelaine, Christophe Ondet, Anne-Isabelle Veillot, *Un projet de décroissance. Manifeste pour une dotation inconditionnelle d'autonomie*, Utopias, 2013.

[23] Tim Jackson, *Prosperity without Growth*, Earthscan, 2009; Jean Gadrey, *Adieu à la croissance*, Les Petits Matins, 2010; Matthias Schmelzer, Andrea Vetter, and Aaron Vansintjan, *The Future is Degrowth*, Verso, 2022, chapter IV; European Environmental Agency, "Growth without Economic Growth," January 11, 2021.

[24] Dominique Méda, "Promouvoir de nouveaux indicateurs de richesse: histoire d'une 'cause' inaboutie," Working Paper n°145, *Fondation maison des sciences de l'homme*, June 2020.

[25] Service d'information du Gouvernement, "Les nouveaux indicateurs de richesse 2017," p. 3.

[26] We see similar initiatives in Iceland (Indicators for Well-being), Wales (Wellbeing of Future Generations Act), Bhutan (Bonheur National Brut), in the Canadian province of Nova Scotia (Quality of Life), in Vermont and Maryland in the United States (Genuine Progress Index), and in the French region Nord-Pas-de-Calais (*Indicateurs 21*).

[27] Éloi Laurent, "Inscrire les indicateurs de bien-être et de soutenabilité au cœur du débat budgétaire," *OFCE*, 2017.

[28] Erich Fromm, *Avoir ou être?*, Payot, 2016 [1976].

[29] *Convivial restraint* (*sobriété conviviale*) (C. Arnsperger, *Éthique de l'existence post-capitaliste*, 2009); *power of restraint* (*sobriété heureuse*) (P. Rabhi, *Vers la sobriété heureuse*, 2010); *frugal abundance* (*l'abondance frugale*) (S. Latouche, *L'Abondance frugale comme art de vivre*, 2020); *alternative hedonism* (K. Soper, *Post-Growth Living*, 2020); *frugal hedonism* (A. Grubb and A. Raser-Rowland, *The Art of Frugal Hedonism*, 2017).

[30] Hartmut Rosa, *Résonance. Une sociologie de la relation au monde*, La Découverte, 2018.

[31] Julie A. Nelson, "The relational economy: A buddhist and feminist analysis," *Global Development and Environment Institute Working paper*, 2010.

8. CONTROVERSY

[1] "Faced with [the urgency of climate change], there is a very quick model: stopping everything. That's the fastest way. I don't believe in it.

I would even say, I am strongly opposed to it. Why? Because everything we've just talked about, here, which is very important does not exist with degrowth. Because we produce to fund a social model and a welfare State. And so, to all those who say 'there is a climate emergency,' and so we must stop everything that pollutes, end our old model from one day to the next for the sake of the climate—I say to them, very well, what is your social plan? Who will fund elder care? Who will fund healthcare? Who will fund education?," Emmanuel Macron speaking to readers of *Sud Ouest* in Pau, March 2022.

[2] Speech by Jean-Baptiste Djebbari: "Lancement de la feuille de route nationale pour le développement des biocarburants aéronautiques durables dans le transport aérien français," January 27, 2020; Bertrand Piccard, "Entre la décroissance qui aboutirait au chaos social et la croissance illimité qui mène au désastre environnemental, il y a une troisième voie," *La Libre*, April 12, 2021; Brune Poirson in a speech before the Assemblée Nationale in December 2019; Michel Rocard, "La décroissance nous conduirait tout droit à la guerre civile," *La Tribune*, May 29, 2015.

[3] Clément Viktorovitch, "La décroissance, un mot mal choisi," *France Info*, September 6, 2021.

[4] Bruno Latour, "L'écologie nécessite de bien définir qui sont les amis et les ennemis," *Ouest-France*, January 23, 2022.

[5] Jean Gadrey, *Adieu à la croissance*, Les Petits matins, 2010, p. 121.

[6] Paul Ariès, *Décroissance ou barbarie*, Golias, 2005.

[7] Vincent Cheynet, *Décroissance ou décadence*, Le Pas de Côté, 2014, p. 45.

[8] Bertrand Piccard, "Ne tombons pas dans le panneau de la décroissance," *Paris Match*, April 24, 2021.

[9] Ferghane Azihari, *Les Écologistes contre la modernité: le procès de Prométhée*, La Cité, 2021, pp. 15-16.

[10] Clément Viktorovitch, "La décroissance, un mot mal choisi," *France Info*, September 6, 2021.

[11] Observatoire des Inégalités, *Rapport sur les riches en France 2022*, June 2022, p. 37.

[12] Philippe Charlez, "Covid-19 et décroissance: un plaidoyer pour le 'monde d'avant,'" *Contrepoints*, February 10, 2021.

[13] Jason Hickel, *Less is More . . .* , *op. cit.*, p. 174-175.

[14] Two works that address moderation as a political challenge: Bruno Villalba and Luc Semal (eds.), *Sobriété énergétique. Contraintes matérielles, équité sociale et perspectives institutionnelles* (Quae, 2018) and Barbara Nicoloso, *Petit traité de sobriété énnergétique* (Charles Leopold Mayer, 2021).

[15] Rémi Godeau, "Pour l'écologie, sortir de la dictature de la décroissance," *L'Opinion*, June 2, 2021.

[16] Michael Liebrich, "Climate action—It's the trade, stupid," *Bloomberg NEF*, June 25, 2021.

[17] Robert Pollin, "Degrowth policies cannot avert climate crisis. We need a Green New Deal," *Truthout*, July 3, 2021.

[18] Noah Smith, "People are realizing that degrowth is bad," *Noahpinion*, September 6, 2021.

[19] R. B. Jackson *et al.*, "Global fossil carbon emissions rebound near pre-COVID-19 levels," *Environmental Research Letters*, March 7, 2022.

[20] Olivier Pastré, "La décroissance n'est pas forcément un choix," *Constructif*, January 2012.

[21] Dominique Seux, "Faut-il déployer la 5G en France? Le débat Éco," *France Inter*, September 25, 2020.

[22] Beth Stratford, "Green growth vs. degrowth: Are we missing the point?," *Open Democracy*, December 4, 2020.

[23] Bruno Le Maire, "La transition environnementale est-elle compatible avec la croissance économique?," *Le Monde*, January 27, 2022, 1:14:48.

[24] Robin Rivaton, "Comment peut-on matérialiser la 'décroissance' prônée par Delphine Batho," BFM Business, September 13, 2021; Arnaud Montebourg, "Dimance en politique—Bourgogne, avec Arnaud Montebourg," September 6, 2021; Jacques Attali, *L'économie de la vie*, Pluriel, 2022, p. 153.

[25] Denix Olivennes, "Décroissance: la seule solution à la crise écologique?," *Public Sénat*, September 21, 2021, 00:17:00.

[26] Under the first estimate ("What does it mean to be rich? Some conceptual and empirical issues," *European Journal of Social Security*, 2018), Pierre Concialdi estimates that, in 2013, 40% of disposable national income was in excess of the national income necessary to satisfy the needs of the entire French population. I contacted the study's author, who shared the results of his latest estimate: the national surplus in 2021 was 44%.

[27] Max Roser, "The economies that are home to the poorest billions of people need to grow if we want global poverty to decline substantially."

[28] Denis Olivennes, "Décroissance: la seule solution à la crise écologique?," *Public Sénat*, September 21, 2021, 00:17:40.

[29] Christine Kerdellant, "La décroissance ou le découplage?," *L'Usine Nouvelle*, October 14, 2021, 00:01:55.

[30] Andrew Simms and David Woodward, "Growth isn't working: The unbalanced distribution of benefits and costs from economic growth," *New Economic Foundation*, January 23, 2006.

[31] David Woodward, "*Incrementum ad absurdum*: Global growth, inequality, and poverty eradication in a carbon-constrained world," *World Economic Review*, 2015.

[32] Jason Hickel, *Less is More . . .* , *op. cit.*, p. 190.

[33] Éric Toussaint and Damien Millet, *La Derte ou la vie*, Aden, 2011, p. 326.

[34] Jason Hickel *et al.*, "Imperialist appropriation in the world economy:

Drain from the global South through unequal exchange, 1990-2015," *Global Environmental Change*, March 2022.

[35] David Harvey, "The 'new' imperialism: Accumulation by dispossession," *Socialist Register*, 2004.

[36] Colin Chambers, "Degrowth: An environmental ideology with good intentions, bad politics," *Liberation School*, July 20, 2021.

[37] Daniel Ben-Ami, "The 'reset' we really need," *Spiked*, December 16, 2020.

[38] Leigh Philips, "Mirages de la décroissance," *Le Monde*, February 2021.

[39] Matthew T. Huber, *Climate Change as Class War: Building Socialism on a Warming Planet*, Verso, 2022, p. 148.

[40] "We don't need aggregate growth to deliver innovation. If the objective is to achieve specific kinds of innovation, then it makes more sense to invest in those directly, or incentivise investment with target policy measures, rather than grow the whole economy indistrimately and hope it will deliver the innovation we want. Is it really reasonable to grow the plastics industry, the timber industry and the advertising industry in order to get more efficient trains? Does it really make sense to grow dirty things in order to get clean things? We have to be smarter than that." Jason Hickel, *Less is More . . .* , *op. cit.*, p. 198.

[41] Thomas Piketty, *Capital et idéologie*, *op. cit.*, chapter XVII, "Revenu de base et salaire juste: le rôle de l'impôt progressif sur le revenu."

[42] Jean-Marie Harribey, *Le Trou noir du capitalisme*, 2020, p. 71.

[43] Frédéric Lordon, *Figures du communisme*, 2021, p. 139 (first citation), pp. 103-104 (second citation).

[44] Daniel Laturo, *Trop tard pour être pessimistes! Écosocialisme ou effondrement*, Textuel, 2020, p. 223.

[45] This argument is explored in depth by Louison Cahen-Fourrot in her doctoral thesis, "La soutenabilité de l'accumulation du capital et de ses régimes," Sorbonne Paris-Cité, 2017.

[46] John Molyneux, "Growth & degrowth: What should ecosocialists say?—Part one," *Rebel News*, March 1, 2021.

[47] Michael Löwy *et al.*, "For an ecosocialist degrowth," *Monthly Review*, April 1, 2022.

[48] Giorgios Kallis, "Socialism without growth," *Capitalism Nature Socialism*, October 17, 2022.

[49] Paul Ariès, *Décroissance ou barbarie*, 2005, p. 27.

[50] Aaron Bastani, *Communisme de luxe: un monde d'abondance grâce aux nouvelles technologies*, Diateino, 2021.

[51] Projet de décroissance, "Les idées de la décroissance infusent la société en silence," *Mediapart*, January 26, 2017.

[52] "I am not a supporter of degrowth. I believe in science. I want it to

have a larger role in public debate and for our decisions to be more guided by it. I know what our country owes to its agriculture and how fortunate we are to being able to count on hardworking and passionate farmers. I love industry, and I stand by that: I admire its employees, factory workers, technicians, and engineers who produce. I believe in a market economy regulated by policy, in innovation, and in the power of growth." (Édouard Philippe, speech before the Assemblée Nationale, June 12, 2019).

[53] Guillaume Duval, "Décroissance ou développement durable?," *Alternative économiques*, n° 221, January 2004.

[54] Marc Simard, "Climat: qui voutra retourner à l'ère préindustrielle?," *La Presse*, May 2, 2019.

[55] Emmanuel Bonnet, Diego Landivar, and Alexandre Monnin, "Crise climatique: 'Nous devons apprendre à désinnover," *Le Monde*, September 3, 2021.

[56] For Pascal Perri, author of *Le Péril vert*, degrowth is a dead end: "Given the world's geography, its political structure, we have no other choice but to pursue the march of progress, which alone will guarantee the safekeeping of our countries' social achievements and foster growth that respects the environment. We must trust in the human genius." (Pascal Perri, "La décroissance, cette écologie triste qui ne résout rien," *Atlantico*, May 9, 2021).

[57] Florent Mengaux, "Un nouveau paradigme de la croissance," Rencontres économiques d'Aix-en-Provence, July 3, 2021, 00:14:55.

[58] Bertrand Piccard, "Bâtir une société durable et désirable," July 6, 2021.

[59] "[. . .] if I can't picture a world without growth, is that proof that we lack imagination? I wonder if we do not lack imagination. For those who preach degrowth, I preach the example. Let them come see a company with six centuries of history, where one its sectors is in decline. From 18 billion letters in 2008 to 3 billion in 2030. That's degrowth. Well, stretch that over a human community of 250,000 people, a country of 70 million, or a planet of 9 billion—the complexity, the tensions, the challenges to the identities of thousands of people—I don't see myself choosing degrowth. So I think we do not lack imagination when we think that growth is the solution for us; for postal workers, growth is the solution." (Philippe Walh, "Un nouveau paradigme de la croissance," Les rencontre économiques d'Aix-en-Provence, July 3, 2021, 00:30).

[60] Bertrand Piccard, "Rencontre avec des passeurs," *Canopée*, Hors-série, 2015.

[61] Xavier Timbeau, "A-t-on encore besoin de croissance économique?," *Mediapart*, March 29, 2019, 00:10:45.

[62] Angus Maddison, *The World Economy: A Millenial Perspective*, Paris, OECD, 2001.

[63] John Molyneux, "In response to Louis N. Proyect on degrowth," *Global Ecosocialist Network*, December 23, 2020.

[64] Luc Ferry, "Décroissance? Ni possible, ni souhaitable!," *Le Figaro*, December 2, 2020.

[65] "14e baromètre de la consommation responsable 2021," GreenFlex & ADEME.

[66] Odoxa for Medef, Debember 2019 and May 2020.

[67] "Les Français, plus 'écolos' que jamais," Odoxa for Aviva, *Challenges*, and BFM Business, October 2019.

[68] Terra Nova, "Les femmes et le changement climatique," June 29, 2021.

[69] Global Commons Alliance, "The global commons survey," August 2021.

[70] Medef, "Le rapport au progrès: regard des Français et comparatif européen," September 2020.

[71] Timothée Parrique, *The Political Economy of Degrowth*, 2019, pp. 500-501.

[72] Géraldine Woessner, "Contention citoyenne: le choix de la décroissance," *Le Point*, June 20, 2020.

[73] Éloi Laurent, *Sortir de la croissance, op. cit.*, p. 15.

[74] Hervé Kempf, *Que crève le capitalisme, op. cit.*, p. 92.

[75] Philippe Charlez, "Décroissance: la pauvreté comme seul menu," *Valeurs actuelles*, July 18, 2021.

[76] Rémi Godeau, "Pour l'écologies, sortir de la dictature de la décroissance," *L'Opinion*, June 2, 2021; Bruno Le Maire, *L'Ange et la Bête, op. cit.*, p. 328.

[77] World Inequality Report, 2022, "France," p. 193.

[78] Julia Cagé, *Le Prix de la démocratie*, Fayard, 2018.

[79] Jacques Ellul, *Le Bluff technologique*, Hachette, 1988, p. 412.

[80] François Perroux, *Le Capitalisme*, "Que sais-je," 1948.

Conclusion

[1] Corey J. A. Bradshaw *et al.*, "Underestimating the challenges of avoiding a ghastly future," *Frontiers in Conservation Science*, January 13, 2021.

[2] "Policy-makers are often mesmerized by the quantity of growth. They need to be more concerned with its structure and quality. Unless governments take timely corrective action, economic growth can become lopsided and flawed. Determined efforts are needed to avoid growth that is *jobless, ruthless, voiceless, rootless*, and *futureless*." (UNDP, Human Development Report, 1996, pp. 2-4).

[3] Jean Gadrey, *Adieu à la croissance: bien vivre dans un monde solicitarie*, Les Petits Matins, 2010.

[4] Éloi Laurent, *Sortir de la croissance, op. cit.*

[5] Romano Onafrio, *Towards a Society of Degrowth*, Routledge, 2019.

[6] Dominique Méda, *La Mystique de la croissance . . . , op. cit.*

[7] Aurélien Barrau, "Que faire? Pour une pensée du déraillement," *Diacritik*, April 11, 2022.

[8] Timothée Parrique, "Sufficiency means degrowth," *Timotheeparrique.com*, April 24, 2022.

[9] Serge Latouche, *L'Abondance frugale comme art de vivre: bonheur, gastronomie, et décroissance*, Payot & Rivages, 2020.

[10] Michael Albert, *Parecon: Life After Capitalism*, 2003; https://weall.org; Kate Raworth, *Doughnut Economics, op. cit.*; Christian Felber, *Pour une économie du bien commun*, Dunod, 2022; Christian Arnsperger and Dominique Bourg, *Écologie intégrale. Pour une société permacirculaire*, PUF, 2017; David Schweickart, *After Capitalism*, Rowman & Littlefiel, 2002; Thomas Piketty, *Capital et idéologie, op. cit.*; Daniel Tanuro, *Trop tard pour être pessimistes! Écosocialisme ou effondrement*, Textuel, 2020.

[11] Internationale convivialiste, *Second manifeste convivialiste: pour un monde post-néolibéral*, Actes Sud, 2020; Sylvain Breuzard, *La permaentreprise. Un modèle viable pour un futur vivable, inspiré de la permaculture*, Eyrolles, 2021; Mouvement pour une frugalité heureuse et créative, *Commune frugale*, Actes Sud, 2022; Fabrice Bonnifet and Céline Puff Ardichvili, *L'Entreprise contributive: concilier monde des affaires et limites planétaires*, Dunod, 2021; Stefano Bartolini, *Pour une société fraternelle: En finir avec l'égoïsme, la compétition et la surconsommation*, Pocket, 2015; Kate Soper, *Post-Growth Living: For an Alternative Hedonism*, Verso, 2020; Harmut Rosa, *Résonance. Une sociologie de la relation au monde*, La Découverte, 2018; Philippe Bihouix, *L'Âge des low tech. Vers une civilisation techniquement soutenable*, Seuil, 2014; Céline Marty, *Travailler moins pour vivre mieux. Guide pour une philosophie anitproductiviste*, Dunod, 2021; Mathias Rollot and Martin Schaffner, *Qu'est-ce qu'une biorégion?*, Wild Project, 2021; Emmanuel Dockès, *Voyage en misarchie: essai pour tout reconstruire*, Detour, 2019; Gerard Endenburg, *Sociocracy as Social Design*, Eburon, 1998; Murray Bookchin, *Pour un municipalisme libertaire*, Atelier de la création libertaire, 2018.

[12] J. K. Gibson-Graham *et al.*, *Take Back the Economy: An Ethical Guide for Transforming Our Communities*, Upress, 2013.

[13] Bruno Latour, *Imaginer les gestes barrières contre le retour à la production d'avant-crise*, AOC, 2020.

[14] Hervé Kempf, *Que crève le capitalisme, op. cit.*

[15] Stéphane Hessel, *Indignez-vous*, LP, 2010.

[16] Des agros qui bifurquent, "Appel à déserter la remise des diplômes AgroParisTech 2022," *YouTube*, May 10, 2022.

[17] Clément Choisne, "Discours remise des diplômes 2018 Centrale Nantes," *YouTube*, 2018.

[18] Anne-fleur Goll, "HED Graduation—Quel rouage serez-vous?," *YouTube*, June 11, 2022.

[19] Célia, "Le discours de révolte des jeunes diplômés de Polytechnique," *Brut*, June 25, 2022.

Acknowledgements

If there is one truth in economics, it's that nothing ever gets made alone.

In the academic spirit of peer review, this book was reviewed by many experts whom I thank sincerely for their critical feedback: Yves-Marie Abraham, Paul Ariès, Fabrice Bonnifet, Benoît Borrits, Louison Cahen-Fourot, Clément Caudron, Mélanie Ciussi, Timothée Duverger, Jean-Marie Harribey, Pierre Kohler, Éloi Laurent, Serge Latouche, Dominique Méda, Antoine Missemer, Gilles Mitteau, Antoine Monserand, Emmanuel Pond, Céline Puff Ardichvili, Cedric Rossi, François Schneider, Luc Semal, Christophe Sempels, Agnès Sinaï, Andrew Sutter, and Franck-Dominique Vivien. I am particularly indebted to Cédric Chevalier for his many suggestions. Of course, I remain solely responsible for any errors.

I also thank my colleagues at the Observatoire de la Post-Croissance et de la Décroissance (OPCD) for taking the time to edit the manuscript: Armel Brouette, Charlotte Burnod, Marceau Challet, Clément Choisne, Jerome Cuny, Thomas Dauphin, Sylvie Ferrari, Fabrice Flipo, Félix Garnier, Stéphane Hairy, Manon Laveau, Vincent Lavilley, Arnaud Levy, Vincent Liegey, Michel Lepesant, Gabriel Malek, Timothé Miot, Emmanual Benoit Raufflet, Benoît Rolland de Ravel, Hélène Rollo, Vivien Starosse, Antoine Tiberj, and Arian Tichit.

I am eternally grateful to my fellow thinkers, friends and colleagues, for their exceptional proofreading work: Yaëlle Amsallem, Anton Beraber, François Briens, Antoine Giraldi, Mathieu Jeanne-Beylot, Quentin Jaud, Céline Marty, Laurent Pagani, and Thomas Wagner. I also thank my mother, Marie-France Parrique, who, even after more than fifteen years of university, still corrects my (many) spelling mistakes.

A big thank you to Salomé Viaud, my editor at Seuil, for her trust and determination through the very end. I thank Louis Jolivet, the main economist to review this book, who went through every paragraph with a fine-tooth comb, always providing invaluable feedback.

And finally, I would like to thank all the people who supported me during the writing of this book: the Club Touchard, which welcomed me with open arms for two years on the beaches of Anglet; Lund University in Sweden, where I finished the book; my parents, who kindly took me in during the first lockdown; and the many strangers who, every week, send the kind words of encouragement that allow me to keep my spirits up and continue digging into such difficult subjects.

And lastly, I would like to thank Romy, my first supporter, to whom I dedicate this book.